Deaf Students in H
current researcl

December 07.
KH.

Deaf Students in Higher Education: current research and practice

Edited by Lynne Barnes, Frank Harrington, Jannine Williams and Martin Atherton

Douglas McLean Publishing
Coleford, Gloucestershire

First Published in Great Britain

by

Douglas McLean Publishing in 2007

ISBN 978-0-946252-64-0

Printed and Bound in Great Britain by

Cpod, Trowbridge, Wiltshire

Published by

Douglas McLean

8 St John Street

Coleford

Gloucestershire

England

GL16 8AR

www.forestbooks.com

Contents

Foreword

This very interesting and well-written volume shares with readers both the good news and bad news regarding inclusion of deaf persons in Higher Education. The good news is that deaf persons are entering institutions of Higher Education in greater numbers than ever before, where they are often quite successful in pursuing their degrees. The bad news is that serious challenges and barriers to this success still exist and that much needs to be done to create full and equal opportunities for this group of students. It is a testimony to the editors and contributors that so much ground is covered in this volume, and in such an honest and direct fashion.

As noted in the introduction to the book, the fifteen chapters cover a range of topics related to Higher Education, including public policy, transition to Higher Education, support services, and post-graduate studies. Within and across each of these topics one finds consistently woven threads that are worth noting.

The first thread is *balance*—between discussions of what is known and not yet known, what is working and not working, what has been accomplished and not yet accomplished, and between theory and practice. This is a great strength in the volume because it speaks to a range of readers including academics and practitioners, researchers and teachers, deaf and hearing students and educators. There is something for everyone in these chapters and hopefully readers who identify predominantly with one group will learn something about the perspectives and work of the others.

The second thread is the inclusion of deaf *first-person accounts*. This is critical in a work such as this because these accounts reflect both engagement with and respect for the perspectives of members of the population that is the focus of the work. Moreover, these accounts are incorporated via a range of strategies, from ethnographic interviews conducted as part of a research study to chapter authors. From the shared stories readers gain insight into the lived experience of deaf students in a mainstream Higher Education setting.

The third thread is the focus on *using what is already known to generate suggestions* regarding what needs to be done to improve inclusion, access, and success of deaf students. Most, if not all, contributors conclude their chapters with a discussion of 'further issues to be considered', 'suggestions for practitioners' or 'questions that remain'. Generally, these are designed to lead readers towards further inquiry or improved practice. Given the range of contributors to the volume, most readers will find something that addresses their needs in these discussions.

Finally, there is the thread of '*touchstone themes*' or educational issues that appear throughout all sections of the book. Some themes that this reader found particularly salient are literacy, accommodations, funding, and isolation. Each of these themes represents a critical aspect of educational inclusion for deaf students, often serving as markers of access and exclusion, success and failure. Further, the degree to which each of these issues is successfully addressed by a particular institution of Higher Education often correlates with student persistence in the programme. The variance across all institutions of Higher Education creates a climate in which choices for deaf students are still de facto limited. Ironically, the more advanced the student's educational pursuits, the more he or she is challenged in each of these areas. Thus the post-graduate student faces an academic culture in which there is often less awareness of the learning styles of deaf students and related accommodations, reduced funding for support services, increased emphasis on literacy as evidence of mastery, and further isolation at a time when incidental learning and peer networking is most critical for academic success. Perhaps this is to be expected, since post-graduate work is the final step in academic studies and thus the last educational frontier for deaf students.

In conclusion, this is a timely volume that addresses a critical area of educational preparation. As teachers, educators, advisers, support service providers, disability coordinators and administrators, perhaps in a second edition of this volume we will be reading about new strategies that enhance success of deaf students in further education, including post-graduate studies. Maybe we will be enjoying the fruits of this effort, including new collegial working relationships with deaf graduates of Higher Education programmes. That would be a wonderful thing!

Professor Susan Foster, PhD
Department of Research and Teacher Education
National Technical Institute for the Deaf
Rochester Institute of Technology
Rochester, NY, United States

Introduction

Despite a growing number of deaf students entering Higher Education Institutions in the United Kingdom, there has not previously been a single book that addresses the challenges posed by this increased access and uptake of educational opportunities. This book brings together for the first time a blend of theory, research and practice relating to the support of deaf students in Higher Education in the UK. The range of contributors, their national and international reputations in this field, and the innovative nature of the diverse materials gathered offers an indispensable resource to all those delivering support to, or receiving support as, deaf students on university courses. Focusing predominantly on the United Kingdom, this book is also relevant to a wider international audience in a field which is actively seeking to promote and establish global networks amongst practitioners and policymakers. Evidence of this interest is provided by a recent on-line conference focussed on supporting deaf people, which attracted 187 participants from eighteen countries (www.online-conference.co.uk).

The model of support which is developing in the UK and described in these chapters represents a significant shift in practice, moving away from that founded on the now widely discredited medical perspective, to one reflecting a social framework. In the United States, the catalyst for this change was the 1990 *Americans with Disabilities Act*, whilst this shift has been mirrored in the UK by the 1995 *Disability Discrimination Act* (DDA). Part IV of the DDA (*Special Educational Needs and Disability Act* 2001, enforced 2002) requires educational institutions to monitor entry, progression and outcomes for deaf students, whilst the 2005 Disability Equality Duty means that they must promote disability actively and take into account the needs of disabled people when making decisions or developing policy. In the wake of this, it is expected that deaf students will enter a wider range of institutions in increasing numbers. The ways in which institutions will need to respond to the consequent demand to become inclusive, proactive, consultative and anticipatory in their support for deaf students are all addressed within this book. With contributions from researchers and practitioners, and including personal testimony from undergraduate and postgraduate deaf students, this volume offers illuminating and fresh perspectives on the many elements of good practice and quality provision.

The idea for this volume originated with researchers and practitioners currently working in UK Higher Education institutions. The volume reflects a concentration of expertise, with contributors bringing together wide-ranging experience gathered over many years in a variety of settings. The book showcases the work of notable practitioners who have either led their institutions in developing tailored services and support for deaf students or who work nationally in the UK via CHESS (the Consortium of Higher Education Support Services for Deaf Students) to support other practitioners in developing their appreciation of the distinct experience of deaf students. Other contributors have a wealth of experience in working with deaf students within Higher Education, whilst the views of deaf students themselves are also represented, giving invaluable service-users' perspectives.

Readership

British disability discrimination legislation now requires all public authorities to make access arrangements for deaf people, including Local Education Authorities with responsibility for sixth form students, Further Education Colleges and Higher Education Institutions. This book is therefore of interest and practical benefit to all those working in this field and includes:

- Disability Coordinators in Further and Higher Education institutions
- Deaf students in Higher and Further Education
- Parents of deaf pupils and students
- Interpreters and interpreter trainers
- Support workers and their trainers
- Careers Advisers
- National deaf Organizations and organizations dedicated to supporting deaf young people
- National organizations for students with Disabilities and Learning Difficulties

In addition, the book will be of interest to researchers and teachers within Deaf Studies, Disability Studies, Sociology and related social sciences, and organizational behaviour and organizational theory academic communities.

Structure of the book

The book consists of fifteen chapters, which fall into three broad categories: policy, accessibility and transition; support services; post-graduate study. The contributors to this book include practitioners, theorists, policymakers and service users, and as such represent a wide range of perspectives and experiences. As well as providing evidence-based analyses and perspectives, each chapter concludes by highlighting key concepts, principles, issues and questions for further consideration and exploration by the reader. To assist in this ongoing analysis, useful further reading lists are provided. These signposts support the reader in considering the theories and practice under discussion in relation to their own contextual circumstances and help to disseminate the sharing of good practice and practical experience to national and international readerships. The book concludes with a discussion on how services and practices might take a more Disability Studies based approach as the basis for future development.

The chapters which comprise this timely and innovative work are outlined below.

1. Students with disabilities in Higher Education in the twenty-first century

Alan Hurst

This chapter considers the development of policy and provision in three sections: national policy and provision, changes in funding, and the legal context (including the amendments made following the DDA 2005). This is followed by a brief overview comparing developments in the UK with what has been happening in other countries. The dimension which makes the UK distinctive is the focus on inclusive learning and teaching. The chapter therefore concludes with an exploration of inclusive pedagogy under five headings, based around the 'Teachability' project in Scotland: information, course design, learning and teaching, assessment, and quality monitoring and enhancement.

2. At a 'Headstart' workshop: developing support services for deaf students in Higher Education

Jannine Williams

This chapter provides an overview of one of a series of workshops organised by the Royal National Institute for Deaf People (RNID) project 'Headstart'. These workshops were designed to support the development of support services for deaf students in Higher Education. The chapter outlines how the workshop aimed to offer participants perspectives from two different universities on working collaboratively to establish services which met each institution's particular support context. The chapter discusses approaches to establishing support services, factors influencing the shape of the services provided and offers practical suggestions to assist readers in developing their own provision.

3. The experience of d/Deaf FE students moving to Higher Education
Rachel O'Neill and Michelle Jones

Examining the experiences of fifteen deaf learners who made the transition from Further to Higher Education between 1996 and 2004, O'Neill and Jones question the experiences and expectations deaf learners accrue in Further Education and how these impact on the practical, academic and social success of their Higher Education. This research, invaluable to both Further Education and Higher Education tutors, offers insights which can be applied more broadly and help institutions to identify why some deaf students progress, some fail, and others simply do not apply to universities at all.

4. Year Zero for Deaf Students: an access course for deaf students
Gary Quinn and Nicola Nunn

This chapter describes the unique access course for deaf students based at the University of Central Lancashire. The authors track the progress of the Year Zero students from pre-entry to post–graduation, exploring how the course affected their study and choice of career. Successes within the programme are highlighted as are some of the issues that arose from its delivery. Students recount their experiences of the course and discuss the benefits of discrete access provision. In providing a rationale and structure for the course, this chapter gives practical guidance to other institutions wishing to develop similar programmes.

5. The naked deaf student
Donna Williams, Gavin Lilley and Paul Scott

Three deaf students describe their differing experiences of university life, outlining the difficulties faced at times in their academic careers, as well as explaining how they overcame some of the barriers to success. These personal journeys have crossed difficult terrain such as the oft-dreaded work placement, foreign exchange visits and learning a foreign language. In this candid and informed discussion, the authors evaluate the support mechanisms that worked for them, and offer insight into areas ripe for improvement. In presenting these stories, the authors afford us a rare glimpse of the real deaf student perspective, which is guaranteed to both enlighten and inform.

6. Can you put that in writing?
Kay McCrea and Paddy Turner

Reviewing the history of the development of notetaking services for deaf people within Higher Education, the authors unpack and explore some of the issues currently facing notetakers within the sector. From the practicalities of provision of service, through the training process and the monitoring of standards and quality, notetaking for deaf students is thoroughly re-evaluated. Using a broad evidence-base, this chapter seeks to develop a template for the inclusion of new technologies in the context of increasing numbers of deaf students, and looks towards the professionalisation of note-taking.

7. Investigating literacy support for deaf students in UK Higher Education
Graham Turner

Drawing upon the academic disciplines of education studies, sociology and linguistics to begin to examine the service provided by Language Tutors, Graham Turner is directly interested in the development of all parties' understanding of the process and its implications, and the generation of relevant institutional policy. The chapter sets out a number of contextual factors, with particular reference to the use of literacy skills. Drawing upon the New Literacy Studies (cf Baynham, Street and Lankshear), the chapter outlines a theoretical framework and illustrates its application by describing a particular, detailed example from the author's own experiences, drawing out key points for service provision.

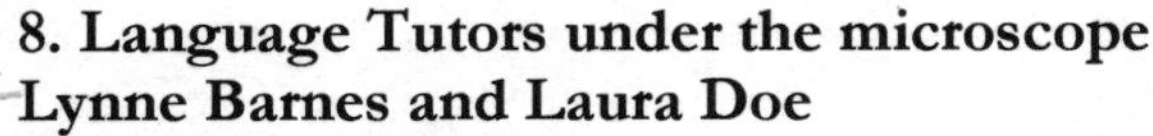

8. Language Tutors under the microscope
Lynne Barnes and Laura Doe

This chapter questions the role(s) and investigates the working practices of Language Tutors, within a consideration of some of the broader issues surrounding inclusive educational practices, such as whether a minimal level of English should be required for deaf students entering university. Reflecting on a number of key questions, notably role definition, the diversity of current practices and what constitutes good practice, the role of translation skills, and appropriate training and qualifications, this chapter seeks to describe and to posit how Language Tutors *do* and *should* respond to the diversity of language fluency amongst deaf students.

9. We've started, but can we finish? Towards accessible assessment for deaf students

Lynne Barnes

Written from the perspective of an experienced adviser for deaf students, Lynne Barnes critically evaluates current assessment procedures, questioning whether deaf students are disadvantaged by Higher Education assessments requiring an ability to understand and respond to written English questions or tasks. The difficulty experienced by some students in effectively conveying their knowledge via written English provides the backdrop to much of this chapter. The practicalities of enabling students to produce their work in British Sign Language provides the basis for outlining potential alternative assessment arrangements for deaf students. Further discussion places these arguments within the framework of increased diversity amongst the whole student population and the need for more inclusive learning and assessment.

10. Integrating technology, improving access
Kevan Williams and John Hodgson

There are many ways in which technology can be utilised to enhance the student experience, and this is particularly valid in relation to deaf students, for whom technology can be harnessed to ensure equality of access to the learning materials readily enjoyed by their peers. In this chapter, the authors address both the development and effective implementation of a variety of learning technologies. These include online communication using Macromedia Breeze web conferencing, the use of icons and images to more effectively access the web, multicast live and on-demand streaming video techniques, and the effective integration of the e-Learning toolset to create co-ordinated content delivery that is simultaneously available to all users. Including user feedback from a number of case studies, this chapter seeks to advance methods of incorporating technology into the support of deaf students in education.

11. Sign language interpreting in Higher Education – a period of progress?
Sarah Obasi

Sign language interpreting as a profession has witnessed a decade of rapid change whist the wider field of interpreting has also been the subject of increased scholarship and research. These academic insights perform a useful role in revealing the role of the interpreter as one which is much more complicated than would first appear. This is particularly true within the interpreted class room which has its own environmental and institutional dynamics adding further complexity to the role. Interpreting has developed into a profession which now has the potential to develop a multitude of specialisms within an established professional footing. This chapter reflects on some of the changes over a twelve year period, and its impact on interpreting, interpreters and their relationships with the deaf community.

12. Hearing education through the ears of others
Frank Harrington

For many deaf students, the principal form of direct access in the classroom is through the services of a BSL/English Interpreter. The first 'in depth' study into the activities of the interpreted classroom in the UK was undertaken between 1997 and 2000, and directly influenced changes not only in the way in which interpreters and deaf students work in educational settings, but also into the ways in which the interpreters themselves are trained. Increasingly, interpreter training is being delivered in Higher Education institutions, with student interpreters being taught in the same environment in which they are supporting deaf students. This paper will draw together some observations of the intricacies of classroom interaction, and its impact on deaf students, before going on to look at the education and training of the interpreters who work in these settings. It will explore the changing nature of the training required for interpreters in a new millennium, and the changing needs of the students themselves.

13. A bridge too far? The issues for deaf students in research education
Val Farrar

Deaf students face particular issues in the research environment. Differing hugely from the undergraduate experience, these differences have real implications for those concerned with support. The author, a seasoned advisor, draws on her experience to examine participation rates for deaf students in research education, together with rates of completion, and transition to employment. Informed by students' own accounts, this chapter seeks to both identify the barriers to access, and describe ways of surmounting them. The student perception of research study, the language of research, the relationship between supervisor and student, the challenges of the thesis and the viva, and entering academic employment are key topics addressed here.

14. The loneliness of the long distance post-graduate student
Steve Emery

This chapter, written by a recent post-graduate student, illustrates the joys and frustrations of one deaf student's experiences of undertaking a full-time PhD. Steve Emery reflects constructively on applying for a research studentship, transferring from MPhil to PhD, interpreting provision, the process of undertaking research, and the experience of research supervision. Helping to pave the way for others to follow, this chapter provides insightful material for those soon to be concerned with the inevitable, impending rise in demand for access to postgraduate education from deaf graduates.

15. Developing services and inclusive practices for deaf students
Jannine Williams and Hayley Quinn

Briefly describing the key factors in the development of support services for deaf students in Higher Education in the UK, this chapter seeks to orientate the novice reader and provide useful background to those seeking to establish a system of support in the current legislative climate. The chapter goes on to suggest that critiquing the Disability Studies literature and employing a narrative approach to researching deaf students' experiences can assist universities and policy makers to reflect upon how they should develop services and inclusive practices across their institutions.

Note on terminology

Within the chapters of this book, the word 'deaf' is written in a variety of forms, including 'Deaf', 'deaf', 'D/deaf' and 'd/Deaf'. This multiplicity of expression reflects the views of the individual authors on the cultural aspects of deafness, all of which are respected here. The capitalised 'Deaf' has particular connotations, as highlighted by Woodward (1972) who introduced this term to denote those individuals who view their deafness not in medical/audiological terms but as a symbol of their social, cultural and linguistic identity. Within this book, 'deaf' is also used as a generic term without implying or assigning any particular status to any individual or group of people.

The accuracy of all references in the 'Further reading' section of each chapter is the responsibility of individual contributors.

Biographies of contributors

Lynne Barnes taught deaf children and supported deaf students in a number of colleges around the country before returning home to Preston to set up the Deaf Studies degree programme at the University of Central Lancashire (UCLan) in 1993. As Subject Co-ordinator she leads a team comprising both deaf and hearing colleagues who individually and collectively have established a national and international reputation for excellence in teaching and research. In addition, Lynne is also an Adviser for Deaf Students within the university, drawing upon her experience within this field. Her main research focus has been on issues relating to deaf students in Higher Education, particularly understanding the particular learning issues faced by deaf students and exploring the pedagogic implications for the deliverer and learner. She has several publications and conference papers to her credit on these key aspects of deaf education. Lynne also has a record of external grants for development and research in this field which have included establishing the first and so far only national Access Course for deaf students wishing to enter Higher Education. She is a member of the CHESS (Consortium of Higher Education Support Services for Deaf Students) Planning Group and is a member of several editorial boards and national councils.

Laura Doe graduated from the University of Central Lancashire with a First Class Honours degree in Deaf Studies in 2006. She now works as a Project Officer with UCLan's Deaf Studies team and is currently working on the SignOn! project which involves developing an online English course for international deaf sign language users. Laura also works as a Language Tutor for deaf students and she lectures on the Deaf Studies course. Laura has a particular interest in the impact of public and government policy on deaf people and she is currently pursuing PhD research opportunities within this field.

Steve Emery, who is deaf, is originally from Brighton, on the south coast of England, and has lived, worked and studied all over the UK and the Republic of Ireland. He is currently based at Heriot-Watt University (Scotland). In 2007 he successfully defended his PhD thesis on 'Citizenship and the Deaf Community'. He is a qualified counsellor and holds a BA Cultural Studies. Other work experience with the deaf community includes advice work and community development work. Prior to his work with the community he was employed for several years as a typesetter and became involved in the socialist and trade union movement. His work projects as a research assistant include research on a sociolinguistic history of British Sign Language, and an exploration of deaf people's attitudes and beliefs in relation to genetics and genetic counselling. Steve has travelled extensively, including the completion of a seven month solo round the world trip, a journey which covered every continent.

Val Farrar has worked for over thirty years as a teacher, adviser and researcher in Secondary, Further, Community and Higher Education. Most recently she coordinated two Higher Education Funding Council for England (HEFCE) projects. The first of these involved setting up a national network of university careers staff (the DDN) in order to develop careers work with deaf and disabled students. The second HEFCE project sought to improve provision across the sector for disabled research students. She now works as a freelance researcher and staff developer in diversity and Higher Education.

Frank Harrington joined the Deaf Studies Team at UCLan in May 1997 as a project officer on a HEFCE funded project looking at deaf students access to Higher Education. Frank is a qualified BSL/English interpreter, and he has researched the use of interpreters in the classroom. Now a Senior Lecturer in Deaf Studies, Frank is Course Leader of the Post-graduate Diploma in BSL/English Interpreting, and has research interests in social policy, social inclusion and exclusion and discourse analysis, particularly in relation to deaf people who use British Sign Language (BSL) as their first or preferred language. Much of his work has focussed on the bilingual BSL/English interpreter and the impact s/he has in various settings where deaf people need to access information. This work has lead to developments in interpreter education at UCLan, as well as continuing to inform discussions around education for deaf people. He is also currently reading for a PhD with Lancaster University in the Department of Religious Studies, looking at the changing nature of the Christian Church in the 21st century.

John Hodgson has been working in IT for thirteen years, specialising in accessibility for seven years. He has championed the technical needs of disabled staff and students throughout the University of Central Lancashire providing a proactive response to their current and future requirements and has responsibility for research and provision of specialist training to deaf and disabled users. John has also campaigned publishers for providing their texts in electronic format and has provided many awareness presentations on internet accessibility and other related subjects.

Professor Alan Hurst was born in Atherton, Lancashire, and holds degrees from Hull, Manchester and Lancaster universities. After teaching history in school he became a lecturer in education at Lancashire Polytechnic. He joined the National Bureau for Handicapped Students (now Skill: National Bureau for Students with Disabilities) in 1978 and remains a Trustee. He investigated access to Higher Education and disabled students for his doctoral thesis, published as 'Steps Towards Graduation' in 1993. The title of Professor was awarded by the University of Central Lancashire for his work with disabled students in the university, nationally and internationally. In June 2005 he was awarded the honorary degree of Doctor of the University by the Open University in recognition of his contribution to developing policy and provision for people with disabilities in Higher Education. He continues to deliver staff training, publish papers, lecture and lead workshops at conferences throughout the world. In 2006 he completed a practical guide on staff development and inclusion, the product of a HEFCE- funded project.

Michelle Jones is a deaf BSL user who grew up with an oral education and developed her BSL skills from the age of 18. She has worked in education since 1998 and is currently employed at City College Manchester as a qualified Teacher of the Deaf, supporting deaf learners with range of skills and abilities, including students with learning difficulties, minimal signing skills, and emotional and/or behavioural issues. Michelle's responsibilities include teaching and assessment of new deaf learners, deaf awareness training, language tutorial sessions and liaising with the Deaf Access Team.

Gavin Lilley joined the University of Central Lancashire initially as a student on the then newly founded Year Zero for Deaf Students, progressing to eventually gain a BA Deaf Studies. He is still at UCLan, working as a Project Officer on the collaborative 'BSL:QED' project funded by a grant from the Fund for the Development of Teaching and Learning. He also teaches BSL on UCLan's various Deaf Studies undergraduate courses and hopes to study for a Higher degree in the near future.

Kay McCrea gained a degree in Applied Social Studies before becoming a qualified Social Worker. Kay went on to specialise as a Social Worker with Deaf People. After a career change in 1994, she began working as an Educational Interpreter at the University of Central Lancashire where later she was asked to expand and develop services for deaf students within the University. As Team Leader of the Specialised Learning Resource Unit (SLRU), a thriving service that includes a long-established transcription service and one of the largest and most highly qualified teams of BSL/English interpreters in any Higher Education institution in the UK, Kay has been proactive in creating a more accessible and inclusive environment for deaf, blind and disabled students at the University. In addition, Kay has been instrumental in setting up a notetaker service at the University, developing training for notetakers, students and university staff. More recently, Kay ran a short course to train electronic notetakers and was involved with the production of the RNID's 'toolkit' for training electronic notetakers.

Nicola Nunn holds a BA Deaf Studies from UCLan, where she has worked as a Lecturer with the Deaf Studies team since 2002. She previously spent many years working in the deaf community, promoting and teaching BSL and actively raising awareness of the deaf community. Since qualifying as an Further Education teacher in 1996, Nicola has gained certificates in BSL Linguistics and Advanced BSL Teaching from City University, London and the Postgraduate Higher Education Teaching Certificate. She is a qualified Assessor for BSL NVQs and has gained the highest possible level of achievement in her own preferred language, BSL. Nicola's research interests are mainly in the field of applied linguistics in the context of language teaching and learning.

Sarah Obasi is the Course Leader for the Masters degree in Equality and Diversity, based in the University of Central Lancashire's Centre for Ethnicity and Health. She is a qualified BSL/English Interpreter and works part-time interpreting mainly within the Higher Education environment. Sarah is of Nigerian origin and grew up in a bilingual, bi-cultural household which fostered her enthusiasm for interpreting. In addition to interpreting, Sarah's research interests are in race, ethnicity and deafness and the interface between the three. She is at present studying for a PhD in Equality and Diversity.

Rachel O'Neill is a lecturer in deaf education at Moray House School of Education in the University of Edinburgh where she trains teachers of deaf children. She previously worked at City College Manchester as a tutor of deaf students. She has an Masters degree in linguistics, experience in Teaching English to Speakers of Other Languages (TESOL) and an interest in teaching English to deaf learners. She is currently working with a group of deaf scientists in Scotland to develop curriculum signs for school science with BSL explanations.

Gary Quinn joined Heriot-Watt University, Edinburgh, in March 2006 as Project Officer for the Training of Tutors (ToT) project, which is funded by the Scottish Executive. He is also involved in a range of smaller-scale and pilot projects in sign language research and application. He previously worked at the University of Central Lancashire for six years, initially as Course Leader of Year Zero for Deaf Students course before taking up a Lecturership in Deaf Studies. He also acted as Research Assistant for the National Lottery Charities Board funded Minimal Language Skills project. After gaining a Post Graduate Certificate in Management in 1999 and a Post Graduate Certificate in Learning and Teaching in Higher Education in 2003, both at the University of Central Lancashire, Gary gained his Masters degree in Linguistics at Lancaster University in 2005. His particular interests and areas of study are historical linguistics, pragmatics, sociolinguistics, applied linguistics and dialect and variations in BSL.

Hayley Quinn has worked with deaf people for the past seventeen years in education, employment and health and social care. She worked as a Disabilities Adviser for deaf students with the majority of her experience grounded in community development work raising the profile of deaf issues, challenging practice and working with deaf people to drive forward service improvements in the public, private and voluntary sector. Hayley currently works as a Regional Development Officer for Skills for Care North East focusing on workforce development within the social care sector and is the lead officer for People Who Use Services, and Carers. She is currently completing an Masters degree in Social Research.

Paul Scott is deaf and a native BSL user, having been born into a deaf family. He attended a mainstream school in Norwich and later moved to Derby College for Deaf people for three years before going to Jordan in the Middle East. In his three years there, he taught English in a deaf school and also worked with the local deaf community delivering culture development training. Paul graduated from the University of Central Lancashire with a BA Counselling and Psychotherapy and Deaf Studies.

Professor Graham Turner has had an international reputation for his work since the 1980s in the fields of Applied Sign Language and Deaf Studies. Entering the field professionally as a member of the research team which produced the first bilingual BSL-English dictionary, he has authored over a hundred research papers and edited two international refereed journals. He has worked closely with a wide range of deaf and hearing colleagues to devise and deliver a number of projects and programmes aimed at enhancing understanding of signed language and deaf communities. Since 2005, Professor Turner has been the Director of the Centre for Translation & Interpreting Studies in Scotland, part of Heriot-Watt University's award-winning Department of Languages & Intercultural Studies. The Department provides a range of research and study opportunities, blending theory and application across many modern languages, and hosts a vibrant doctoral programme in intercultural studies and applied linguistics.

Paddy Turner currently works for Sheffield Hallam University as a manager within their Disabled Student Support Team and as an Assessor for deaf Students within Sheffield Regional Assessment Centre. He is a Director of NADP Ltd (The National Association of Disability Practitioners) and has been an active member of HECFE (The Consortium of Higher Education Support Services with deaf Students) for nearly ten years. He has organised and presented at many conferences and workshops during that time. Paddy successfully completed a degree in Sign Language Interpreting from Wolverhampton University although management commitments have now put a stop to his interpreting career. He has been assessing the needs of deaf students since 1998 and finds it a deeply satisfying and fascinating process. He believes firmly in keeping the aim of creating an inclusive student experience as the guiding principle in all that he does. Paddy received some of the earliest notetaker training in 1993 and has taught many courses in notetaking including electronic notetaking (ENT). He initiated one of the first in-house ENT services in the country at Sheffield Hallam University and took an active part in the development of the ENT software Stereotype.

Donna Williams is a graduate of the University of Central Lancashire, gaining a BA Deaf Studies and Philosophy. She now works as a freelance journalist and 'Plain English' translator, and has written and performed material with *Deafinitely Theatre* and *Shape Arts*. She hopes to continue her studies with an Masters degree at the Centre of Deaf Studies in Bristol and her ambition is to become a recognised deaf writer.

Jannine Williams began working with young deaf people in 1997, developing a regional programme of events, projects and training and development activities for deaf, hard of hearing and hearing young people to encourage partnership working and personal development. Jannine has worked in a range of Higher Education institutions developing services for deaf students, disabled staff and diversity and equality initiatives and was Convenor of the CHESS (Consortium of Higher Education Support Services for Deaf Students) Planning Group. Jannine is currently researching disabled academics' experiences of career and organisation at Newcastle Business School.

Kevan Williams has worked at the University of Central Lancashire since 1996, designing and developing multimedia content for campus-wide use. His expertise is in the area of video, audio, online interactions and the institutional support of strategies designed to embed technology in teaching and learning, primarily with a focus on issues of accessibility. He also develops CD/DVD titles to support various academic disciplines with a view to enhancing the learner experience.

Section One:
Policy, accessibility and transition

CHAPTER ONE

Students with disabilities in Higher Education in the twenty-first century – policies, provision and progress?

Professor Alan Hurst

Introduction

Sometimes those working to support disabled students in Higher Education become frustrated and disillusioned by what might be perceived to be slow progress. Nevertheless some progress has been made. The number of students declaring that they have an impairment either on entry or during their time in Higher Education has grown year by year.[1] However, there is still the need to improve participation rates generally in some institutions as well as within particular faculties and departments. At the level of policy and provision, there has been a shift in focus since the mid 1990's. From improving access and increasing student numbers which appeared to be the major focus of the first national survey of disabled students in universities (NIC, 1974), the major concern has now become the quality of the Higher Education experience, especially in learning, teaching, and assessment. This can be demonstrated by considering the projects and initiatives supported by both the English and Scottish Higher Education Funding Councils.

[1] The overall number of applications from those disclosing a disability was 15,997 in 1995 and 37,700 in 2004, of whom 16,746 took up places – source UCAS Statistics

In England, some of the Higher Education Academy Subject Centres have published very useful guides about the inclusion of disabled students into their curricula (e.g. in engineering, geography, and social work). In Scotland, the excellent 'Teachability' project has prompted all teaching staff to review their classroom practices in order to evaluate the extent to which there are barriers to inclusion. In both England and Scotland, there have also been important research projects which have tried to explore the quality of the learning experience from the students' perspectives (Fuller et al 2004, Riddell et al 2005).

Models of disability and conceptions of independence and equality

There have been important developments in the theoretical approaches within the field of disabilities since 1975 which have led to consequent changes in policies and practices. Thirty years ago, the position adopted could be described as the individual/medical/deficit model, which sees all problems and challenges faced by people with impairments as their own. Impairment was viewed as an illness; people were seen as being deficient in some attribute such as hearing, mobility and vision. It was left to the individuals to try to resolve any difficulties themselves, often with the help of charities, social services, and the medical profession. Within Higher Education in the early days, this was reflected in the close involvement of university medical staff in the development of policy and provision (Hurst 1993). In the late 1970's/early 1980's, a group of disabled people proposed the replacement of the original model with what was described as the social/educational/political model of disability. From this perspective, any difficulties and challenges faced by people with impairments result from the social construction of society. For example, for people with mobility impairments, problems of access to public buildings and public transport are created by the design of these facilities. This has now become recognised more widely; in the UK, anti-discrimination legislation has tried to ensure that access to public facilities is guaranteed. In more recent times, there have been criticisms of the social/educational/political model; for example, because of its lack of recognition of the impact of an impairment on individuals. One instance of this is the lack of consideration for the pain and discomfort experienced by individuals (Shakespeare and Watson 2001). There has also been some suggestion that this model has become the new orthodoxy and is not open to challenges (Low 2001).

Within Higher Education there are still remnants of the individual/medical/deficit model. For example, the standard application form used by the majority of those wanting to enter universities asks applicants to indicate the nature of their impairment by using a numerical coding system. They can indicate whether they are blind, D/deaf etc. Were the system to move towards a genuine social/educational model the categories would need to be written to allow users to say if they have difficulties with print materials, oral work etc. Institutions would then need to consider how these difficulties might be addressed and minimised. The onus of responsibility shifts from individual students to the institutions and the staff they employ.

With regard to conceptions of independence and independent living, two principles in particular are important: the principle of having choices and the principle of having the right to take decisions about one's own life. Firstly it is important to ensure that disabled students experience the same levels of choice regarding what and where to study as their non-disabled peers. Occasionally, in connection with choice, a case is proposed for establishing 'centres of excellence'. This would mean that in every region one institution would develop high quality policy and provision for those with a particular impairment, whilst its neighbours would choose a different impairment on which to base their support facilities. Such an approach has a particular appeal when there is a focus on supposed cost effectiveness. However, the approach is unsound and unacceptable. It places restrictions on choices. It assumes also that studying the same subject in different universities is identical in relation to subject content, core knowledge and available options. Secondly, disabled people have the right to take decisions about their own lives. It is no longer acceptable to inform students that the institution does not think they can complete the course for which they are applying. The situation has changed, since new laws make it illegal to discriminate solely on grounds of disability. So, if an applicant is rejected for a place on a course, it is necessary to provide sound reasons for the decision if the institution wishes to avoid possible litigation. This does not mean that there is unlimited access for those with disabilities. What it does mean is that institutions need to be very clear about why an application has been rejected. One approach to this is to identify the core requirements of a study programme, to investigate whether the applicant might meet these with some modifications to the course. This point will be explored further in a later section of this paper.

Finally, as will be seen, there has been an important focus on the concept of equality. Yet, it might be argued that this is not really at the core of the changes. Rather, the latter are about equity. It is the difference between treating people the same (equally) and treating them according to their situation (fairly). Taking the simple example of a cake which has to be divided between a group of people, if slices are based on equality, all would get the same irrespective of whether the size of each slice is appropriate to the context and the individual. For instance, dividing a small sponge cake between a large group would result in everyone getting little more than crumbs. In this instance, equal treatment for all could be unfair to some. Moving to the principle of fairness, it might be agreed that, because of their position, some will be given more than others. Some of the recipients may not have eaten for some time so it is agreed that they may deserve more than others. Perhaps, this is really what is at the core of the legislation and the policies to be discussed below.

Disabled students and the law

Whilst groups such as women and people from minority communities have had anti-discrimination laws protecting them since the mid-1970's, it was not until 1995 that legal protection for people with disabilities was provided.

The Disability Discrimination Act 1995

The Disability Discrimination Act 1995 (DDA) begins by defining 'disability'. According to the law, this is 'a physical or mental impairment which has a substantial and long term effect on the person's ability to carry out normal day-to-day activities' (DDA 1995, Appendix II). It also defines discrimination as treating an individual unfairly compared to people without disabilities because of the person's impairment. Organisations have to make 'reasonable adjustments' in order to allow and facilitate access to their goods and services for disabled people. They also have to act in anticipatory ways rather than responding in an ad hoc reactive manner to a situation when it arises. For instance, whilst there might so far never have been the need to provide printed information in various formats, organisations need to plan for a future in which they will encounter people with visual impairments. When the Act was passed by Parliament, the main concerns were access to employment, and to goods and services. Policy and provision in education was not covered by this law although it did require institutions to devise and publish Disability Statements. This was an attempt to improve the quality of information available to disabled people.[2] It took another six years for

---

[2] For a detailed review of Disability Statements see Higher Education Funding Council for England 1998. This is also relevant to the discussion on the Disability Equality Schemes which follows shortly

the law to be extended to embrace policy and provision in schools, colleges and universities.

The Special Educational Needs and Disability Act 2001

The Special Educational Needs and Disability Act (SENDA) became law in 2001. In effect this is really Part Four of the DDA. It uses the same definitions of disability and of discrimination and the same requirements for 'reasonable adjustments' and anticipatory duties are now placed on schools, colleges and universities. The first stage of implementation began in September 2002, auxiliary aids and services were covered from September 2003, and the physical environment from September 2005. Within Higher Education, all services are covered by the law including learning, teaching and assessment, distance and e-learning, and partnership and overseas provision. Discrimination can be avoided by making 'reasonable adjustments' and also by complying with the anticipatory requirement of the SENDA. Changes should not be made as a direct result of enrolling a student with a disability; rather, those responsible for the course should have planned in advance for what they need to do to make the course accessible and inclusive. There is a key role here for staff training and the development of high levels of disability awareness since the provision of such training could be central to any defence if discrimination is alleged.

Rejecting applications from disabled students

Within the law it remains possible to refuse entry to a student with a disability on a number of grounds. Firstly, the decision might be based on the need to maintain academic standards. However, in order not to put themselves at risk, course teams and admissions tutors need to be clear about criteria used to select students. Secondly, the decision might stem from there being parts of courses which are a basic requirement but which some students with disabilities might be unable to complete and where 'reasonable adjustments' cannot be made. This is often linked to the involvement of external professional and regulatory bodies Thirdly, the decision might result from 'reasonable adjustments' that would be 'material' and 'substantial', perhaps involving high costs within a very restricted budget.

Has discrimination occurred?

If discrimination is alleged to have taken place, there are key issues to consider. Firstly, the individual needs to have a disability as defined by the law. Secondly, are the services covered by the law? Thirdly, has there been either less favourable treatment or lack of 'reasonable adjustment'? Fourthly has the student disclosed a disability? If the institution can prove that the individual did not disclose, it is unlikely that the allegation can be proved. However, institutions have a responsibility to ensure that students have several opportunities to disclose information about their disability. In itself this raises further questions, since there are issues about who the information is disclosed to and whether the individual asks that the information remains confidential since confidentiality requests are seen as 'reasonable adjustments'. Specific guidance on matters relating to disclosure has been issued (Department for Education and Skills 2002) as well as some useful general information (Learning and Skills Council 2003, Rose 2006, Skill 2005).

There have already been disputes between students and universities but so far they have been resolved by the Disability Rights Commission (DRC) before any action in courts of law. The DRC has provided some information on its website about the kinds of issues raised. However, both the DDA and the SENDA do seem to reflect much more the approach of a social/educational/political model of disability with the focus on changing the context rather than the individual.

The Disability Discrimination Act 2005

The most recent legislation is the Disability Discrimination Act 2005. This was passed by Parliament in March 2005 and passed into law in stages by the end of 2006. It includes changes to access to employment and to goods and services as well as revising the definition of disability to cover more impairments. There are general duties, such as the ending of discrimination and of harassment, and more specific duties. The Act covers both students and staff and so it might be seen as a 'whole institution approach' to eliminate discrimination. The most important point for colleges and universities is that they have a Disability Equality Duty (DED). This means that they must promote disability actively and take into account the needs of disabled people when making decisions or developing policy. For example, they will need to monitor the admission, retention and achievements of disabled students. They must also each produce a Disability Equality Scheme (DES) (a three year plan) which must involve disabled people in its compilation and which must demonstrate how policies and provision have had an impact on disabled people and how the scheme will be checked. Impact assessments will have to be done on all existing policies and procedures to ensure that universities and colleges take into account any poor quality decisions they have made in the past (see Skill 2005 for a more detailed outline of the legislation).

There are a number of concerns regarding the DED. In some ways the requirement to devise and publish a DES is a threat to the progress made in many HEIs with developing inclusive practices and mainstreaming procedures. Overall it is retrograde in that it is a return to making disability special. This could lead to more onus again being placed on specialist advisers rather than distributing responsibilities amongst all staff.

To begin with, there are concerns about some concepts and definitions. As suggested earlier there are concerns about the concept of 'equality'. Perhaps what is being sought is 'equity' in the sense of being fair. This could lead to some unequal treatment in the sense of what in the USA is called affirmative action. Indeed the DDA 2005 suggests that there might be unequal treatment in that HEIs must take into account disabled people's needs even if this means treating disabled people more favourably. In that sense the DDA contains a contradiction. Perhaps we should follow the example of Australia where an important report was called 'A Fair Go' and where institutions publish equity plans to obtain funding.

Secondly, the 'involvement' of disabled people - what does it mean? Can it be measured and quantified? What is it that people are involved in? Being 'involved' will mean disclosure so what about those staff and students who prefer to keep information about their impairments confidential? This might be more significant for people with unseen impairments but if people with unseen impairments are not involved then the process of meeting the DED and devising a DES will contribute to the continuation of stereotype images of impairment such as wheelchair users and blind people using seeing dogs.

There seem to be a number of approaches to 'involving' disabled staff and students. For example there might be elected representatives; there could be co-options; getting 'involvement' could be accomplished randomly; on the other hand, they might be selected. The guidance from the Equality Challenge Unit (ECU) reminds us of the dangers of self selection:

> 'Institutions may find that they have previously relied on a small group of active disabled staff and /or students for feedback. These individuals will continue to be of great importance in the preparation of a DES but it would not be wise for a handful of individuals to represent the full range of concerns within an institution's

disabled community'. (Equality Challenge Unit 2005b)

Not all NUS branches in Higher Education Institutions have disabled students' officers in post, and for those who do, having annually elected representatives caused issues with continuity.

If disclosure for both staff and students is confidential there are issues about how the initial approach and invitation to be involved is handled and who is responsible for the first contact. It would be interesting too if nobody wants to become 'involved'?

Thirdly there is the notion of 'impact'. Impact assessments have to be carried out but how is impact to be measured and evaluated? How will distinctions be made between short term and long term and between temporary and permanent?

If one looks in detail at the DED and the DES it appears that there is a wide range of variables potentially impacting on experiences of both staff and students with impairments. Will these be recognised and taken into account? For example there is:

- the size and scope of the HEI;
- the subject/course/programme in which staff are employed and students enrolled;
- the mode of employment /study (part-time, full -time);
- the type of impairment;
- the gender of the individual;
- the age of the individual;
- the community background of the individual.

The conclusion must be that the field is too broad to provide meaningful data. This seems to be acknowledged in guidance from the ECU (2005b). Paragraph 20 states:

> 'Disabled people are not a homogeneous group. They have multiple identities and other aspects of their identities may influence outcomes. Data on the number of disabled people with a black or ethnic minority background, the number of disabled women or the age of disabled staff, for example, will potentially be very useful when pursuing lines of enquiry about discrimination against particular groups'

Another concern is the ease or difficulty of contacting prospective students and applicants who it is suggested should be part of the process of compiling a DES. There are also the implications of any differences between staff interests and student interests. Questions also arise about the use of surrogates or disability 'experts' and experienced consultants and whether this might be acceptable in some circumstances. We must remember that the Disability Rights Commission (DRC) Code of Practice says:

> 'Involvement is particularly important given the under-representation of disabled people in positions which determine policies and priorities of public authorities'. (paragraph 2.19)

It is not clear what will happen when the DES are published. Will they go to the DRC? There is a danger that the DES from HEIs might sink without trace. If the situation is compared to the requirement for Disability Statements which was the case some years ago, at least the HECFE reported on good practice. Will the DRC will do something similar and if so what will the criteria be? What happens if a DES is unsatisfactory? What does 'unsatisfactory' mean?

Finally there is the fluidity of data. The ECU quite rightly reminds us:

> 'Disability is dynamic and relative to environment so data relating to the percentage of disabled people within an institution needs to be dynamically collected and maintained' (ECU 2005b: Paragraph 11)

Perhaps there is a need to consider the relative significance/importance of the DED. Many disability advisers feel that the main focus of the work in HEIs now should be on learning and teaching yet the DES could focus on broader environmental concerns such as physical access – a retrograde step. Even if this does not happen, the actual effort of compiling the DES will deflect attention from other perhaps more important concerns for example:

- the effectiveness and efficiency of the current system of DSA;
- the auditing of the use of the HECFE additional premium;
- the need for a new investigation of what might constitute base-line provision given the progress made since the original study published in 1999;
- the desirability of revising Section 3 of the QAA Code of Practice.

There will be considerable demands on the time of somebody which might be used more effectively in other ways.

It is no use being critical without suggesting something to take its place. One answer is that we make more use of existing procedures - for example the National Student Satisfaction Survey which could be modified further to include better feedback from disabled students. Secondly, we could use existing structures - for example the national funding councils, the Higher Education Academy, and especially its network of subject centres and in doing so replicate what is happening at national policy level in terms of making disability less special. Thirdly we could use existing systems in the HEIs- for example when new courses are to be validated and old courses renewed, it should be made a routine standard responsibility of validating panels to check on level of inclusiveness - this is about learning and teaching.

This suggestion leads into a consideration of developing learning, teaching and assessment which is genuinely inclusive of all students. A passing reference was made to the 'Teachability' project at the start of this chapter. It is time now to look at this in more detail. The 'Teachability' project began in Scotland in the mid-1990s. It is intended to prompt academic staff to consider ways in which their current classroom practices may help or hinder the full participation of students with a range of impairments in their subjects, courses and programmes of study. In doing so, it might be useful to bear in mind that some barriers might stem from the requirements and nature of the subject, course and study programmes themselves. Others might be created as a result of the strategies chosen for use in routine approaches to teaching and learning. Finally there are those barriers to participation which result from an unconscious approach to what is done in classrooms as part of the routine daily practices and which might be changed by maintaining heightened levels of sensitivity and awareness.

The project is based firmly on two key principles. First of all, academic staff are the most appropriate to take decisions about learning and teaching. Secondly, in adopting pedagogic styles which are inclusive, the actual practices involved (whilst being effective for students with a range of impairments) are usually effective for all students. In simple terms, what is being proposed is universal course design which would result in only a minimum of individual adaptations being necessary. In effect, what is being proposed is more efficient use of time rather than a significant additional workload or burden.

The 'Teachability' project worked with staff from different academic departments, who were asked to do the following tasks:

- identify ways in which the subject, course or programme for which they have responsibility or with which they were associated closely is accessible to students with a range of impairments (for example impaired hearing, mobility, vision, intellectual functioning);
- identify any barriers which might prevent the participation of students with a range of impairments;
- suggest how these barriers might be overcome;
- suggest what needs to be done in order to implement the strategies identified for overcoming the barriers;
- indicate ways in which attention can be drawn in an honest way to the possibilities and challenges posed by the current subjects, courses and programmes of study.

Experience in Scotland suggests that sometimes staff need some assistance at the start of the task. If this is the case then the key question to be addressed is: 'What can be considered to be the core requirements and core skills which all should have on completing the subject, course or programme of study successfully?'.

In order to assist staff in this audit of their courses, the project provided guidance on relevant topics: provision of information, design of courses, learning and teaching, assessment, and monitoring and evaluation. There are a series of short booklets which embrace these aspects and cover some specific dimensions of courses such as e-learning, work placements, study abroad etc.

In fact, undertaking an audit of provision based around tried and tested approaches such as 'Teachability' is one way of addressing the legal requirement for impact assessment. In this instance it is the impact of policies on pedagogy which are in focus.

Developments in England and the wider international context

Finding out about what is happening in other places is helpful in four ways. Firstly, it can be used to develop and enhance the policies and practices already in place. Secondly, it can offer reassurance about possible progress. Thirdly, it involves gathering information for staff and students who might wish to take part in exchanges. Finally, it gives the opportunity for comparative analysis based around some common themes.

Common themes

a: Anti-discrimination laws

There is a growing number of countries where there are anti-discrimination laws. Perhaps the best known are those of the United States of America which started legislation in the 1970s and more recently the Americans with Disabilities Act 1990. Other countries have followed suit; in New Zealand, a group of students successfully used the Human Rights Act against the University of Wellington.

b: Codes of practice

A code of practice on working with disabled students was published in Australia in 1998. This contains examples of good practices in several aspects of provision in named institutions. The Code of Practice published by the Quality Assurance Agency for Higher Education in England appeared in 1999 and offers general advice based around a collection of basic precepts.

c: National co-ordination

Probably the first country to appoint a national co-ordinator was Sweden in 1996, followed shortly afterwards by Scotland. The approach in England was to appoint a small team of experienced staff whose main responsibility was to monitor the special initiative projects funded by the HECFE. This developed into the National Disability Team which was disbanded at the end of 2005. The funding, development and monitoring of provision is to be embedded into mainstream approaches.

d: Specialist professional organisations for staff

Again it was in the USA that the first specialist organisation, the Association on Higher Education and Disability – AHEAD developed. Other countries followed this example, with the UK establishing the National Association of Disability Officers – NADO.[3]

e: Organisations of and for disabled students

In the UK in 1974 a conference was held, the outcome of which was the creation of the National Bureau for Handicapped Students, now known as Skill: National Bureau for Students with Disabilities. Trying to involve students working alongside professional has been taken up in many other countries. One of the most recent is 'Gaudeamus' which has been established in Moldova, a former Russian satellite country in which the

---

[3] Now the National Association of Disability Professionals (NADP)

general cultural context of disability and the levels of poverty make for a very challenging environment.

f: Voluntary organisations
Some countries have set up voluntary organisations such as Relais, Handicap and Sente in France, Handicap and Studie in the Netherlands and AHEAD in Ireland.

g: Provision and quality
Taking a global view, the development of policy and provision is patchy and uneven. This is evident at a number of levels – within countries and within continents (e.g. Northern and Southern Europe, Western and Eastern Europe)

h: Information
There has been a growth in the amount of information available about disabled students in Higher Education and this has occurred alongside the development of easier access to that information. Whilst there are signs of growth, relatively speaking there remains a lack of research on disability in Higher Education – for example about the experiences of disabled staff.

i: Questions for further attention
In some countries, there is the need to focus on increasing the participation rates of disabled people. In those places where there has been progress with this, attention has switched to the exploration of inclusive learning and teaching. Once progress has been made in this, a further stage would be to focus on including the topic of ' disability' in the curriculum of as many subjects/courses as possible

Closing comments

Looking at the legislation and its gradual development, the Further and Higher Education Act 1992, was followed by DDA 1995, Human Rights Act 1998, SENDA 2001 and most recently the DDA 2005. Despite the number of Acts relating to disabled students, it is questionable whether these laws have contributed significantly to those changes that have been made.

The *Guardian Special Supplement on Disability* said:

> 'Even ten years on from the establishment of the DDA 1995, the

figures are stark. Only 50% of disabled people of working age are in employment, compared with 81% of non-disabled people – and they earn 30% less when they are working. Disabled people are twice as likely to have no qualifications and are more likely to live in unsuitable housing that their non-disabled counterparts.' (Friday December 2nd 2005)

Indeed, are there ways in which the laws might have had a negative impact? For example, in fostering a reluctance to innovate and experiment, given the threat of litigation should things not work out as planned? Many of what have now become standard procedures to support disabled students began as 'experiments'; due to their success there were no problems. However, now that there are laws in place, staff might be less willing to be adventurous in introducing innovations, which, if they are not successful, might result in litigation.

It is worth considering whether there have there been other more powerful agents of change. I think that there have – the Institute for Learning and Teaching in Higher Education, the Higher Education Academy and the Learning and Teaching Subject Networks especially with their focus on learning and teaching, the Higher Education Funding Council for England and the Scottish Higher Education Funding Council with national co-ordination and funding both via special initiatives and the additional premium. Let us also not forget SKILL with its successful dissemination of information and good practices.

The momentum for positive change is there but meeting the requirements of the new legislation constitutes a danger and could check this progress and slow it down. There is the possibility that institutions will develop policy and provision which meet only the basic requirements of the law and will take no initiative to go beyond the minimum level. If this is the case, then it could be unlawful and does not meet the spirit of the law. However, it is essential to remind ourselves of the limitations of the law. In the words of Mary Johnson (2003) 'A law cannot deliver what the culture does not will'.

Some key issues for further discussion

1. To what extent is it true to assert that the social model of disability has been too neglectful in terms of recognising the impact of an impairment on the individual?

2. Why should institutions compete to recruit specifically students with

disabilities – which might then lead to the creation of 'centres of excellence'?

3. When should students disclose their impairment and what information should they reveal?

4. In what way might the shift to a more legalistic system affect the development of policy and provision for disabled students?

5. What are the strengths and shortcomings of [providing additional funding to individual students (through a system such as the Disabled Students' Allowances) or to institutions (like the Additional Learning Support money provided for further education institutions)?

6. What value is there in making a distinction between 'learner support' and ' learning support'?

7. Why should students who are Deaf or hard-of-hearing remain within the responsibilities of an institution's disability service?

8. In view of the changing focus of policy and provision for disabled students, is there now a stronger case for agreeing on a common title for the role and position occupied by staff working to support these students?

Further reading

Department for Education and Science 2002 *Finding out about people's disabilities: a good practice guide* London, DfES

Equality Challenge Unit 2005 *Promoting equality – the public sector duty on disability: suggested first steps for HEI* London, ECU

Equality Challenge Unit 2005a *Update 06/05* London, ECU

Equality Challenge Unit 2005b *Disability Equality Schemes: Collecting and improving baseline data and the importance of involving disabled people* London, ECU

Fuller, M., Bradley, A. and Healey, M.2004 'Incorporating disabled students within an inclusive Higher Education environment' *Disability and Society* 19, 5: 455-468

Higher Education Funding Council for England 1998 *Disability Statements: a guide to good practice* Bristol, HECFE

Hurst, A. 1993 *Steps towards graduation: access to Higher Education and people with disabilities* Aldershot, Avebury

Johnson, M. 2003 *Make them go away: Clint Eastwood, Christopher Reeve and the case against Disability Rights* Louisville, The Avocado Press

Learning and Skills Council 2003 *Disclosure, confidentiality and passing on information* London, LSC

Low, C. 2001 'Have disability rights gone too far?' *Insight* Lecture, City University, London April 2001

National Innovations Centre 1974 *Disabled students in Higher Education* London, NIC

Riddell, S., Tinklin, T. and Wilson, A. 2005 *Disabled students in Higher Education: perspectives on widening access and changing policy* London, Routledge Falmer

Rose, C. 2006 'Do you have a disability – yes or no? Or is there a better way of asking?' *Guidance on disability disclosure and respecting confidentiality* London, LSDA

Shakespeare,T. and Watson, N. 2001 'The social model of disability; an outdated ideology' *Research in Social Science and Disability* 2: 9-28

Skill 2005 *A Guide to the Disability Discrimination Act for Institutions of Further and Higher Education* (revised Summer 2005) London, Skill

CHAPTER TWO

At a 'Headstart' workshop: Developing support services for deaf students in Higher Education

Jannine Williams

Introduction

In 2003 the Royal National Institute for Deaf People (RNID), launched a national project, 'Headstart', with the aim of:

> '... promoting greater accessibility to higher and further education and working closely with universities and colleges to make learning environments deaf aware and inclusive, we hope to encourage more deaf and hard of hearing people to enter higher and further education and successfully complete their degrees.' (Wight 2003)

As part of this project, a series of workshops were offered to encourage and support Higher Education Institutions (HEIs) to consider their approach to meeting the access requirements of deaf people. The following case study outlines one part of the workshop series, which aimed to support workshop participants to reflect upon the factors which influenced the development of services for deaf students across two universities. The case study is included as a chapter in this publication to offer HEIs who are reviewing their services an opportunity to review the workshop materials as an aid to their deliberations. The case study below is a recount of a half day workshop including the aim of the session, the materials used in the workshop and the activities workshop participants undertook.

In the first part of the workshop participants considered the development of the Joint Universities Deaf Student Support Services (JUDSSSS) Project, a collaborative programme of service development between two HEIs between 2000 and 2003. Following this participants were encouraged to reflect upon the experiences of the JUDSSS development worker, and consider the factors which are affecting the development of provision for deaf students within their own institution. In particular participants were encouraged to consider the situational and circumstantial factors they might need to consider, and the strategies and tactics needed to successfully negotiate for service developments to meet the access requirements for deaf students.

Throughout the first part of the workshop my experiences as the project development worker was shared, my journey in developing services for deaf students, the factors that influenced me and the tools and techniques I used to manage myself in relation to the project.

The materials presented at the workshop are re-presented here with a brief introduction to indicate how they were used to support workshop participants' reflections, with the aim of offering readers an opportunity to reflect upon how they might develop services within their own institutions.

Case study of JUDSSS

Background

The first part of the workshop was to outline the background and aims and objectives of the JUDSSS project to collaboratively develop services for deaf students between two universities, and to present my experiences as the project development worker.

The JUDSSS project was developed in response to a Higher Education Funding Council for England (HEFCE) funding initiative to improve provision for disabled students in Higher Education. The 2000 to 2003 funding round included three strands, of which the third was focused upon encouraging collaboration between institutions to make effective use of existing resources and available funds. A Russell Group and a post 1992 university bid for funding to establish a collaborative service for deaf students was successful, providing funding for one development worker and small sums of money for service developments.

There were significant differences between the two institutions, the post 1992 university had a long established disability support service, the Russell Group institution was in the process of establishing a disability service, where previously disabled student support was offered by an Assistant Registrar, as one/tenth of their overall role responsibilities.

JUDSSS project aims and objectives

JUDSSS aims were to encourage more deaf people to gain access to HE, promote wider access to, and understanding of, issues related to deafness within the partner universities, and ensure deaf students are fully integrated into learning processes. Overall, the aim was to create and embed a quality support service for deaf students at each institution.

To achieve these aims, JUDSSS objectives were to develop of day to day advisory services for applicants and students, develop support workers registers, carry out a feasibility study to consider British Sign Language as a module in a modern languages department, and offer staff development and deaf awareness training.

First considerations

The aim of the first part of the workshop was to outline the first stages undertaken to explore the feasibility of the JUDSSS Project, the tools used to carry out this feasibility review and the outcomes which influenced the priorities set.

As the development worker and new member of staff to the two universities, I underwent a process of aligning myself with the project, aiming to marry my values and beliefs to the project, and establishing where the focus of activities could or should be. I carried out an analysis of the internal and external factors which might affect the success of the project and which would help me align myself to the project, initially using a 'SWOT' and 'PESTEL' analysis.

This was followed with a check on the project outcomes being 'well-formed'. That is I ensured I was clear about how I would achieve the outcomes and the factors that I needed to take into account in terms of understanding what the successful achievement of the project objectives would be like.

The outcomes I sought from these analyses were:

- What situational and sector factors will impact on the project?;
- Which of the project objectives seem feasible in this context?;
- Which objectives should be prioritised?;
- Who should I consult or seek support from?;

- How would I know the objectives had been successfully achieved?;
- What do the aims of the project mean to me?

The analysis identified there were differences between the two institutions in terms of structure and culture. In addition, there were significant differences in the stage the disabilities services had reached (one established and growing, one in the process of becoming established). The student profile at both institutions was dominated by hard of hearing students, with very low numbers of Deaf students ever having attended either institution. Initial management feedback suggested the priority for JUDSSS was to meet the access requirements of the current student profile.

Early student feedback identified a preference for choices in arrangements for, and providers of, communication support which suggested a range of approaches to service development may be necessary. Finally, I took into account my belief in the importance of offering choices to deaf students in relation to the types of services and support available, especially in relation to the provision of communication support. All of these key factors were to be important in shaping how the project aims would become service developments and sustainable projects outcomes. To support the workshop participants in identifying the key factors likely to affect the development of their services we carried out a SWOT and PESTEL exercise and reviewed the outcomes against a project well-formed outcomes model. Copies of these exercises are included in the appendix for this chapter.

JUDSSS project outcomes

As a result of this analysis direct services were prioritised which reflected the needs of the student profile at both institutions and which would gain support from the management teams at both institutions. This led to the main achievements of JUDSSS being a successful collaborative support worker service across the two universities, the establishment of a day to day advisory services for deaf students and the provision of staff training sessions on deaf awareness.

Two key aspects of the project were not fully achieved due to this focus, and which the universities agreed would be developed at a later point once the day to day services were well established and functioning well. These were the feasibility study into British Sign Language as a modern language module and a British Sign Language/English Interpreter option within the support worker service.

Learning outcomes

What did I learn as the JUDSSS Project development worker when developing the collaborative services across two HEIs? Student involvement was essential when attempting to prioritise service developments and to ensure services meet their needs. To make progress with the project objectives it was important to employ negotiation skills when developing new services, and being patient when attempting to bring about positive changes to current practices. Overall, as the development worker I found my most important learning point was the need to be very clear about my understanding of appropriate access arrangements for deaf students, and that whilst compromise was necessary at times, it was essential to be willing to negotiate across and between the two institutions for the priorities identified in the early analysis.

To explore the issue of negotiation further, the 'Headstart' workshop participants were introduced to a negotiation model outlined by Gennard and Judge (2000) which demonstrates the principle of negotiation as a process over time. Gennard and Judge outline the importance of carrying out an analysis of the factors likely to influence your negotiations, to be clear about the aims you want to achieve and to develop a strategy and tactics to achieve these, and to be prepared to negotiate over a series of meetings to achieve your aims.

Figure 1: Negotiation - the reconciliation of differences over time (Gennard and Judge 1999)

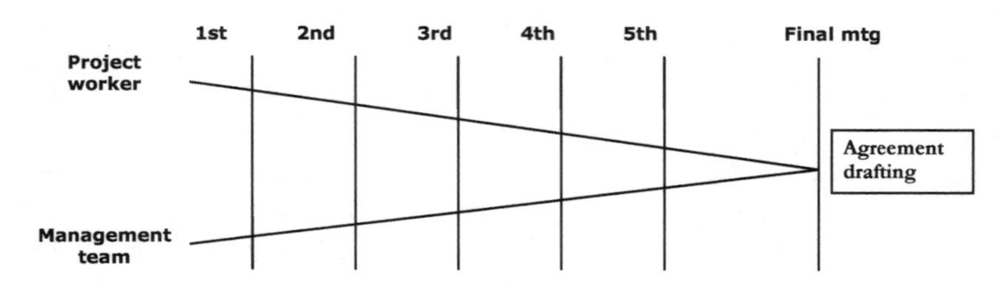

To explore the potential use of this approach to negotiating, workshop participants were encouraged to prepare an approach to negotiating for an aspect of service development within their institution using the model. The exercise is included in the appendix for this chapter.

Closing the first half of the workshop

To bring this part of the workshop to a close we reviewed the implications of the Special Educational Needs and Disability Act (2001) upon our practices within Higher Education and the participants identified a range of good practice to adopt.

The following issues were raised by participants on how the Special Educational Needs and Disability Act 2001(SENDA) might influence our approach to service development and delivery.

Post SENDA participants discussed the potential benefits of:

- Working with deaf students to inform service and university developments;
- Aiming to have deaf student access issues included in university deliberative processes;
- Using the Commission for Racial Equality impact assessment model to ensure policies were not having an adverse impact upon deaf students;
- Building principles of reasonableness and auxiliary aids and services into policy reviews/development;
- An annual review of policy, procedure and practice in each area of student services activity;
- Encouraging a task group/working group approach across institutions to develop provision and share good practice;
- Monitoring sector developments and disability discrimination cases;
- Expecting a 'rising bar' of access provision;
- Identifying special interest groups;
- Health Care Practitioners web pages and guidance on deaf students in health related learning environments;
- Support available from the Consortium of Higher Educational Support Services with Deaf Students (CHESS);
- Advice available from the Royal National Institute for Deaf People (www.rnid.org.uk).

The aim of this chapter has been to outline the content of a 'Headstart' workshop on developing services for deaf students which was informed by my experiences as development worker of the JUDSSS Project. In addition to provide the resources used by workshop participants to assist the chapter reader in developing their own institution's services. By discussing my experiences and approaches it is hoped to encourage readers to reflect upon their own experiences, their and their institutions priorities and draw upon lessons learnt in the JUDSSS project.

.

Chapter appendix

Activity One

Reflect upon and make notes about the factors that may influence your approach to developing support services for deaf students. Then carry out a SWOT analysis, noting any internal factor you identify as important in your university context which may impact upon your project plans.

- Strengths;
- Weaknesses;
- Opportunities;
- Threats.

Strengths	Weaknesses
Opportunities	Threats

PESTEL analysis

A PESTEL analysis assists you in identifying and considering external factors (outside of your institution), which may otherwise be overlooked by a SWOT analysis. Consider the following areas, noting any external factors you identify as important for your project.

- Political:
  - Local;
  - National;
- Economic;
- Social (or socio-cultural);
- Technological;
- Environmental;
- Legislative.

Activity Two

Reviewing your project outcomes to ensure they are well-formed may help you to increase the likelihood of the outcomes being successful, and help you to clarify what this success means to you and that your outcomes are both believable and realizable.

For each of your project outcomes work through the following questions:

1. What is your outcome? - Is it specific and stated in positive terms; that is worded to identify what you do want to achieve rather than what you don't?;
2. Is achieving the outcomes within your control? - If you will rely upon others, do you have their understanding and support?;
3. How will you know if you are achieving your project outcomes? - What criteria will you use to evidence the outcomes you want, what will you see or hear when you are successful?;
4. Are you aware of the context in which you are working?;
5. What resource requirements do you have, and are they available to you?;
6. What impact would this objective have on other project objectives if it were achieved?;
7. ecological -When you achieve your outcomes what will change for the project and for you? There are usually advantages and disadvantages to achieving change. Being clear about how change will affect the project and yourself will help you to anticipate how these may affect how the project progresses;
8. What are the first steps you need to take to achieve the outcome you are aiming for?

Activity Three

Consider how you would approach the negotiation process in relation to developing access within your institution to better meet the access requirements of D/deaf students:

- Selection and admissions practices;
- Enrolment, registration and induction;
- Accommodation;
- Teaching and learning;
- Examinations;
- Central services support;
- Estates.

Make some notes on how you will prepare to negotiate for improvements to your institutions access arrangements for D/deaf students.

Gennard and Judge (2000) suggest that in preparing for negotiations you may want to consider:

- Carrying out an analysis of the situation;
- Developing and clarifying your aims;
- Preparing your strategy and tactics.

Analysis

- What facts or sources of information do you need to consider?;
- Are there any relevant rules or regulations you should take into account?;
- Are there any relevant precedents or comparisons to take into account?;
- What do you know of the other party's position on the issues?;
- What issues are tradable to you and/or the other party?;
- What is the significance of the issues for students or their representatives?

Aims

- Ideal (what is it you would like to achieve?);
- Realistic (what do you hope to achieve?);
- Fall back (what must you get to ensure the project is a success?).

Strategy

- Decide who will lead in negotiations;
- Can you anticipate the other side's arguments and prepare your counter argument?;
- Ensure you are familiar with the meaning and intent of agreements, procedures and rules of your organisation.

Additional resources

Research reports on deaf students:
Deaf Students in Scottish Higher Education, Scottish Funding Council Report 2005:
http://www.ssc.education.ed.ac.uk/resources/deaf/deafstuds/intro.html

Chapter Four of the Sequal Report 'A valued part of the workforce?':
http://www.surrey.ac.uk/politics/cse/sequal-reports/sequal-final-report-bristol.pdf

Premia, a resource base developed to highlight disabled postgraduate research student experiences and examples of good practice:
http://www.premia.ac.uk/

An excellent change management toolkit developed by the National Health Service for groups wanting to bring about change. This includes a simple guide to carrying out a SWOT and PESTEL analysis.
http://www.informatics.nhs.uk/download/795/part4.pdf

An example of a PESTEL and SWOT analysis carried out by Cornwall County Fire Brigade:
http://www.idea-knowledge.gov.uk/idk/aio/751740%20

An example of different approaches to developing well-formed outcomes:
http://www.wendwell.co.uk/Resources/outcomes.htm

Further reading

Gennard, J., Judge, G., 1999, *Employee relations.* IPD, London

Hall, J. & Tinklin, T. 1998 *Students first: The experiences of disabled students in higher education.* Glasgow: Scottish Council for research in education,

(Scottish Council for Research in Education Report No 85) [Online]. Available at: http://www.scre.ac.uk/resreport/pdf/085.pdf (Accessed: 12th July 2006).

Rachel Wight 2003 'RNID/Barclays launch new initiative to help universities improve access for deaf students' Available at: http://www.rnid.org.uk/mediacentre/press/2003/rnid_barclays_launch_new_initiative_to_help_universities_improve_access_for_deaf_students.htm

CHAPTER THREE

The experience of d/Deaf Further Education students moving to Higher Education: a tale of transition

Rachel O'Neill and Michelle Jones

This study examines the views of fifteen d/Deaf people who have all studied at a large metropolitan Further Education college over the period 1995 to 2005. All of these students had the qualifications needed to enter Higher Education and thirteen of them went on to an Higher Education course. We followed the students to find out about their own views of the process of transition. The aim of the study was to explore the reasons why d/Deaf students decided to apply to Higher Education or not, their experience of transition into Higher Education and their views about this process. We wanted to find out how the transition could be made easier so that more d/Deaf students stay and succeed at university.

Through discussions, the participants reflected on the contrasts between their college and university experiences, they discussed the processes they went through to decide on a university and how far this was determined by the possible access arrangements. The participants also reflected on their experiences of friendship and social support at university and of studying alongside hearing and d/Deaf students. Finally, they discussed their views about the qualities needed by a young d/Deaf person to succeed in the hearing-controlled space of Higher Education.

Four of these students have completed their degrees, four dropped out and five are still studying at university. We cannot give a true figure of the achievement rate yet, because five are still at university, but the present situation is that 31% of the thirteen d/Deaf students who applied to Higher Education dropped out. This compares unfavourably with a non-completion rate in 1998 of 18% across the UK (Yorke 2000). There are even higher rates of non-completion in America; research from 1987 and 1997 found that in the USA there was a non-completion rate of 75% for d/Deaf students on both two and four-year degree programmes (Stinson and Walter, quoted in Lang 2002). By means of semi structured interviews and questionnaires the researchers wanted to find out more about the educational culture of Further Education in the UK and how it helped or hindered d/Deaf learners as they moved into Higher Education.

The researchers had personal knowledge of the students' experiences: the hearing researcher taught all these students in the Further Education college and the Deaf researcher had gone through the transition from deaf school to mainstream Further Education college and onto university. This means that our attitudes and view of the students have influenced the design of the questionnaire and the outcomes of the face to face interviews (Sarantakos 1994:194). Our view of d/Deaf students' place in the education system is that they experience serious discrimination in the workplace. By gaining higher qualifications, d/Deaf students have more opportunities to secure employment that is more appropriate to their ability level. For this reason, the Deaf Access Team in the Further Education college has promoted access to Higher Education for the past decade. More recently, over the period 2002 to 2005, d/Deaf students from the college have been involved in 'Headstart' events both inside the college and at other universities (RNID 2003). This was a programme in England which promoted visits to universities, seminars about access arrangements and residential experiences with other d/Deaf students in a university setting.

The three sectors of school, Further and Higher Education are all funded differently, have different teaching and learning cultures and have, in the past, operated largely independently of each other (Haydon 2002: 265). Students who negotiate a path from school to college and on to Higher Education often take a very different route from the traditional one of taking three or four academic A levels in a sixth form.[4]

[4] A sixth form is for pupils aged 16 – 18 and is often attached to a secondary school. The UK also has a large number of sixth form colleges which are not attached to schools. In both cases the curriculum is largely academic and most pupils are aiming for university entrance at eighteen.

Students who fail to achieve the five GCSE (General Certificate of Secondary Education) grades A to C at school often find they can succeed on more vocationally orientated courses in Further Education.

Table 1: Routes through Further Education to Higher Education

Route	Level One	Level Two	Level Three	Level Four
Academic	National Curriculum level five, expected of school pupils at age twelve.	GCSE A – C grades achieved by 57% of sixteen year olds in England (DFES 2006b)	A levels (AS / A2) Access	Degree
Vocationally orientated		GNVQ BTEC First	AVCE BTEC National	HND
Vocational	NVQ 1	NVQ 2	NVQ 3	NVQ 4

NVQ: National Vocational Qualification
GNVQ: General Vocational Qualification
AVCE: Advanced Vocational Certificate of Education
BTEC: Business and Technology Educational Council
HND: Higher National Diploma
Access: An intensive one or two year course for adults without qualifications
A levels: subjects at advanced level
AS / A2: first and second year of Advanced Level

Students can achieve points for their Access or vocational qualifications with the Universities and Colleges Admissions Service (UCAS) to gain university entrance; an AVCE grade C for example is equivalent to two A levels at grade C. This alternative route into Higher Education is a feature of the British education system which is very different to the USA, for example, where university entrance is determined by scores in English, maths and science tests (Bochner 2005:232). Students from Further Education colleges made up 22% of successful Higher Education applicants in 2005 (UCAS 2006) and most of these entrants probably do not enter with the traditional three AS/A2 levels. None of the fifteen d/Deaf students in this study gained A levels.

Table 2: Qualifications of the fifteen d/Deaf students in the study

Qualification gained by students in the study	Level of course	Number of students with these qualifications in the study
BTEC National	3	7
GNVQ Advanced / AVCE	3	3
Access	3	2
NVQ 3	3	2 (to Year Zero)
GCSE Grade D	2	1 (to Year Zero)

d/Deaf students negotiate paths through Further Education which are often similar to other groups of learners who have not achieved academic success at school: working class learners, those who have English as a second language, learners who have arrived in the UK in childhood and students with disabilities. The mean age of entry to Higher Education for the thirteen d/Deaf learners in this study was twenty five and only two were adult returners. The mean length of time in Further Education for these fifteen learners was 4.8 years. This is significantly longer than the two years usually spent in FE by hearing students.

The funding mechanism to provide access for students with disabilities to sixth form colleges and Further Education in England and Wales has been very favourable since 1992. The Further Education Funding Council (FEFC) and now the Learning and Skills Council (LSC) fund additional support on the basis of assessed need rather than a fixed local authority budget which is a financial constraint in school services. A survey by the National Association of Tertiary Education for Deaf People (NATED) found that 80% of colleges supported d/Deaf students, but only 65% of these colleges employed a tutor specifically to work with d/Deaf students and only 29% had qualified tutors of d/Deaf students (O'Neill et al. 2002;105). The assessment depends on knowledge of the needs of d/Deaf students which is best provided by a tutor for d/Deaf students. The NATED survey also found that most Communication Support Workers (CSWs) were not qualified and 62%

did not have fluency in British Sign Language (BSL).[5] In this context, 'being fluent in BSL' is taken to mean having a level of fluency equivalent to the NVQ3 qualification of the Council for the Advancement of Communication with Deaf People (CACDP).[6] So despite needs-led additional support funding in Further Education in England and Wales, there are very variable standards of access to learning for d/Deaf students.

Access arrangements at the college

The d/Deaf learners in this study all attended one mainstream Further Education college and received a standard level of access: CSWs who had a minimum of NVQ3 BSL (most of whom also held the Edexcel CSW certificate) and manual and electronic notetakers all trained to CACDP standards. The college trains CSWs and notetakers and is unusual in having a large pool of electronic notetakers. Language tutorials were provided by qualified tutors of d/Deaf students. Other facilities available to these learners included speech and language therapy, weekly radio aid and hearing aid checks, technical tutorials with subject tutors, additional English, Maths and British Sign Language courses taught in BSL and a programme of preparation for Higher Education taught as part of the language tutorials. Handouts and assignment briefs are modified into plain English for students reading at Level One or below. A reading programme is available for d/Deaf students to boost reading skills by working one to one with hearing or Deaf tutors; this service was used by three of the participants in this study. The input from Deaf tutors is an important feature of this college's access team, for example teaching language tutorials, technical tutorials, reading programmes and English, Maths, Information Communications Technology (ICT) and BSL classes.

The study

The methods used in this study were a questionnaire (eight participants) and a semi-structured interview (seven participants). Participants who lived further away used email to reply to the questionnaire.

Over the period 1995 – 2005 there were twenty four d/Deaf students who left the college to enter Higher Education or who gained qualifications which would have allowed them to enter Higher Education.

---

[5] A Communication Support Worker works in educational settings in the UK and provides interpreting and notetaking access for deaf students. There is a qualification to train CSWs accredited by Edexcel.
[6] CACDP is the national awarding body for British Sign Language qualifications

Attempts were made to contact all twenty four students, but we were unable to make contact with three of them. Of the twenty one students who we were able to contact, there was a 71% participation rate in this study.

Table 3: Language use of students in the study

	BSL users	English speakers
All 24 students we tried to contact	14	10
15 students who responded to questionnaire or had an interview	12	3

The response rate in this study was significantly higher for BSL users. This may reflect the way that Deaf BSL users feel a sense of community connected to their college which d/Deaf people who use speech may not feel. The initial contact letter was from the Deaf researcher and explained that she was profoundly Deaf and could sign and use lipreading; this may have led some students who used speech not to respond.

The questions used for the interviews and in the questionnaire were designed by the Deaf researcher to be open-ended and to give participants the opportunity to reflect on their educational journey. The schedule was devised in BSL then translated into English for the written questionnaire and as a memory aid in the face to face interviews. As Gregory et al (1995:349) point out, the language in which the questions are devised can influence the responses and the way the interview goes. 24 prompt questions were used, covering college experience, the decision about whether to go to university, the experience of transition, access arrangements at university, relationships with hearing and d/Deaf friends at university, the course itself and future plans.

Both researchers have BSL skills at CACDP Level Four or equivalent so they felt confident about conducting the interviews in BSL. Six of the face to face interviews were conducted in BSL and one using spoken English. The interviews lasted from thirty to sixty minutes each.

We discussed the use of video with all interviewees before the appointment. All except the participant who used English had regularly used video cameras whilst at college and felt quite comfortable with the camera. All students were happy to be recorded. Five of the interviews were conducted in college and two in students' homes. The camera did have some effect on the participants; for example, one waited till the camera was switched off at the end to report something that had happened at college which she wanted to complain about.

As Sarantakos points out (1994:194) trust is promoted if the interviewer is similar in background to the participants. In this study the Deaf researcher conducted four of the seven face to face interviews. The participants all knew the hearing researcher well, which may have improved trust but could also have encouraged participants to give answers which they thought researcher wanted to hear.

All interviews were transcribed from the video tapes, with each researcher comparing the translations of the other researcher with the original videotapes. The transcript of the student who used speech was checked against the tape by a hearing colleague. The data was then analysed using headings determined by themes which emerged from the interviews and questionnaire responses.

In the following sections we used the participants' exact words if they used spoken or written English. Responses from BSL users have been translated into Standard English, which as Skelton and Valentine note (2003:460) may miss some of their meaning and marginalise them, though this was not our intent.

Participants will be offered a paper and BSL copy of this report when it is published.

The participants

Ten of the participants are profoundly deaf, four are severely deaf and one is moderately deaf. The definitions used are the UK audiological descriptors (BATOD 2006) not necessarily the self definition provided by participants in interviews. Participants sometimes referred to themselves as fully Deaf meaning completely aligned with the Deaf community and its values rather than audiologically profoundly deaf. Twelve of the participants use BSL as their preferred communication mode and three use speech. Six of the fifteen participants (40%) had a disability which affected their learning.

The level of English qualification held by the participants ranged from Entry Three in the Skills for Life Framework (DFES 2006b) to Level Two. The mean English level was between Level One and Two and the modal level was Level Two. Entry Three is equivalent to National Curriculum level three, expected for school pupils aged eight; Level Two is equivalent to GCSE C English or above, achieved by 62% of pupils aged sixteen; the level of English is equivalent to National

Curriculum levels five to eight, expected for pupils from eleven to fourteen.

Seven of the fifteen participants (47%) are black or minority ethnic (BME). There is a correlation between the levels of English and ethnicity in this study: White British or Irish participants were more likely to have Level Two English or above; 75%, compared to only 14% of BME students. However, three of the participants who were BME had come to the UK in late childhood, had had very interrupted education or developed their first language very late.

Eleven participants worked with CSWs and electronic or manual notetakers for their Further Education courses. The other four participants used notetakers and/or radio aids in the Further Education classroom. This type of access was generally maintained when the thirteen participants moved to Higher Education, except that more reported manual rather than electronic notetaker (ENT) access.

The participants had experienced a range of school placements before starting at college: 53% had been to a deaf school as their main secondary placement, 33% had been to a resource base in a school and 13% had been mainstreamed without contact with other d/Deaf students.

53% of the participants had close family at, or who had attended, university. The questionnaire/interview did not ask about the socio-economic status of their families.

Themes identified by the research findings

The research identified the following themes from participants' accounts: access to college:

- finding out about university and deciding whether to go;
- deciding not to go;
- learning independently at university;
- experiences of Further Education;
- access at university;
- British Sign Language, friends and social support at university;
- English and tutorial support; self-advocacy and persistence

a: Access at college

Eleven out of the fifteen participants commented favourably on the high quality of access to learning at the Further Education college. Particular mention was made of the standards of CSW and notetaker support provided. One respondent who had experienced a lack of support at another college was amazed to find she had full time one to one CSW support. When the respondents compared their Further Education access to Higher Education they noticed that in Further Education they had more consistent staffing and were able to book a CSW or notetaker for extra sessions more easily:

> '[At college I found] that I was capable of being successful at obtaining qualifications with great (notetaking) support.' (female, uses speech)

Participants liked the fact that Deaf students in Further Education could learn English in groups with other Deaf classmates:

> 'I do think I have most positive experience at (college) is studying English with Deaf Adults and tutor which I have learnt a lot such as seminar, writing a report, etc. though I only have studied it for a year.' (male, uses BSL)

Having Deaf tutors was mentioned as very important by several respondents. The students' positive sense of their own identity as Deaf people grew over the years spent in Further Education:

> 'I saw fantastic role models of Deaf tutors of Deaf students. That had a big impact on me. They used sign language to teach and they were very visual. I felt I was getting full information and it came directly from the tutors…I realised they were Deaf professionals and that's why I had learned so well.' (male, uses BSL)

One respondent was particularly pleased with the speech and language therapy support which taught her how to communicate with hearing peers. This service at the college could be extended to BSL users on level three courses:

> 'I saw a speech and language therapist during my AVCE too…. From the beginning to the end I improved dramatically with her, and I needed more. She helped my confidence and she helped me say some words. She taught me how to actually start communicating…It really helped me with this whole world, about communicating.' (female, uses speech)

b: Finding out about university and deciding whether to go

Half the students who decided to apply to university mentioned that they looked at a wide range before choosing and that they made several visits before applying. Participants mentioned the benefit of 'Headstart' events, being able to watch presentations from different universities in the college and working with their language tutor to investigate different options.

One issue for d/Deaf students was whether to choose a university known to have a good support team for d/Deaf students (for example the Universities of Central Lancashire, Wolverhampton or Sheffield Hallam) or whether to prioritise the more usual concerns of hearing students such as the particular course or location of the university. In fact 62% of the participants who went to university chose one that had specialist support for d/Deaf students:

> '(I did a) lot of research before I applied for the course. I am glad that I am on the right course so far!' (male, uses BSL);

> 'I went to a "Headstart" event at Sheffield Hallam. We stayed for four days ... It was about deciding whether to go to university and they explained the positive and negative things about it. I met lots of new people.... We had a really good time. There were trips to different university buildings round Sheffield, we looked at the halls of residence .... we went to see an interpreted play in Leeds....Before I went to university I visited Preston, Wolverhampton and Sheffield. I accepted [names university] because it was the best course for me.' (female, uses BSL);

> 'I met with my language tutor and also my course tutor explained about the different universities that do multimedia and we looked at a list on the internet. I used the internet and the prospectuses too. I visited Preston, MMU, Derby and Wolverhampton. ... We looked round the department, met the lecturers, things like that.' (female, uses BSL)

c: Deciding not to go

The two participants who decided not to go to university explained why it was not possible: one had two young children and the other had to work and was not confident enough about her English:

> 'My English is not that brilliant. I gave in an assignment (at college) and I would have to redo sections to make them clearer. Sometimes a friend would proof read my work for me. I think that university would be harder again. Maybe I'll go later – I've put it off.' (female, uses BSL)

d: Learning independently at university

Five of the thirteen participants found a difference between college and university because they had to learn much more independently. In some cases this was because the student felt unprepared academically:

> 'I hadn't practised enough at college about how to learn useful skills like writing reports and essays of a thousand words, about doing presentations and research.' (male, uses BSL)

The amount of work was a shock to some students and three hour lectures led to eye strain for one respondent who has a visual impairment.

Some respondents found the level of the work too difficult despite having a reasonable level of English:

> 'It was a real leap. The work was much more difficult and the reading level was much higher. I didn't know a lot of the word meanings.' (male, uses BSL)

Respondents with weaker English skills found university level work a real struggle:

> 'It was a complete culture shock at university. I have good BSL but written English is my second language. It took me a long time and many hours hard work to understand what was going on at university. I had to plan much more so that I could meet the deadlines. I … spent hours on research. It's risky going to university.' (male, uses BSL)

Two respondents found the transition from college to university quite straightforward and thought their Further Education course had helped them to prepare:

> 'At college I learned to manage my studying on the Access in IT course as it was designed for anyone to preparing to enter Higher

Education. I cannot believe how lucky I am that I got that excellent course as it made a huge difference in my first year, because I kept ahead of the other students … at university.' (male, uses BSL)

Some concerns are probably similar to hearing students moving from Further Education to university: the large number of students and individual timetables:

'It's not the same timetable every week. There are lots of people coming in and out for modules. College was a bit monotonous with the same people all the time, but I found it quite a shock coping with all the changes of people at university.' (female, uses BSL)

Participants were evenly divided about how helpful university tutors were. Generally they were more positive about the amount of time they had from their tutors at the three well-resourced universities:

'Many of my lecturers had experience in working with d/Deaf students and I feel I received a positive response from them all. They were able to support me during lectures and make sure I was able to follow. All my lecturers welcomed me if I approached about certain issues concerning me.' (female, uses speech)

However, this was not always the case:

'I found some tutors had a bad attitude toward me because they did not understand my Deafness.' (female, uses BSL)

e: Access at university

All the students who chose universities with established deaf access teams were generally happy with the level of interpreter, notetaker and language tutorial or subject tutorial support available at university:

'I get a notetaker, BSL interpreter and sometimes two interpreters if we have a presenter. Sometimes I get different interpreters and sometimes they sign in a different style, too fast or too slow.' (female, uses BSL);

'[I get] communication support - an interpreter and note taker-plus weekly subject tutorial support on Maths and Technical issues (in BSL with a Deaf tutor) and extra time in examinations. (I get this) without fail apart from health reasons e.g. the interpreter or note taker is unwell at short notice. That's life!' (male, uses BSL);

'I was lucky to receive one to one support from a tutor who worked with the disability team. We met once a week and went through my course work and she would often advise me on my work. I also had a notetaker in lectures which enabled me to follow discussions and take part, as well as understand the lectures more effectively. I feel that the support has contributed to me successfully completing my degree. I lived in student accommodation and my room was adapted for me, for example flashing doorbell light, rumbler fire alarm, a phone socket for using a minicom.' (female, uses speech)

The three students who were unhappy with the access arrangements chose universities which had few d/Deaf students. In some cases they wished they had chosen one of the three universities with well-resourced d/Deaf access teams. These three participants were resentful at the amount of time they had to spend organising their own access arrangements, which ate into their study time. The shortage of qualified staff was a common theme:

'At college if I had a last minute request for a CSW it was possible to book an extra one, say for a changed lecture date or a student social event. When I tried to book an interpreter for extra events at Higher Education it was too late, I couldn't get one. They were all booked. It was very frustrating and I had to rely on hearing classmates at those times, so I didn't get the full information.' (male, uses BSL);

'At college my needs were met by the unit's arrangements whereas at Higher Education I had to organise how my needs could be met by myself through Disabled Students' Allowances. I don't agree that a Deaf person should be arranging all that on his / her own.' (male, uses BSL)

The participants were uniformly satisfied with the assessment arrangements for Disabled Students' Allowances (DSA) at university. DSA is a non-means tested allowance used to fund access support for students with disabilities in Higher Education:

> 'They had already seen other students who were in the same position as me so the paperwork went smoothly. I got a new computer system at home with funding from DSA. My LEA was helpful too.' (male, uses BSL)

f: Friends and social support at university

Most participants said they had mainly Deaf friends at university, or that they had hearing friends on their course and Deaf friends for their social life, sometimes outside the university:

> 'I mixed well with Deaf and hearing students. I prefer Deaf students as I enjoyed learning and sharing information and skills with them.' (male, uses BSL);

> 'There were hearing students at university but they all wanted to learn to sign and I just didn't have the time....There were some other Deaf students (who).. used to ask me to go to the Deaf club with them sometimes, and I did, so we could support each other.' (male, uses BSL);

> 'In the day I get on with my work by myself, doing my assignments. I don't need to be with Deaf people all the time. Only in the evening I meet up often, say hello, catch up and have a chat. In my shared house in the halls of residence all the other students are hearing. We get on very well. There are quite a lot of overseas students at university which is interesting.' (female, uses BSL)

The two students who had mostly hearing friends use speech to communicate:

> 'I had a mixture of friends. I mixed with other students on my course but I developed a close relationship with those whom I lived with in my first year in hall. All my peers were hearing.' (female, uses speech)

Five participants mentioned difficulties in communicating with hearing peers. They often felt that their relationships with hearing students were superficial and unequal. Several mentioned that hearing students did not approach them to talk about work or social issues:

> 'Sometimes if I have any problem with the assignments and if they have a problem, they always hesitate to tell me because I'm Deaf. When I see their faces, I talk to them and they are happy. But I told them many times to ask me if they had any problem but they did not respond at all.' (female, uses BSL);

> 'Well I'm the only Deaf person on my course and I found the other students a bit reluctant to talk to me. They talk amongst themselves. I kept approaching them and said 'hi'. I won't give up. I was really pleased and surprised when my tutor started to learn to sign. Then some of my friends decided to learn to sign. That was great.' (female, uses BSL);

> 'I didn't mix with hearing students. I found it too stressful having to explain myself and communicating with them. I found students preferred to be friendly with my interpreters.' (female, uses BSL)

Several participants discussed strategies they had found for communicating better with hearing students. Some used the interpreter and notetaker to join in conversations with hearing students and found that later they could communicate without these staff being present. Others taught basic BSL to their peers to improve communication in class and used the interpreter for higher level discussions:

> 'In my group, there are eighteen students but I often work together with four or five students. They learned how to deal with an interpreter and note taker and how to include me in conversations without any problems...including dirty jokes!' (male, uses BSL);

> '[I mix with] both Deaf and hearing. I use the interpreter to communicate with my hearing friends in class. And I teach some of the friends on my course some sign too, just basic. For higher level discussions I use the interpreter.' (female, uses BSL);

> 'There was no problem for my HND. I was mixing with all hearing students, especially a lot of foreign students....The overseas students were very friendly and they introduced me to a lot of restaurants. We went to the cinema. I really got on well with all of them.

At break time and dinner time we all talked and I had no problems talking to them.' (female, uses speech)

Two participants were particularly pleased at the new independence they found at university and moving away from home:

'The best thing about going to university was] independence! My friends and family at home have seen so much change in me since I've been to uni.' (female, uses speech)

g: English and tutorial support

Three respondents found the language tutorial support at university helpful but four did not think it was adequate and in one case there were none available. They found that the language tutors did not have fluent BSL skills and they were waiting in tutorials while tutors read their work. There is considerable variation between the number of hours of tutorial support being offered by different universities, varying from a whole day a week to an hour a week. Several respondents commented that they did not need language tutorials but liked the additional subject tutorials:

'I can manage so far but can email staff if I need it. However for my subject or maths, I have a weekly tutorial with (a Deaf tutor) who is great!' (male, uses BSL);

'[The language tutorial] is completely different from college. At college I had two hours a week. At university there's just one hour a week. The rest of the time you have to go off by yourself and write. It's much worse at university compared to college. One hour just isn't enough. The language tutor doesn't use BSL, she uses SSE[7] and she's too slow at reading the work. It's not acceptable really. You have to book your session on a big timetable and a lot of the sessions are already taken.' (female, uses BSL);

'[At college I liked] to meet [name of language tutor] for a study support tutorial. It was good because I had the chance to understand what was going on in the lectures. This does not happen in university, which is a struggle.' (female, uses BSL);

---

[7] Sign Supported English is a method of communicating with deaf people often used by hearing people; it uses signs from BSL but with English word order and grammar.

'My English is not perfect but it is not important because when I have finished my draft essay, my language support tutor checks it then I give it the lecturer by the deadline.' (male, uses BSL)

h: Self advocacy and persistence

Five of the respondents discussed how they found it difficult to persist with the course, and three of these people dropped out. Some could not meet all the criteria to pass a module or did not feel part of the university, partly because of living a long way from the campus:

> 'A lot of it I found really boring. I felt I should keep going because I didn't want to waste my money. I felt guilty about wasting it. If the interpreting and notetaking support had been there all the time I would have been much more enthusiastic about the course. I felt it was so unfair that the hearing students could go out and have a good time and they didn't have any of these extra responsibilities to arrange support, or put up with limited access to the course.' (male, uses BSL)

Several respondents felt that although they found the course hard, they did not think that they found it harder than the hearing students.

> 'I definitely found e-studying (the hardest part) as there is lots of English and lots of navigation to do with e-studying. I can see that is my weakness but will work on it in my second year. I know my fellow hearing students said the same things but they often ask me for help by SMS[8], like 'which folder is that file in?'' (male, uses BSL)

Several respondents found ways to support other Deaf students or found that positive ideas came out of their negative experiences at university:

> 'I bought lots of books. But what I really would have liked is a service to translate the books into BSL in digital format so I could access them properly. I'd really like to see that in the future to help other Deaf students.' (male, uses BSL);

> 'One of my (Deaf) friends was bullied at university and got de-

[8] Short Message Service: a method of sending and receiving text messages using mobile phones.

pressed. She was thinking about transferring to a different university but I encouraged her to keep going. She was worried that her English was holding her back. In the end she listened to me and kept going.' (female, uses BSL);
'A positive outcome for me personally was learning to stand up for myself and challenging the discrimination I received.' (female, uses BSL)

Discussion

Our presupposition as researchers and tutors who worked in this college was that the level of access our team provided was adequate and that it would provide a sound basis for preparing students for university (May 1993:131). The CSWs at this college work as interpreters with most students on Level Three courses which we thought would prepare students well for working with interpreters at university. This assumption was not entirely borne out by the responses. Even respondents who attended universities with well-established access teams were disappointed with the inconsistency of the communication support in Higher Education and did not find it easy to change from a language tutorial where they reviewed the week to a tutorial where they handed in their written work for amendment.

Language tutorials at the Further Education college in this study are not just about language. They include a review of communication access during the preceding week, discussion of lecture content, translation support with reading and guidance on research skills. Respondents in this study noticed the difference at university where language tutorials were focused on modifying their written English. Research from the USA (Lang et al 2004) confirms that students prefer active involvement in tutorials. The few students who received subject specific tutorials in Higher Education were very satisfied with them. Over the past five years at the Further Education college most of the language modification of students' assignments has been provided by email, leaving time in the language tutorial for more discussion and tuition; the tutorials are largely student-led. The amount of language tutorial available and the teaching and learning methods used in these tutorials appears to vary widely both in Further Education and Higher Education.

Students who had studied on more academic courses at Further Education (e.g. Access courses or AVCE) were better prepared and happier about university level work than students who had studied on very vocational courses or Further Education courses at below Level Three.

This study shows that a much wider range of d/Deaf students can achieve at university than has previously been thought (Jarvis & Knight 2003:62; Bowe 2003:487). Students with Level One English and above appear to cope fairly well, provided that the university has effective language or technical tutorials in place. Powers (2003:63), in common with most education researchers, uses five GCSE grades A to C at age sixteen as the standard measure of academic success. However for d/Deaf students academic success may come much later, after four or five years of Further Education.

The more investigation respondents did before going to university, the happier they were when they got there. There were five types of preparation: tutorials with the tutor for d/Deaf students, university visits, 'Headstart' activities, work with their Further Education course tutor and sessions with the college guidance workers.

Respondents who used speech had better experiences at mixing with hearing peers at university. Those who used BSL found having a Deaf peer group valuable and many had developed ways of managing communication with hearing students. The questionnaire could have explored more the relationship between d/Deaf and hearing students while they were at college. It may be possible within Further Education to prepare students better for interacting with the hearing students on their course, perhaps by CSWs working at break times. This would need even more CSWs, a scarce commodity in the Further Education sector. There could be more explicit teaching of communication techniques for BSL users on Level Three courses.

Many of these respondents were resilient and persistent and had a positive view of themselves as d/Deaf students. One of the features which several mentioned was having Deaf tutors at college and a feeling of solidarity with other d/Deaf students. Reay (2001:337) interviewed working class hearing students who studied on an access course in Further Education before going to university. She found that the students were trying to negotiate a difficult balance between investing in a new identity and holding on to a cohesive self that retained a secure link to their past. Her research shows (Reay 2001:340) that the students negotiated a balance between safety, risk and challenge. Safety was the main priority because these students had experienced a dislocated schooling. She suggests that risk is not individual for these students but a collective class risk for working class students. One of the respondents in the present study discussed the sense of risk he felt in entering a university which did not have many Deaf students. This sense of danger does not come across from those students who chose a well-resourced university. They have a well established identity as deaf students which they have built through their years in Further Education and have not lost their sense of solidarity with each other or the wider Deaf community. The BSL users who were happiest at university had regular contact with Deaf tutors.

This study was not able to explore in great detail the reasons why people dropped out of university, however, from the evidence in this study there were several factors identified:

- Inadequate academic preparation;
- Not enough research on the range of universities or transition activities;
- Choosing a university which did not have specialist access for d/Deaf students;
- Having a mental health problem.

One of the aims of this study was to explore the reasons why some well-qualified students did not go on to Higher Education. In one case, the very first student who was qualified in 1996 did not go partly because there was no tradition to follow. She was not able to keep in contact with d/Deaf peers who had successfully made the transition while she was in Further Education. This first student remained unconfident about her English, whereas for students who followed her, this was not such a worry. Some respondents who studied at Further Education over the period 2000 to 2005 may have had weaker English skills but their self confidence as Deaf students and their knowledge of the system of transition was much better.

Summary

The study showed that this group of d/Deaf students was generally optimistic about transition to Higher Education if they had researched the course and access available in the university of their choice. Issues of access to interpreters, notetakers and language tutors affected all students, but those who chose universities with a large d/Deaf peer group experienced less personal pressure in arranging access. A d/Deaf peer group was also important at college to encourage students to apply to university.

Issues for practitioners

1. How can the Further Education sector provide more consistent access arrangements for d/Deaf students so that more are able to progress to Level Three courses?
2. What transition activities can be built into d/Deaf students' experiences at college so that they explore the issues which will face them at university?
3. Should Further Education tutors provide language tutorials more like the ones they will experience in Higher Education, or could Higher Education language tutors learn from Further Education practice?
4. Could tutors of d/Deaf students in Further Education provide more focused tuition on academic writing skills to prepare their students for Higher Education?
5. What can we do to facilitate the employment of more Deaf teachers to work in Further Education and Higher Education with d/Deaf students?

Further Reading

BATOD 2006 Audiometric descriptors for pure tone audiograms [Internet], High Wycombe: British Association of Teachers of the Deaf. Available from: <www.batod.org.uk/content/articles/audiology/audiometric-descriptors.pdf > [Accessed 22 December 2006].

Bochner, J. & Walter, G. 2005 'Evaluating deaf students' readiness to meet the English language and literacy demands of post secondary educational programs' *Journal of Deaf Studies and Deaf Education* 10, 3, 232–243.

Bowe, G. 2003 'Transition for deaf and hard of hearing students, a blueprint for change' *Journal of Deaf Studies and Deaf Education.* 8, 4: 485–493.

Davis, A., Fortnum, H. & Bamford, J. 1998 'Epidemiologic issues associated with newborn hearing screening' in Bess, F. H. (ed.) *Children with hearing impairment: contemporary trends.* Nashville, Vanderbilt Bill Wilkerson Center Press, 1 - 10.

DFES 2006a 'School and college achievement and attainment tables 2005 GCSE (and equivalent) results: Manchester' [Internet], London: Department for Education and Skills. Available from: < www.tinyurl.com/fmelr> [Accessed 22 December 2006].

DFES 2006b 'Adult literacy core curriculum: Entry 3, The national standards and level descriptors' [Internet], London: Department for Education and Skills. Available from: <http://www.dfes.gov.uk/curriculum_literacy/level/e3/ > [Accessed 22 December 2006].

Gregory, S., Bishop, J. & Sheldon, L. 1995 *Deaf young people and their families.* Cambridge, Cambridge University Press.

Haydon, A., Paczuska, A. (eds.) 2002 *Access, participation and Higher Education.* London, Kogan Page.

Jarvis, J. & Knight, P. 2003 'Supporting deaf students in Higher Education' In: Powell, S. *Special Teaching in Higher Education.* London, Kogan Page.

Lang, H. 2002 'Higher Education for deaf students: research priorities in the new millennium' *Journal of Deaf Studies and Deaf Education* 7, 4: 267–280.

May, T. 1993 *Social research.* Buckingham, Open University Press

O'Neill, R., Mowat, P., Gallagher, J. & Atkins, P. 2002 'Deaf students and their support in Further Education in the United Kingdom: Results from the NATED Survey 2000' *Deafness and Education International* .4, 2: 99–114.

Powers, S. 2003 'Influences of student and family factors on academic outcomes of mainstream secondary school deaf students' *Journal of Deaf Studies and Deaf Education.* 8, 1: 57–78.

Reay, D. 2001 'Working class relationships to education' *Journal of education policy* 16, 4: 333-346.

RNID 2003 'RNID/Barclays launch new initiative to help universities improve access for deaf students' [Internet], London, Royal National Institute for Deaf People. Available from:<http://tinyurl.com/vdmcm> [Accessed 22 December 2006].

Sarantakos, S. 1994 *Social research.* London, Macmillan.

Skelton, T. & Valentine, G. 2003 'It feels like being Deaf is normal': an exploration into the complexities of defining D/deafness and young D/deaf people's identities' *The Canadian Geographer* 47, 4: 451–466.

Stinson, M., Walter, G. 2000 'Persistence of deaf and hard-of-hearing students: what the literature tells us' Quoted in: Lang, H., Biser, E., Mousley, K., Orland, R. & Porter, J. 2004 'Tutoring deaf students in Higher Education: a comparison of Baccalaureate and Sub-baccalaureate student perceptions' *Journal of Deaf Studies and Deaf Education* 9, 2: 190.

UCAS 2006 *Educational background: applicants and accepted applicants as percent (%) (2002-2005 entry)*. Universities and Colleges Admissions Service. Available from: <http://www.ucas.com/figures/ucasdata/background/ed1.html> [Accessed 22 December 2006].

Yorke, M. 2000 'Smoothing the transition into Higher Education: what can be learned from student non-completion?' *Journal of Institutional Research* 9, 1: 36-47.

CHAPTER FOUR

Year Zero for Deaf Students: an access course for deaf students

Gary Quinn and Nicola Nunn

This chapter describes a unique access course for Deaf students introduced by the University of Central Lancashire in 2000. The authors track the progress of students from pre-entry to post-graduation, exploring the impact of the course on their study and choice of career. The successes of the programme and the issues arising from its delivery will be addressed, supported by students' accounts of their experiences of the benefits of discrete access provision. By outlining the rationale and structure of the course, it is hoped this chapter will offer practical guidance to other institutions considering the development of similar programmes.

Rationale for the programme

As the current trend within education generally is towards the inclusion of Deaf students, rather than offering discrete provision, it is perhaps necessary to explain the motivation for establishing a specialist course for Deaf students. Although the course begins in a discrete setting, it culminates in a gentle introduction to the inclusive Higher Education experience. As such, the course draws on the strengths of both approaches, whilst hopefully avoiding some of the weaknesses inherent in each.

In Britain, the way in which education has been provided for Deaf people has historically proved inappropriate and problematic. This is in part because the predominantly oral system reduced access to learning; a situation often exacerbated by an effective ban on the use of sign language in educational settings. The effect on Deaf people has been that many have not received a full education (Powers et al, 1998), which in turn has resulted in low academic achievement, a lack of confidence in academic settings, and difficulties in coping at Higher Education level (Barnes 1997). Low academic achievement denies Deaf people access to Higher Education, and the resultant lack of academic qualifications leads to lower social status (Quinn and Barnes 2004). One consequence of this is that traditionally there have been very few Deaf professionals in Britain. Deafness *per se* does not signify intellectual impairment yet few Deaf people gain high status jobs, and ingrained attitudes persist that Deaf people are unable to 'cope' or to function at a professional level (Quinn and Barnes 2004). This means that Deaf people suffer not only from reduced educational success; they also experience a higher level of unemployment and underemployment than the general population (Quinn and Barnes 2004).

Students in Further and Higher Education who are classified as disabled are entitled to claim Disabled Student's Allowance (DSA).[9] DSA provides financial assistance to pay for human and technological support for disabled students, in order to provide equality of access and opportunity. In the case of Deaf students, DSA pays for such support as interpreter and notetaker services, language tutors and any necessary assistive technology, such as radio hearing aids. As a result, the number of Deaf students in British universities has risen considerably since 1993. Despite this, there is a high drop-out rate amongst Deaf students attending universities, as highlighted in the Green Paper 'The Learning Age: a renaissance for a new Britain' (DfEE 1998). This situation has arisen despite the framework for encouraging disadvantaged students outlined in the 1999 White Paper 'Learning to Succeed: a new framework for post-16 learning'. Prior to the introduction of DSA, poor support was identified as a key contributor to low retention rates amongst British Deaf students (Olohan et al, 1995). Even after support was provided, students still suffered from a lack of academic experience and continued to face a general absence of 'Deaf friendliness' on the part of institutions (Olohan et al, 1995).

In the United Kingdom, universities are literate environments, where spoken and written English are the basis of academic life. Lectures, tutorials, and seminars are all spoken, whilst lecture notes, reading texts

---

[9] DSA is a centrally funded grant provided to disabled students by their Local Education Authority. The amount awarded to individual students is based upon an assessment of need and is paid directly to the students themselves. DSA is not intended to give disabled students an unfair advantage over non-disabled students.

and research are all in written English. There is an explicit expectation that students' work be submitted in written and spoken English of an appropriate academic standard, no matter what the native language of individual students. Thus, whilst Deaf students are as intelligent as their hearing peers, Deaf BSL users face a formidable barrier within Higher Education, as they cannot easily access texts and complete written assignments. This disadvantage is a linguistic one, rooted in the fact that English and British Sign Language are different languages. For many Deaf students, English may be a second or third language, and they enjoy a culture different to that of their hearing peers (Quinn and Barnes 2004). Many lecturers do not understand this difference, nor do they appreciate the nature of their Deaf students' particular language needs. In effect, both university staff and fellow (hearing) students are not fully aware of what being Deaf really means.

In 1999, the University of Central Lancashire (UCLan) applied to the Higher Education Funding Council for England (HECFE) for funding to develop a discrete access course that would meet the specific needs of Deaf students wishing to read for undergraduate degrees. The Deaf Studies team at UCLan was subsequently awarded funding under HEFCE's 'Widening Participation' strand for a three-year project. The project was to establish the Year Zero for Deaf Students course, which aimed to bridge the gap between Further and Higher Education for Deaf students. The first cohort of students was enrolled in September 2000.

The course was the first of its kind in the UK, and represented a positive step forward for Deaf students in realising their academic potential. Before the inception of the Year Zero for Deaf Students, such students had, of necessity, to either enter the first year of undergraduate study or take an Access course that did not cater for their particular needs. Subsequently, it was recognised that many Deaf students were unprepared for the demands of undergraduate study, and needed extra time to develop confidence and improve literacy and study skills. Perhaps unsurprisingly, many Deaf students were unable to realise their potential to succeed at Higher Education level, as evidenced by the low numbers of Deaf students entering universities and the high withdrawal rates of those who did. For many Deaf students in the UK, the Year Zero for Deaf Students course afforded the first real opportunity to achieve academic success in an Higher Education setting. The Year Zero for Deaf Students was able to draw on the existing Year Zero Access course at UCLan, whose main aim is to ensure the university's courses were fully accessible to all. Therefore, it seemed logical to combine the successful approaches used on the generic Year Zero courses with the expertise within the Deaf Studies team as the basis for creating the Year Zero for Deaf Students course.

The aim of the Year Zero for Deaf Students was not to provide a 'back door' or 'fast track' route into Higher Education for Deaf Students. Deaf students had to meet the same academic standards as hearing students in order to pass the course and progress to undergraduate study. The only difference was in the way the course was structured and delivered to meet the specific needs of Deaf students.

Course structure

Students on the Year Zero for Deaf Students followed a course of study that provided them with a mixture of modules delivered in both discrete and integrated settings. The emphasis in Semester One was on developing students' study and academic skills, whilst in Semester Two, they had the opportunity to learn more about particular subjects alongside hearing students, as a precursor to choosing subjects for their undergraduate studies.

Figure 1

Year Zero (generic): semester 1	Year Zero for Deaf Students: semester 1
ASB012 Introduction to study ASB004 Introduction to IT ASB013 Introduction to subjects MSB003 Numeracy ASB009 Valuing diversity Plus one of the following:- ASB010Reflection on experience ASB011 Supplementary study skills	*DFB001 Introduction to study skills* *DFB002 Access to Higher Education* *DFB004 English skills for Higher Education* ASB013 Introduction to subjects MSB003 Numeracy ASB004 Introduction to IT

Figure 1 above shows the course structures of the two Year Zero courses during the first semester. In the left-hand column, the modules studied by hearing students on the generic Year Zero course are listed. The right-hand column shows modules taken by students on the Year Zero for Deaf Students programme. Modules listed in italics indicate discrete modules delivered exclusively to Deaf students through the medium of British Sign Language (BSL). This discrete provision was a result of research that indicated that when Deaf students were taught alongside hearing peers, they tended to struggle considerably in subjects such as Study skills and English. When these courses were delivered in spoken English, some Deaf students did not have access, did not understand and, consequently, did not learn. Even with the provision of a BSL/English interpreter, the message was not always clearly relayed, and second-hand learning was not always effective (Traynor and Harrington 1999).

As this comparison shows, the content of both courses is very similar, with the discrete modules for Deaf students matching those of their hearing counterparts whilst addressing the particular needs of Deaf students. For example, generic Year Zero English classes tend to focus on literature, or on improving the existing skills of native English users. As Deaf students usually have low levels of English language competence, there is a greater need for specialist teaching to develop their English language skills to the standard required for undergraduate study. For this reason, a specialist *English Skills for Higher Education* module was developed for the Year Zero for Deaf Students and was taught via British Sign Language.

Similarly, the development of study skills was identified as a key issue in providing Deaf students with the necessary tools for success in Higher Education. The existing Year Zero Study Skills modules were based on spoken English and texts prepared for hearing students. In its place, a specialist *Introduction to Study Skills* module, taught in BSL and taking Deaf culture as its reference, was introduced. This was more accessible to Deaf students and proved very successful in developing these key academic skills.

The *Access to Higher Education* module provided insights into the support systems available to students at UCLan, such as how to book and cancel interpreters, notetakers, and so on. Some Deaf students are overwhelmed by university culture, whilst at the same time having to grapple with the intricacies of DSA budget management and the organisation of support networks. This module proved invaluable in addressing these problems, as BSL/English interpreters were engaged to provide first-language access when representatives of the various support agencies of the university explained their specialist areas. The remainder of the modules in semester were integrated with the generic Year Zero programme, with interpreters and notetakers providing *in situ* support. Students used additional language tutorials outside the classroom to clarify any queries arising from materials provided in written English and to support them in preparation for classes and the writing of assignments.

A vitally important factor of the Year Zero for Deaf Students was that the course tutor was a Deaf person with direct experience of the issues faced by Deaf students within Higher Education. As well as providing a positive role model for the students, the course tutor was also able to hold group and individual tutorials with the students in their first language. This gave students the opportunity to discuss all aspects of their course and the tutor was able to check individuals' progress without the need for any third parties being present. There was a considerable amount of compulsory tutorial support during the first semester, to ensure that any problems were identified and dealt with quickly and effectively.

Semester two

During semester two, a more integrated approach was taken, with only two discrete modules provided for the Deaf students; the remainder were taken alongside hearing students. Deaf students still met for modules in extended study skills and *Critical Thinking.* This latter module was an extension of the earlier *English Skills for Higher Education* module, with the aim of developing the students' awareness of how to argue and debate at academic level. The two discrete modules aimed to give the students a deeper awareness of degree level study, through developing their analytical skills and in presenting cohesive arguments. The remainder of the Semester Two programme followed the pattern of the generic Year Zero programme, by allowing students a free choice of four subjects from the undergraduate Combined Honours programme. These modules provided students with opportunities to practise their developing skills within a rigorous academic environment. Deaf and hearing students mixed within the classroom and all were taught in the same style with the same assignments to complete. All students (Deaf and hearing) were introduced to the issues of working with interpreters and notetakers in lectures and seminars. Deaf students also had access to additional language support for assignment writing and lecture preparation. An additional benefit of these integrated modules was the raising of awareness of the needs of Deaf students amongst fellow students and academic staff.

In Semester Two, the group tutorial was withdrawn, in order to promote greater academic independence amongst the students, although individual tutorials were retained. In effect, students were given more responsibility for managing their own programme of tutorial support, whilst still being actively encouraged to make full use of the support available from the course tutor.

Evaluating the course

When the first cohort of Year Zero Deaf students graduated from their degree courses, a longitudinal evaluation of the three-year project was undertaken. Students from all three cohorts were interviewed individually and collectively about their experiences on the Year Zero course and its impact on their studies at undergraduate level. Their experiences prior to joining the course were also taken into consideration. The students were interviewed in BSL, and the interviews were recorded on video. A total of fourteen students were interviewed, from an overall body of twenty-three students who had completed the Year Zero for Deaf Students.

Some of the responses and feedback received from students on what they considered the best features of the course are given below:

> 'Learning about things that would be useful for me for university life!';
>
> 'A Deaf teacher! It's easy to have someone who I can talk to in my own language and I find it easier to follow';
>
> '...good learning about future in University, what I will do when I am step 1st year';
>
> 'I do found the intro of Study Skills very interested, I have learned a lots of Study Skills';
>
> 'The availability to have tutorials with a Deaf tutor';
>
> 'Having practice with writing skills, answering questions before going on to Year One';
>
> 'Everything explained clearly, step by step which was good and easy to follow';
>
> 'The method of teaching and the 'freedom' – the ability to write or read anything. No restrictions'.
> (Cited in Quinn and Barnes 2004)

Developing the course content

Following the completion of the first year of the course, the entire course was evaluated and some important changes were made, in order to improve the content further. The most important of these changes affected the key topics of numeracy and English.

Numeracy

The first cohort of Deaf students studied numeracy alongside hearing students in the generic class, supported by sign language interpreters. The lecturer, who has extensive experience in teaching numeracy at this level, reported that using an interpreter meant the Deaf students were always slightly behind their hearing peers in accessing and contributing to whole-class activities. This was especially problematic as the lecturer often demonstrated numeracy principles on a whiteboard, and talked through these at the same time. The Deaf students were unable to watch the interpreter and follow the examples being given on the board simultaneously. In addition, many of the course materials were written in an idiomatic form of English that the Deaf students reported to be often incomprehensible. The course was subsequently altered to include a discrete numeracy group for Deaf students, delivered in BSL by a Deaf lecturer. The lecturer retained the module content but amended the delivery and resources, using PowerPoint presentations to achieve a visual approach that was more suited to the needs of Deaf students.

English

For the first year of the course, English was offered for one semester, followed by a module in *Critical Thinking* in the second semester, to extend and develop students' literacy skills. However, it soon became clear that a regime of two hours per week for one semester was insufficient to provide the necessary English literacy skills to cope with the demands of a degree course. The *Critical Thinking* module made new and different demands on the students and the need for additional practical literacy development was evident. Student feedback was unanimous; they all wanted more English of the kind offered in the first semester. The module tutor confirmed that a bare twenty-six hours of tuition was not enough to bring Deaf students' literacy skills up to that required for degree entry level.

The English module was extended to a full academic year, which enabled the tutor to extend the scope of the module and include some of the basic grammar tuition the students demanded, though the emphasis remained on applied academic English. In addition, literacy was afforded the same amount of tutorial time as numeracy. This revised approach proved more successful, and provided a more satisfactory module offering a wider range of essential literacy knowledge and skills.

Issues of integration and awareness

Through their involvement in the Year Zero for Deaf Students course, some academic staff who did not normally encounter Deaf students had the opportunity to experience working in such an environment for the first time. A lack of Deaf awareness amongst some lecturers did lead to some initial difficulties but these were largely overcome following discussions with the course tutor and the Adviser for Deaf Students. These experiences ranged from lectures that were delivered too rapidly for interpreters to keep up, to grave misconceptions about the role of support workers. For example, one lecturer had to be persuaded that the notetaker was there for legitimate reasons and was not 'doing the work' for the Deaf students. Some lecturers avoided eye contact with Deaf students (a necessary aspect of communication), digressed, or failed to give explanations or allow for questions. The important difference to the students' previous experiences of educational settings was that they now had the knowledge and confidence to inform lecturers of the effects of these situations and thereby increase awareness.

It is noteworthy that the Deaf students also gained 'hearing awareness'. The Deaf students gained insight into the workings of the University in the first semester, and by the second semester entered integrated classes knowing how to make best use of their support workers. Armed with this, they approached integrated classes better able to cope with academic work, and student confidence in working with interpreters and notetakers improved. Some students reported that they now enjoyed working with hearing students and lecturers, and felt that the situation had been eased by their gentle introduction to academic life in the first semester. They no longer felt afraid to ask for advice and support, and felt more able to contribute without fear or apprehension. What Deaf students had previously seen as the 'attitude problem' of hearing people was recognised as the result of unfamiliarity, lack of resources, and lack of awareness, all of which could be remedied.

Student experiences on the course

Students were asked for their overall feelings about studying as a Year Zero Deaf student. Many of them said that the opportunity to experience university life enabled them to build up a wealth of essential information and knowledge, such as 'university jargon', the range of available support systems, degree course options and the techniques and culture of study. 'Full access' was mentioned frequently. Having lectures delivered in BSL was seen as a real advantage, and students reported that they appreciated having Deaf lecturers who shared and understood their experiences. They reported feeling more independent and confident by having direct access to education in their own language. They felt that the structure of the course helped them to prepare for integration with hearing students, and that the direct access through BSL in the first semester had built up their confidence, knowledge and understanding ready for the step into integrated classes in the following semester. In their previous educational experiences, the students had encountered enormous barriers. By removing these in the first half of the course, the Year Zero enabled the students to enter Higher Education with more confidence, and with insight into ways to work within the system and make optimum use of the support available.

Conclusion

In an ideal world, there would be no need for a course of this nature, as all students, regardless of background or personal characteristics, would enjoy equal opportunities in an equal environment. The reality is that many Deaf people have had poor educational experiences at schools and colleges, resulting in a subsequent lack of success in Higher Education. Although educational opportunities are increasing for Deaf people, access for Deaf BSL users remains in dire need of improvement. It will take time for improvements in educational philosophy and practice to take effect.

In the UK, literacy remains at the heart of the debate on educational standards. In order to achieve academic success, a high level of literacy is required and this poses problems for many profoundly Deaf people. Courses such as the Year Zero for Deaf Students will help to address the difficulties in entering Higher Education posed by the barrier of literacy. The Year Zero for Deaf Students made the first moves towards bridging the access gap. Until there is full access and equality, courses such as the Year Zero for Deaf Students will be necessary. In disseminating these experiences and examples of good practice, it is hoped that similar courses will be established and secure the future of access to Higher Education for Deaf students.

Key issues to consider

A number of examples of good practice were evident in the course and these are identified here as key issues for consideration by other institutions wishing to set up a similar access course for Deaf students. These illustrate the appropriateness of the provision offered by the Year Zero for Deaf Students course in meeting the needs of Deaf students entering Higher education (see also Quinn and Barnes 2004).

1. First language delivery

All the discrete modules were taught in BSL, either by Deaf tutors or by tutors with experience of teaching Deaf students. For example, the English tutor was a specialist in Deaf literacy with a good command of BSL, and had long experience of teaching literacy and language at this level.

2. Advice and support

- Tutors provided guidance and advice to students, helping them to make informed decisions, whilst at the same time encouraging the students to take responsibility for all aspects of their own learning;
- During the first semester, the students were provided with a lot of personal individual support, with scheduled individual and group tutorials;
- The course staff worked together with the university support services to ensure the provision of high quality support, with appropriately qualified interpreters, notetakers and language support tutors all available.

3. Promoting independence

Some Deaf students were accustomed to being very dependent on others for help with study; many had been given one-to-one help throughout their previous studies. This was not necessarily good preparation for the university environment. The Year Zero for Deaf Students gently eased the students into independent study, slowly reducing the amount of tutorial direction and support as their confidence grew. The students developed their own skills, and from being dependent upon others, gradually became confident and independent self-learners.

4. Managing inclusion and integration

Deaf students were gradually introduced to a more integrated educational environment. Deaf students, especially those placed in mainstream education, have often experienced isolation in education (Quinn and Barnes 2004). On the Year Zero for Deaf Students, they had a group of Deaf peers with whom they could feel comfortable, and who could be mutually supportive. Deaf undergraduates at the University were also part of this supportive network and became important role models. UCLan also has several Deaf staff, and this proved very important in affording the students the opportunity to see Deaf BSL users in responsible, professional roles, thus encouraging their aspirations and fostering ambition.

5. Promoting Deaf awareness

If the experience of coming to university is daunting for young Deaf students, having Deaf students in their courses for the first time can be equally daunting for lecturers and hearing students. All hearing lecturers and students coming in to contact with Deaf students at UCLan are offered Deaf Awareness training sessions, and it is hoped that they will also absorb some Deaf awareness naturally, through a form of cultural osmosis. At the same time, it must not be forgotten that the Deaf students gain greater awareness of the ways of the hearing world. This is especially useful for those who attended special Deaf Schools and may not be used to mixing with hearing people.

Further reading

Barnes, L., 1997 'Supporting deaf students in Higher Education: a service model' in *Neįgaliųjų asmenų socialiniai poreikiai, jų tyrimoiir tekino problemos* [Report on International Conference on Disabled Students in Higher Education, Lithuania]

Department for Education and Employment 1998 *The Learning Age: a renaissance for a new Britain*. London, Her Majesty's Stationery Office

Department for Education and Employment 1999 *Learning to succeed: a new framework for post-16 learning*. London, Her Majesty's Stationery Office

Traynor, N. and Harrington, F. J. 1999 'Second-hand learning: experiences of deaf students in Higher Education' in: *Proceedings of the Deaf Nation symposium 2: pathways to policy part 2*. [video] London, London Deaf Access Project

National Union of Teachers 1979 *Special education needs: the NUT response to the Warnock Report.* London, The National Union of Teachers

Olohan et al 1995 *Access and communication support for deaf and hearing impaired students in Higher Education.* Nottingham, Nottingham Trent University Press

Powers S, Gregory S, and Thoutenhoofd E D 1998 *The educational achievements of deaf children.* London, Her Majesty's Stationery Office

Quinn, G. A. and Barnes, L. 2004 'Year Nought for Deaf students at the University of Central Lancashire. Opening doors to Higher Education: Developing and enhancing study skills for Deaf Students'. In C. Storbeck, ed. *Building bridges to literacy.* Witwatersrand, University of the Witwatersand

CHAPTER FIVE

The naked deaf student

Gavin Lilley, Paul Scott and Donna Williams

Introduction

This chapter is not so much an academic account of life at university as Deaf students, as a series of reflections of our student experiences from our individual perspectives as Deaf individuals. We are each from very different backgrounds, and we have had very different experiences of growing up, going through our formal education and coming out the other side, wondering where life would take us. Donna was brought up in a English speaking family and went through an oral education in a PHU, Gavin was educated bilingually, and taught to speak as well as to sign, while Paul has always used BSL as his native language.

Although we are each very different, we hope we have demonstrated that the experience of coming to University has had a real impact on our lives, and that there are at least some common themes running through our experiences.

Donna Williams

My background is similar to that of hundreds, if not thousands of other young Deaf adults. I was eventually diagnosed as being deaf when I was three and a half years old, after having apparently lost my hearing some two years earlier when I was 18 months old. I am told that the fact that it took two years for even that to happen is not that uncommon, but I digress. I was given hearing aids, and as I learned to talk again with minimal encouragement, this was taken as a positive sign and I was sent to a mainstream school with a Partially Hearing Unit (PHU) when I was four. I stayed in mainstream school for all of my education, and emerged at 18 with good GCSE and A level grades, but almost totally unprepared for the hearing world. This was in spite of my Local Education Authority who twice tried to cut my funding because I was doing 'too well' – make of that what you will. I would describe my abilities as 'functional' in that I can function in the hearing world just enough to get by; I can speak and lip-read well enough to get me past interviews (which are generally face to face in a quiet environment) and I can lip-read well enough to understand most people so long as they are directly in front of me. But in a hearing social situation I was lost. Lost. Group conversations, noisy places, forget it!

Little did I know that the university I had chosen to go to in September 2003 would change my life.

How had I chosen this university? Quite by accident, in fact. I was in the last year of my A Levels and in the sixth form at my school it was expected that we would apply for university. Entire tutorials were devoted to the subject. Among other things, we were taught how to use the UCAS website which allows you to browse all the possible courses you can take, in alphabetical order - if one clicked on the letter 'P', one would get all the courses beginning with P, and so on. This is precisely what I was doing, as I was planning to take a course on Philosophy … but I got bored and I started clicking on other letters just to see what was there. Quite by chance, I clicked on the letter 'D' and scrolling down, I came across 'Deaf Studies'. It would be an understatement to say that I was surprised. Most of my life, I had been taught that being hearing impaired was an unfortunate thing, but something that could be overcome if one worked hard enough to fit in. Now here was an entire academic university course devoted to being Deaf? What? Out of curiosity, I clicked on it and it came up with four universities: UCLan, Bristol, Wolverhampton and Durham. For no particular reason I clicked on UCLan. The rest, as they say, is history.

I arrived at University with no idea of what to expect. I met my first UCLan Deafies[10] on the first night, at the Welcome induction at the Guild Hall, where all the first years are rounded up and the Vice-Chancellor officially welcomes us to UCLan. I had of course asked to be at the front and all of a sudden I was in the midst of true Deafies, all signing away. There was an interpreter. And I, again, was completely lost. All of those people I met, who are now my friends, say that they laugh

---

[10] My use of the term 'Deafies' here is intended only as a term of endearment, and is my way of referring to my deaf fellow students and friends who see themselves as culturally and lingually Deaf. It is not in any way intended as an insult.

when they remember meeting me for the first time, because I was so lost but still trying to keep up nonetheless. One or two have said that what impressed them was the fact I even tried, albeit probably too hard and that I was willing to try.

As eager as I was pleased, it was still a huge culture shock. I remember wondering why everybody kept hugging me to say hello and goodbye, even wondering if perhaps I looked ill or something and that was why people kept hugging me? After a while I realised that this was just Deaf culture, hugging friends and occasionally people you have only just met. I remember trying to get someone's attention, eventually touching their chin to try and get them to look at me, and being told off soundly for it. I found out later that this was a child's mistake, that Deaf/CODA children who try this get told off as well; is that an indicator of how much I knew about Deaf culture at that time? [11] Was I that clueless? Apparently, yes I was, since once, in a nightclub, after a toast of 'Deaf Power!' I added 'Deaf oral power!' jokingly referring to myself - and was rewarded with a group of stunned stares.

I had started learning to sign, in earnest. I even started, almost unconsciously, signing a little while I was talking. But then, one of my lecturers actually told me not to do it, saying that I did not need to sign. I wonder if she realised that when she said that, I could hear an echo of a former PHU teacher who had some strong views about how to educate Deaf children and who made my life a misery. This didn't put me off at all, however, and I carried on going to where the deaf folk were, going to social events like the Preston Fancy Dress, trying to fit in with these Deaf people. There were a few cultural lessons to learn along the way, some the hard way, some the easy way. By January 2004 I could sign well enough, albeit very SSE, to consider joining the Deaf Society Committee at their AGM. Someone suggested to me that I could become the Secretary, making notes of what happened in meetings, because of my command of English. I wasn't sure how other, slightly more militant, Deafies would feel about me – an oral Deafie - taking over what was essentially a position of power in the committee, but at the AGM I was voted in without a word of protest. In fact, I received support from some unexpected places.

So it was that I became Secretary, and in some cases an unofficial English tutor, helping out here and there with spelling and meanings of long words. I learned how to type up the notes in Plain English and because I was Secretary, I could justifiably interrupt a meeting and bring

---

[11] CODA – Child/ren of Deaf Adults

it to a standstill in order to ask what a particular sign meant, because otherwise, how I could write down what was being said? This helped me learn BSL at an accelerated rate, albeit at the cost of occasionally annoying the entire committee after I had halted the meeting for the umpteenth time. Once, someone did say something along the lines of 'oh for God's sake, do you have to do this every time?' which I simply countered with 'Do you want to write the notes? Do you? Do you?', but apart from that one little incident I would say that my time as Secretary was highly successful. The next year, I decided to try and become Vice-Chair. Again, I wasn't sure how Deafies would feel about me apparently muscling in on a position of more power than Secretary, but again, I was supported wholeheartedly and this time I was voted in almost unanimously.

Towards the end of my third and final year, I learned that the Students Union was holding its yearly elections for the council. Among various other minor positions, they were looking for new officers, technically vice presidents, for certain key positions, such as communications, entertainment and equal opportunities. The Deaf and BSL Society has always tried to be close to the Students Union, often dealing with the then-equal opportunities officer, Jen, who suggested to me that maybe, as I was in my final year, I could run for equal opportunities. At first, I laughed it off, but my friends said I could do a good job and I started to take it seriously. It did seem like a good job. I would be making a difference. And I could stay in Preston, where all my friends were. I couldn't think of any reason not to have a go. Even so, it took some words of encouragement from one of my best friends to persuade me to at least try. So I ran for election. I made a manifesto, I campaigned, I did Question Time, I did an interview on the radio, I was featured in the student newspaper, and every spare moment I had for a whole week I dressed up as a gangster and handed out leaflets saying: 'WANTED: Donna Williams for Equal Opportunities Officer'. The Election Party on Friday evening when the results were announced was one of the best nights of my life. All of my friends turned out to support me, and we had the whole area in front of the announcer's podium all to ourselves; twenty-odd Deafies had descended and taken it over! Those who couldn't come sent messages of support and even the interpreter who had interpreted my Question Time and my radio interview came along to help out. I had asked a hearing friend, a trainee interpreter, to interpret the election announcements, so strictly speaking the interpreter didn't need to be there, but she came anyway, which reminds me; I still owe her a drink!

I lost. By under 40 votes out of over 700 votes cast. It was a near-run thing between myself and my closest rival. But even so, I wouldn't give up the experience for anything; campaigning helped boost my self-confidence as it forced me to get out there and persuade people to vote for me, and the impromptu post-election party that the Deafies held in my honour was fantastic! My hearing trainee-interpreter friend later said that we were getting funny looks from all the other hearing candidates; no-one could understand why we were celebrating when I had just lost! Deaf Power!

One thing that really helped me though, was my final year dissertation. I decided to write my dissertation on 'The Modern Deaf Identity Crisis', discussing how Deaf children are nowadays often brought up in hearing culture. When, as young adults, they are suddenly exposed to Deaf culture, it can start an identity crisis as the ingrained hearing identity becomes usurped by and fights against the new Deaf identity. I chose that title and that topic because it is understandably close to my heart, and researching and writing it really helped me understand more about myself and why I felt the way did when I was first learning about Deaf culture. It also helped me address a number of questions about myself. Why I feel the way I do now – as if I am split and that part of me is hearing (in that I come from and at the moment live in the hearing world), yet part of me is Deaf (in that I sign, and often prefer to sign), and that I feel part of the Deaf community. I got a high score for my dissertation and hope one day it will be published, so that other people can see it and understand more about what it feels like to be trapped between two different worlds.

I have graduated now; in July 2006 I donned my gown and mortar-board and accepted my degree. I had a great day: the sun was shining, I didn't look too bad in the outfit, my friends were there, my parents were there, and I felt proud of myself – not just for graduating with an Upper Second Class Honours degree, but also for accomplishing what I had set out to achieve in my first year: securing my place in the Deaf community.

Gavin Lilley

I'd had enough of college. Truthfully, I didn't feel I was going anywhere – most of my time (and money) was spent on parties and going out with Deaf mates. I felt like I was the only Deaf person at the college – there were a few others, but most of them had learning difficulties and were on different courses, I couldn't really interact with them. There was an army of Communication Support Workers (CSWs) at the college all bearing minimal qualifications in BSL, with an exception of one or two. So most of my time there was pretty dull, as you can imagine. My fellow classmates in the GNVQ Advanced Media Studies course were all hearing and the longest sentence I ever shared with any of them would probably have been, 'Have a good weekend, see you Monday'.

It is no fault of theirs, or mine. It is just how things are. I am firmly embedded within the Deaf community. My parents are both Deaf and BSL is the main form of communication at the Lilley household. True, I was brought up bilingually - this means I have access to both English and BSL, and having been subject to oral torture at school I am able to speak (not at hearing levels, obviously) but I have chosen not to continue this. One could say I have taken a vow of silence. It is a belief of mine that if all Deaf people speak (or attempt to do so) with hearing people, how can these people learn Deaf awareness or even BSL?

That was the main driving force that led me to Preston. A few friends of mine had told me about the Deaf Studies course there and that there was an access course available – 'Year Zero for Deaf Students'. This was perfect - I had pulled out of the course at college, holding only my GCSEs without even a key to enter the world of Higher Education. I would be studying with a number of other Deaf students.

It was early August when I decided to go to UCLan. A quick minicom call, a train journey up north from the suburbs of Greater London and a meeting with the Course Leader of the Year Zero course. He looked through my GCSEs, asked me a few questions. At the end, he seemed to be happy to offer me a place on this course. I remember him saying 'This is a very last minute application, you've got to find a place to live within a month!' UCAS sent me a number of forms, to enable me to fill in more forms. The amount of paperwork was chaotic but I managed, somehow, to complete all the forms, securing my position at UCLan and arranging interpreter and notetaker support as well as student loans and fees. I told my parents (much to their surprise) that I'd be moving to Preston in a month, and they were truly fantastic in their support. Fortunately, a friend of mine was applying for the same course and she had found a place to live and there was one vacancy. I grabbed it with both hands. Things were going well.

It was one early September evening when my train pulled up in to Preston. Laden with a number of bags I emerged out of the station to embrace the air of Preston and to take a moment to admire the place where I would be spending four years of my life (or so I thought), making new friends and life-altering decisions and all that. Guess what? It was raining. Cats and dogs. Welcome to Preston!

The first week was very intimidating. The weather was awful, my house was miles from the city centre and everybody else seemed to know what they were doing. Luckily I had a handful of friends who were a great help. The second week was when things improved. Lectures started and I met a number of other Deaf students. We began to get to know each other as well as the lecturers within Deaf Studies, the interpreters from the Specialised Learning Resource Unit (SLRU) and the local pubs.

The Year Zero for Deaf Students course was fantastic, with an excellent lecturer and I began to see things in a more academic way.[12] I learnt how to be critical of things (to some extent!) and established a network of career contacts and in the north-west Deaf community. I was involved in the campaign for BSL recognition, organised BSL marches, affiliated myself with the Federation of Deaf People as well as the Deaf Liberation Front, an activist group that aims to gain equality for Deaf people through direct action. The University supported me throughout and on several occasions the lecturers asked me to share my experiences via presentations and seminars. I felt appreciated.

I passed the Year Zero course and decided to continue at UCLan. I chose to do BA Deaf Studies and Journalism. After the first year, I decided not to continue with Journalism – for a number of reasons. To summarise my reasons, I just felt that it wasn't the right path to follow. I was now a BA Deaf Studies student. The whole course is provided in BSL (either directly or via interpretation) and many of the lecturers are Deaf, so I had plenty of role models at UCLan. After three fantastic years, my final year was looming. I decided to go on a student exchange abroad for a semester – this was an opportunity too good to miss. I would broaden my horizons and learn many new things.

It was decided. In September 2004 I went to Pohjois Savon Opisto in Kuopio, Finland. I studied Finnish Sign Language and did work placements with the World Federation of the Deaf (WFD) in Helsinki and at Haukkaranan School in Jyväskylä. These work placements were truly fantastic and I learnt a lot about the structure of Deaf organisations and education in Finland. I even picked up on written Finnish during my stay there.

I enjoyed it so much that I decided to stay another semester. I remember when the Course Leader of Deaf Studies came to visit me in Kuopio and we had to walk for miles through snow to have coffee and discuss my dissertation! She fully supported my decision to stay in Finland longer and I remain grateful for this. That three extra months

[12] The Year Zero for Deaf Students course is described in Chapter Four of this publication

gave me the opportunity to learn much more Finnish, their sign language (Suomen Viittomakieli) and to meet my current girlfriend, Tuija! We've been together for over three years now. When I returned to Preston to finish off my final year and to work on my dissertation, I knew that I would return to Finland someday – I loved it so much there. Tuija also came to England to study BSL.

In June 2005 I graduated and it was a proud moment for me, my family and friends (especially for my mum who wept at the ceremony). I had applied for a job to be a project officer at UCLan – to work on the design of a new BSL curriculum in Higher Education. I remember that I graduated on Tuesday and the following Thursday was my job interview! I got the job, and much to my pleasant surprise, a fellow Deaf student and a very good friend of mine, Ricci got the same job! We were students together, even housemates for some time and now we'd be working together!

Indeed, it was the right decision to come to UCLan. When I look back to that naïve Gavin who arrived at Preston that rainy day, expecting to stay for just a few years and then go back to grey London to continue maybe with some kind of dead-end job, without a girlfriend, it is clear that through the wealth of experiences achieved both in Preston and Finland, a number of brilliant friends and colleagues, the memories of many drunken nights, spending many an hour doing assignments at the break of dawn, establishing a sturdy platform from where I can start my life, I am a very different person now. I just have to laugh.

Paul Scott

As I am writing this, I am in the third year of a BA Deaf Studies and Counselling & Psychotherapy at the University of Central Lancashire (UCLan).[13] I will explain a little about myself. I am culturally Deaf, and my first language is British Sign Language, (BSL). I grew up in a Deaf family and it is from here that I have developed my identity. Also I am politically and socially active in the Deaf community in UK and round the world. I went to mainstream school in Norwich, Norfolk, and there I obtained my GCSEs and afterwards went to mainstream college to study for a GNVQ in Health and Social care (Foundation level). Once I had completed the course I moved to Derby College for Deaf people, which is a specialised college for Deaf people. I have to say that it was here that I discovered more about myself, I gained confidence and I learned about

[13] Editor's note: Paul was awarded an Upper Second Class degree in Deaf Studies and Counselling in June 2007.

different aspects of the Deaf world. I became involved in different committees, campaigns for the college, and I began to discover my own Deaf identity in more depth.

When I finished my course at Derby, I stayed on for another three years and studied GNVQ Intermediate Health and Social Care, after which I went on to do a BTEC in Animal Care which I also passed. It was at that point I began to think about my future and what I wanted to do with my life, I also wished to gain more experience in the international Deaf community and to explore different cultures, because I believed that it would help me to achieve a better sense of myself and become mature enough to go to university.

It was then that I went to Jordan in the Middle East. Originally I was meant to go be for just one year, as a gap year before university, but I ended up staying for three years. There I undertook a wide variety of work from teaching English to Deaf children, Deaf community and cultural developmental work, and I worked in a residential school. Going to Jordan was the best thing I could have done, because I explored different sign languages and met different people from different walks of life, and I also helped to produce a book to enable Jordanian Deaf people to teach other Teachers of the Deaf from different Middle Eastern countries about Deaf culture and community. This should enable the culture and language of Deaf people to be enriched in different parts of the Middle East, and in some sense help to raise the recognition of Deaf people as ethnic minority communities with their own language.

During my time in the Middle East, I did do some travelling to Lebanon, Egypt and Syria, and found that lots of Deaf people struggle to get a better chance in life. Some were fortunate but others were not. Perhaps it was due to the political issues that were happening in the region at the time. I had experienced a number of world changing events at that time, in particular September 11th and the Iraq war. It made me want to take more control of my own destiny, and to fight for better equality for Deaf and hearing people. With my family's help and this inspiration and self motivation, I manage to live there for three years and gain invaluable life experiences which have helped me in later times.

After three years, I was advised to pursue my education further, at university, so it was then that I applied to UCLan. I was overseas at the time I applied, so my contacts were mainly through email. I was accepted onto the Combined Honours programme to study a degree in Deaf Studies, Counselling & Psychotherapy, and Social Policy. Having been away all this time, I flew back to England and moved to Preston to begin my studies. When I started my first year, I studied Social Policy for two weeks, but I quickly found that the course was not for me. I believe it was because I had been out of the political and social environment of the UK for three years, and that had affected my personal views. So I decided to withdraw from that subject and in its place I chose to study Arabic.

It was at this point that I came up against an enormous barrier. The course tutors were hesitant about me doing the Arabic course, but I was determined so I went to see the Adviser for Deaf Students, who supported me in my attempt to get onto the course. We had meetings with my language tutor, interpreter, the Adviser for Deaf Students, the course leader, and the lecturer herself, and we talked about how I would be able to access the subject. The course was very aural in the way it was taught, but I felt that I could do it and that there would be another way to be able to achieve this. In the end the Course Tutor agreed to let me take the course as long I managed to pass the first semester. I was under a lot of pressure from that decision, because I wanted to prove them wrong.

When the first semester finished, I managed to meet all my deadlines for coursework, and so I was permitted to continue until the end of the year. The final assessment consisted of three different exams; oral, aural and a reading/writing exam. Another meeting was held to discuss the aural exam and what 'reasonable adjustments' would be made. It was eventually agreed that this element would be dropped, but that I would have to do the oral exam. This didn't sit easily with me, as I have strong moral views over oralism, but to do this course, I had to put them aside and take the oral exam. When I started my oral exam, I was signing in Jordanian sign language under the table, which helps me to speak in Arabic. It was very challenging and exhausting too. In the end I passed the whole subject and felt a real sense of achievement that a barrier had been broken down and that future Deaf students now have the opportunity to study a language course at university.

Over the year, I was offered to an opportunity do advanced Arabic, but I decided that I needed to focus more on my other academic work, and continued with Counselling and Psychotherapy as my Major subject, with Deaf Studies as my minor subject. It was then that I joined the University's Deaf and BSL society (DBSL) which is a society for people who are learning BSL and also for Deaf people to meet up and socialise. DBSL ran a campaign to teach basic signs to people working in the local pubs, so that they could communicate with sign language users better, and this was filmed by for the Television programme 'VEE TV' in 2005.

During my second year, I was elected Chair of DBSL and I was very pleased to take on this role as it gave me an opportunity to grow and gain more experience, and with the support from the Deaf people in the university. I enjoyed doing this role. However I was again faced with a barrier to my academic career, this time in my Counselling and Psychotherapy course. I was informed that I could not do a post-graduate course in Counselling due to the close focus group issues. A close focus group is a setting in which everyone can speak freely and the group is strictly limited to a small number of people. Because I was Deaf and required an interpreter to translate for me, I was told that this was not possible, because it was believed the presence of the interpreter would disrupt the group. I was very disappointed by that decision because I felt that I had not been given the choice, and that the decision was made and imposed on me before I had had the opportunity to explore and consider post-graduate study for myself. Again I enlisted the help of the Adviser for Deaf Students who helped me to find out the reason behind this decision. At that time I was doing triad work - three people practising counselling skills with each other - and I decided to go on strike, refusing to use my interpreter for the triad work, or to communicate with my lecturer. I did this to make a specific point. It is my belief that there should be equality for all people, regardless of their background or ethnicity to be part of the close group, and allowed to at least apply for a postgraduate course in counselling.

The Adviser for Deaf Students arranged a meeting with the senior lecturers to discuss the situation, and I was pleased that, as a result, the senior lecturer raised the issue with the BACAP (British Association for Counselling and Psychotherapy). They are now looking into ways in which the course can be modified to meet the differing needs of different students.

In conclusion, I feel that I have faced a lot of barriers in my time as a student, but I have faced up to them and challenged them, with the help and advice of those around me. University is all about exploring yourself, finding your potential achieving what you want to achieve, regardless of the barriers you face, and the negative attitude and lack of awareness of the wider society around you.

Some conclusions

It is clear that our lives have been very different, but there are two things that we have all experienced as a result of going to University. The first of these has been the development of our own personalities and identities. For Donna in particular her discovery of herself as a member of the Deaf community has been a very important by product of her University life, while for Gavin and Paul it has been an increased involvement in the life, not least the political life of the Deaf community.

The second has been our growth in terms of our academic achievement. For Paul, there have been real strides forward in terms of the types of courses that Deaf people have access to in Higher Education. For Gavin the university experience has taken him abroad, taught him a new language and resulted in a job as a researcher. For Donna there is hope that her academic work so far can lead to a possible publication, and, who knows, maybe even further study.

There are still barriers to be broken down, not least in terms of the attitudes and lack of awareness of contemporary society towards Deafness and Deaf people, but we continue to strive for our equality, not only within society, but in terms of our education and our life opportunities.

Key points

- University can be an accessible, positive experience for Deaf students;
- Attitudes are changing, and courses not traditionally available for Deaf students are becoming increasingly accessible;
- With SENDA, DDA 2005 and increasing awareness of the needs of Deaf people within Higher Education institutions, this can only continue to improve.

Section Two
Support Services

CHAPTER SIX

Can you put that in writing?

Kay McCrea and Paddy Turner

Introduction

In this chapter we will begin to unpack and explore some of the issues that currently surround notetaking within the sector. We will do this initially by reviewing the history of the development of notetaking services for deaf people within Higher Education (H.E) then we will discuss the practicalities of service provision, the training process, the monitoring of standards and quality and finally, the possible future of notetaking services.

Using a broad evidence-base, we seek to challenge the idea that the traditional provision of notetaking services gives students equal access to their learning and teaching and begin to develop a template for the future of notetaking services which both empowers and re-positions deaf students on a more level playing field with their hearing peers in the classroom.

In the context of increasing numbers of deaf students entering HE and the fact that we are now in the post SENDA (Special Educational Needs and Disability Act 2001 or Part IV of the Disability Discrimination Act 1995) era, we will also take the opportunity to explore what new technologies might become available to promote inclusion and discuss what benefits there are to the professionalisation of notetaking services for providing quality services.

Part I

Why have a notetaker?

It is widely recognised that taking notes is a vital component in the process of learning. Reasons given for this range from the notes acting as a simple but vital aide memoir to the act of notetaking actually reinforcing the learning as it happens. (DiVesta & Gray, 1972)

For most of us, taking notes is a process we take for granted. Listening to the message being delivered whilst simultaneously recording information about it for our own benefit is something we do, to a greater of lesser extent, without instruction. For deaf people though, to varying degrees, it can be a struggle.

In order to receive and understand information delivered through sound, deaf people rely on their eyes - whether it be by looking at a professional sign language interpreter or lip-speaker, or by lip-reading the speaker directly to support their lower levels of hearing (this continuum runs from reliance on lip-reading with minimal support from hearing, to reliance on hearing with low levels of support from lip-reading). Consequently, once a deaf person looks away to write notes, they can not continue to receive the information being delivered and so will miss information.

Additionally, lip reading involves high levels of guesswork: ' ... lip-reading is not just a visual skill – 75 percent of it is a sort of inspired guessing or hypothesizing, dependent on the use of contextual clues' (Sacks, 1989:70), which leaves the deaf person especially reliant on additional clues to help decipher the message accurately.

Thus, the penalty of missing information whilst writing notes is further compounded by the potential for losing track of the context and thereafter finding it even more difficult to make sense of the lip patterns seen.

When lip-reading, message context, body language and facial expression are all brought to bear just to ensure receipt of the message – processing the message and thus learning from it has to take place in addition to of these other activities. This means that the levels of concentration required by a deaf person to receive, process and extract learning have to be much higher to achieve anything remotely close to parity of experience in the classroom or other learning environment.

Given this, not only can the role of a notetaker be seen as critical in this environment, but also, for most deaf learners, the absolute minimum provision towards achieving equality.

What is a notetaker?

A notetaker is a person employed to take notes for an individual who, as a direct result of their disability, requires support to enable them to access their course.

The manual notetaker

A manual notetaker must posses a number of necessary skills. These include: speed, clarity and organisation of writing, the ability to both précis and paraphrase.

Note-takers are also required to modify language where necessary, adapt the layout of notes to suit the student, adapt the content of the subject to the student's needs, become acquainted with subject-specific language and knowledge, work both independently and as part of a team, build rapport with clients and organisations, perform critical self analysis in order to assess and develop their skills and keep accurate records. It is also necessary for notetakers to have legible handwriting, good language skills including a wide vocabulary and accurate spelling, good interpersonal skills, deaf and disability awareness, educational qualifications appropriate to the setting in which they are working, good time keeping and a commitment to equal opportunities (http://www.wmin.ac.uk/ccpd).

With these skills, a notetaker should be able to tailor their service to meet the needs of the individual. For example, in the case of a deaf student, the role of the notetaker maybe to produce a comprehensive written record of the session for the student to use as a revision aide, or alternatively, it maybe to produce a summarised script of what is being said simultaneously enabling the student direct access to the information.

How the role of the notetaker developed

Initially, and for many years, notetakers came in various guises from relatives and friends to peers and professionals.

Prior to 1990, funding in Higher Education was limited to a small award of no more than £750 to spend on resources to support access to learning. As a result deaf students had to rely on a service provided by their local social worker for the deaf/welfare officer at best or at worst, encouraged by the disability services of the time that willingly provided deaf students with carbon paper, ask for a copy of another student's notes (Green and Nickerson, 1992).

The communication support worker

As part of the Student Loans Bill 1990, the Government modified the existing Disabled Students Award (Hurst, 1996), and this initiated a significant turning point in the development of notetaking services for deaf students in Higher Education. Full-time students in Higher Education were now able to claim an additional set of allowances, the Disabled Student's Allowance (DSA), to recover costs towards the provision of specialist equipment and 'non-medical helpers', such as notetakers, if they could demonstrate that their disability would affect their undertaking of the course. The new grant of £4,000 per year was a vast improvement on what had been available.

With this increased funding came the opportunity to introduce a new breed of support worker to Higher Education, the Communication Support Worker (CSW). This role, initially developed in the mid-1980's to support deaf students in further education, involved individuals being trained to provide a range of direct personal support services, such as communicating (using sign language), taking notes and tutoring students. It is interesting to note, that at this time a 'Communicator' could be:

> ' ... a person with limited or considerable academic attainment, vastly experienced or inexperienced in industry or commerce. What they [shared] in common [was] a limited period of similar training ... ' (Green and Nickerson 1992:186).

Although at the time providing training for these individuals to deliver a professional service was seen as a step in the right direction, in essence the various roles provided by the CSW meant that the individual was often a jack-of–all-trades but a master of none.

Need for discrete services

The classroom environment prevalent in further education meant that the CSW could switch between 'signing' and notetaking without excluding the student. However, in the Higher Education environment, where information delivery is more often one-way and continuous, it quickly became apparent that deaf BSL users were having to choose between live access through interpreting but no notes, or notes but no live access . Interpreting and notetaking cannot be practised simultaneously by one individual yet it is vital for equality of access for the deaf learner in HE that both functions do occur simultaneously. To ensure that deaf students received quality access to their learning, these roles needed to be redefined as discrete functions and therefore it was necessary to provide training to individuals in distinct specialist roles rather than concentrate on one person providing a generic service.

Of course, the role of a CSW provided HE Support Services with a highly cost effective resource. Paying for one person in the classroom as opposed to two is clearly much cheaper. The £4,000 available from the DSA, whilst welcome, was now clearly insufficient to pay for both an interpreter and a notetaker to be present in all sessions. HE Support Service managers had to make a choice between quality of access on the one hand and pleasing budget holders on the other and in order to ensure that students were provided with a service relevant to their level of study it was necessary to pay for appropriately trained and qualified individuals.

Development of notetaker training

During the mid-eighties, notetaker training was merely a module within the umbrella of the Communication Support Worker qualification. Later staff working at the University of Derby revamped the module to create an entirely new and distinct qualification which later became nationally recognised as the CACDP Level 2 Certificate in Note-taking for Deaf People. The specialist role of the professional manual notetaker had been born.

Electronic note-taking

Although not the primary focus of this chapter, an additional form of notetaking service that is becoming increasingly popular with students is that of electronic note-taking. It was initially developed as an alternative live access tool for deaf people who either did not have sign language skills or who preferred to receive information in English. The main advantage for its introduction in Higher Education is that it enables both live access and notes for revision, in one package.

In contrast to manual note-taking, electronic notetaking is a computer assisted method of providing notes. The notetaker (Operator) is able to provide access to the spoken word by typing notes directly into a laptop; these notes are then simultaneously displayed on the student's (Receiver's) own laptop. These notes may also be projected onto a large screen via a data projector so that they are visible by the whole audience which is particularly useful when there are a number of individuals within the same setting requiring this form of access.

In addition to the live access element, for many deaf students, there are additional advantages of using electronic notes, over and above that of the manual notetaker.

Speed: the operator is trained to work at a minimum of 60 words per minute enabling them to produce a far more detailed and comprehensive account of the spoken word than a manual notetaker. (It should be noted here that the electronic notetaker, unlike a Palantypist or speech to text reporter, does not record verbatim).

Accuracy: dedicated software enables the operator to be prepared for specialist terminology by entering a glossary of relevant terms into the laptop prior to the session. These can then be simply produced by typing an abbreviation.

Choice and Inclusion: although in some cases the Operator's and Receiver's laptops may be connected by cable, more often, laptops can be set up wirelessly, enabling the student to choose, like every other student, where they sit in the classroom whereas if the student is working with a manual notetaker and relying on the notes for direct access, they are obliged to sit alongside the notetaker for access.

Flexibility: the system is set up to be used, by the student, as a tool for them to record their own thoughts thus encouraging the student to become more actively engaged in the process of learning. Finally, by the end of the session, it is possible to save a complete electronic record of the session (including both the Operator's and the Receiver's notes) so that these notes can be further worked on by the student and/or kept as a revision aid.

For some students electronic notetaking is their first and preferred method of access to communication. For others, who ordinarily prefer to work with an interpreter in class, electronic notetaking may be used as an alternative method of access. Of course the employment of this service, as with any other, very much depends on individual student preference, whether they have a good command of written English and whether the session is one that lends itself to this method of access. Given the right blend of these elements, some deaf students will choose to work with an electronic notetaker in place of having both an interpreter and a manual notetaker present.

Part II

Issues in note-taking

Having established the genesis and need for notetaking as a vital and recognised support mechanism for many deaf students, we will now examine the numerous issues that exist in the field of notetaking as it applies to Higher Education.

We will discuss the issue of creating and maintaining the quality of notetaking services, question the effectiveness of notetaking per se and ask whether it can ever replace the experience of taking notes for oneself. We will also explore the appropriateness of manual notetaking as a tool in a rapidly developing learning and teaching environment.

Quality of notetaking

Although the role of the notetaker is now one that is both recognized and accepted by deaf students, service providers and Assessment Centres alike, there are still huge variations in the quality, range of provision and accessibility of notetaking services across the country (LB Elliot et al, 2001).

In addition to nationally recognised qualifications in notetaking such as those awarded by CACDP or the London Open College Network (LOCN), other qualifications and courses are also run in a variety of institutions with locally agreed assessment criteria. However, there are still no nationally agreed and recognised quality guidelines stipulating that notetakers must be of a particular standard or recognising any specific qualification before they are employed to work with deaf students.

The Department for Education and Skills (DfES) offer extensive guidance to Local Authorities (LAs) regarding the administration of the DSA (http://www.dfes.gov.uk/studentsupport/administrators/dsp_section_112.shtml). There is however no guidance which refers to the qualifications required of a notetaker before the DSA can be released. Thus LA Officers have no option but to approve provision and thereafter, payment for that provision, merely based upon evidence that the service is offered and has been provided.

The specially formed quality assurance body for the DSA (DSA-QAG) has an extensive quality assurance framework for DSA Assessment Centres and a Service Level Agreement for the suppliers of specialist assistive technology for deaf and disabled students (http://www.dsa-qag.org.uk/content.asp?ContentID=1). Once again, however,

Assessors, charged with the responsibility for recommending notetaking services in Study Aids and Strategies Reports for students, are given no guidance as to how to ensure the quality of those services and no service level agreement exists for this aspect of DSA-funded service provision. As a result, providers can deliver notetaking services entirely according to their own constraints and objectives.

However, assuming such guidance did exist, it is still questionable whether the quality of notetaking would be enhanced by it. At present the recognized award to become a qualified notetaker is a Level 2 Certificate awarded by the Qualifications & Curriculum Authority (QCA). Although this award is accredited on the National Qualifications Framework (NQF), it is not sufficient for notetakers who are expected to provide a service for students reading for a degree or higher level qualification.[14] Current qualifications are designed to assess a person's ability to take notes in a range of settings both within education and without and it is therefore perfectly feasible to become qualified without having had any experience of Higher Education.

We would argue that for someone to work as a notetaker in HE specifically, high entry level qualifications and additional skills are necessary to ensure that the individual is appropriate for the role. This should include the notetaker themselves to have at least studied at HE level and preferably to have obtained a degree. An alternative would be for notetakers to be able to demonstrate an ability to process a range of HE level information adequately.

Assuming such improvements in nationalising standards were to take place, there still exist, both for service providers and notetakers themselves, inbuilt constraints which compromise the aims of professionalism and the quality of provision.

A notetaker in HE has to be prepared to work for no more than 30 weeks a year, be flexible about the amount of hours they are offered each week, (and thus the income they may receive) and be committed enough to work with little or no support, often in isolation from other professionals. It is not easy to find someone who meets the necessary criteria of being a graduate (or possibly a post graduate) and a qualified notetaker, who is prepared and able to work under these conditions.

[14] At the time of writing, CACDP have validated a new Level 3 Certificate accredited by the Qualifications and Curriculum Authority (QCA) which will sit within the National Qualifications Framework. It is not possible to say, at this stage, how this will affect the quality of those newly qualified on this route, though concerns still exist that the level 3 Certificate still only equates to FE level.

The levels of pay a notetaker will take home are of particular concern and a significant barrier to the establishment of career notetakers.

It is axiomatic that in order to recruit and retain suitably qualified individuals there needs to be appropriate levels of pay. Presently, although rates do vary across the country, the rate of pay for a notetaker is anything from £6 to £15 an hour, dependant upon experience and qualification. The nature of the work, the timetabling and co-ordinating variables and the limited working year make it impossible for a notetaker to earn more than £12,000 per annum (and most will earn significantly less than that), which, when compared to an average starting salary that can be anticipated by graduates of £18–£22,000, (http://www.prospects.ac.uk) clearly falls short of an attractive remuneration.

Presently, pay rates are constrained by the maximum levels of DSA available to a student (For more information see 'Bridging the Gap: a guide to the Disabled Students' Allowances in Higher Education' (available at www.direct.gov.uk/studentfinance). For service providers to pay a more appropriate level to notetakers, therefore, would require them to pay out much more than they could recoup from the students' DSA. In short, a service provider would be likely to have to subsidise upwards of £10,000 (not including employer on-costs) per notetaker to make up the difference between what can be reclaimed from the students' DSA and what will constitute an attractive salary. Combine this with the fact that some universities will be employing anywhere from 20 to 60 people in this position and the true scale of this financial barrier starts to emerge. Note-taking as a career profession will not emerge at all, unless something is done to unlock this economic imbalance.

In summary, current working conditions ensure that notetaking is a part-time short-term role which leads to high staff turnovers, inconsistency for students and a lack of experienced professionals able to mentor others, develop the profession, and work across the full range of academic settings.

Effectiveness of notetaking

Although there are many excellent notetakers doing a very professional job across the country for a large number of students, it is important for us to consider the actual effectiveness of notetaking itself as a device to ensure the deaf student is given parity of access. This question is best understood by looking at the issue of 'message decay' illustrated by what we have termed the 'Decay Model'.

Figure 1: Decay model

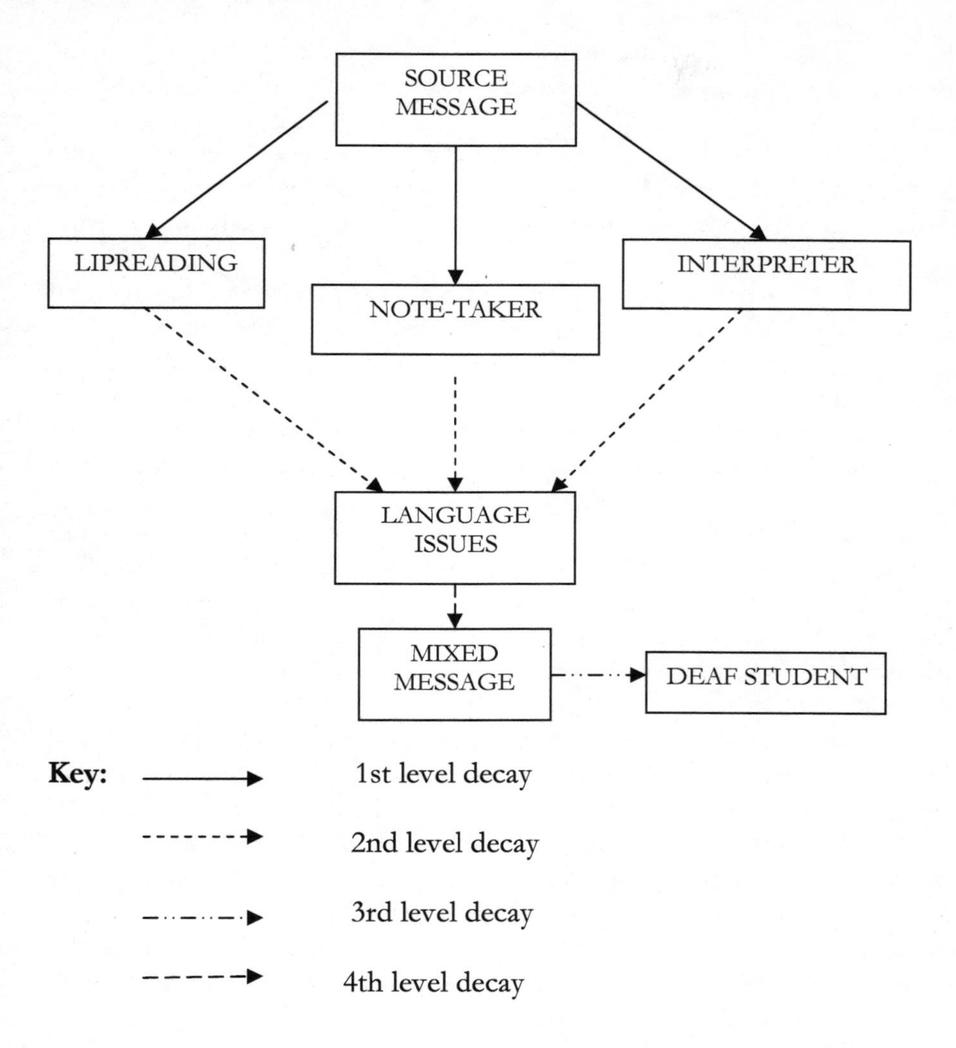

Once any message is delivered there exists an element of decay between the meaning of the message as it is intended by the source (speaker/signer) and the meaning of the message as it is perceived by the target (listener/watcher) (Pregnier, 1978). Words combined into sentences have a wide range of potential meanings which depend on a combination of many other factors (body language; tone of voice; social, cultural and personal context; facial expression and so forth) and, as a result, frequent misunderstandings can, and do, occur (Brien, 1992).

The perfection of a message as it is conceived, intended and delivered by the source will therefore have gone through a level of decay by the time it is processed by the target. This is true for all of us, but for the deaf person the level of decay will be compounded by a variety of factors.

Deaf students accessing a session directly have a much greater likelihood of receiving a decayed message compared to their hearing peers due to the inaccuracies inherent in the act of combining hearing with lip-reading.

However, for a Deaf student receiving the message through an interpreter, then the decay process will take place twice. There will be some decay of the message that is delivered when it is processed into BSL by the interpreter and then again there will be further decay as the message is received from the interpreter by the deaf student.

Similarly, when a deaf student accesses the message through a notetaker two levels of decay will occur.

In the situation where a deaf student is supported both by an interpreter and a notetaker, the student is faced with two, doubly-decayed versions of the original message which may well lead to problems of mixed messages. Which message is right? Are either of them right? Can the student have any confidence in the accuracy of the message at all?

This may be at the extreme end of the 'decay spectrum', but it is nevertheless true that significant decay will have taken place by the time the deaf student sits at home looking through his/her notes.

And it does not end there; a further level of decay is likely to affect most deaf students to a greater or lesser degree depending on their confidence and ability with the English language. It is not the intention or remit of this chapter to discuss in detail the language issues faced by deaf people, most particularly those with profound deafness from birth or occurring during the early years of language acquisition. (see Mole and Peacock, 2007). Suffice to say that acquiring spoken languages and subsequently their written forms depends heavily on the ability to hear. Take away that ability and language becomes a learned process rather than an acquisition, compounded by the ongoing difficulties posed by the phonetics of written language having no meaning. Deaf people simply have to remember the visual shapes of letters and words. It is these difficulties, which again affect deaf people to varying degrees, which lead to the often quoted statistics regarding the low average reading age of deaf school leavers (Gregory & Hindley, 1996).

In other words, the significant decay already experienced by deaf students may be further compounded as a result of them having to interpret the message that has been recorded in a language that they already have difficulties with.

Note-taking content choice

It is self-evident that since average speaking rates in words per minute far exceed that possible when writing, a notetaker must engage in significant amounts of précising. Whilst the aim of the notetaker will be to create a set of notes that reflects the fullest possible content, the notetaker will inevitably be forced to engage in a significant amount of choice over what to leave out of the notes. These decisions will be the notetakers' alone and cannot involve any serious or effective negotiation with the student. It is highly probable, therefore, that the notetakers prioritising of what to include and what to leave out, will not fully coincide with the choices the student would have made and therefore another area of disadvantage arises for the deaf student when compared with his/her peers.

As a consequence, deaf students are likely to be working with a significantly decayed message which may cause confusion and a lack of confidence both in themselves and in the accuracy of the materials they are working with. They may also have a level of difficulty processing the written language and will, therefore, be engaged in significantly higher amounts of reading time. This can be further compounded by the greater volume of notes a trained notetaker will take compared with the average student.

Active versus passive learning

There is a significant volume of research providing evidence to support the idea that students in education tend to learn more effectively through taking (or being encouraged to take) a more active approach to their learning (Modell, 996; Prince, 2004).

This might involve class-based discussion through organised or improvised interaction with tutors and pupils or it might involve the simple act of the student reprocessing the notes that have been taken by the notetaker and reworking the content into their own words following the session.

Most students' learning benefits through the act of taking notes because it assists in the 'encoding' process (DiVesta & Gray, 1972):

> 'the encoding process that occurs during note taking can alter a learner's cognitive process since it forces the student to listen, organize ideas, and relate material to his/her existing knowledge, and [...] the student is able to retrieve the information based upon his/her unique organization and structure for later review.' (Brazeau, cited at http://www.pubmedcentral.nih.gov/articlerender.fcgi?artid=1636926)

Thus, although never anticipated, it seems likely that the provision of a notetaking service itself can be a barrier to deaf students' academic success in that it serves to close down a more active style of learning.

Since deaf students do not, as a rule, benefit from the encoding process, empowering students to actively engage in their own learning by working alongside support services would certainly be valuable. This may involve training students about how to work with their notetakers to get the best out of the notes that are taken, or by encouraging students to rework notes with their language tutors outside of the classroom. Unfortunately, when introducing the notetaking service to students, most service providers tend to focus on the role of the notetaker - advising them where to sit to optimize their ability to take notes; informing them of their boundaries; ensuring that they will work confidentially and impartially and so forth - and neglect the provision of training, instruction or guidance to students about ways that they may make their own notes or become a more active learner in the classroom

Changing academic environment

We should not forget that advances in technology will have an impact on the academic environment as we know it. Digital technology, remote access to courses, distance learning and on-line learning are creating new and varied classroom (and virtual classroom) environments and involve activities for which the more traditional notetaking model is becoming redundant.

Increasingly, extensive lecture notes are being placed on University Virtual Learning Environments (VLEs) as a matter of course. Some lectures are being recorded and placed on the same site either as video or sound files. Many courses are making use of additional on-line facilities as teaching tools, partly to reduce the tutor contact hours required and partly to experiment with the potential for a more varied, exciting and engaging learning experience. These can include limited discussion boards where a discussion is set running and students are required to make a minimum number of contributions over a period of several days. Interactive 'live' tutorial/seminar 'chats' require students to log on at the same time and register as if in the classroom itself. Some modules (and indeed courses) are attempting to go fully on-line. All these developments will reduce the volume of notetaking required overall and if extended much further could have a very significant impact on the requirement for notetaking as a service.

Conclusion

As we have discussed in this chapter, there are a number of issues surrounding the traditional model of providing a manual notetaker to support a deaf student; the levels of training, the lack of quality standards, the unattractive terms and conditions of employment, the effectiveness of note-taking, the effect of message decay and the effects of passive learning. We are now left with the inevitable questions over the future of notetaking as it currently exists. Taking into account its failings in 'levelling the playing field' sufficiently to enable deaf students to experience an equal opportunity with their non-deaf peers, do we accept that this is the best service deaf students can expect or are there untried avenues, perhaps involving new technological advances which were not available when the current support models were developed? Have we become 'locked in' to a pattern or template for supporting deaf students and by focussing solely on improving the quality and provision of the model, failed to recognise sufficiently the unavoidable inadequacies of it? In so doing, are we missing opportunities for developing different models which may reduce the levels of dependence for deaf students and hand back to them a level of control and empowerment to engage them in a fully active learning process?

Furthermore, advances in technology have led to large-scale developments in learning and teaching theory and practice. These advances involve new and varied classroom (and virtual classroom) environments and activities for which the more traditional notetaking model is becoming redundant.

In light of these points, therefore, we will ignore the obvious recommendations surrounding the quality improvements to existing services which are implicit in the body of this chapter but rather concentrate on a limited number of possible solutions to the problems we have identified.

The fledgling introduction of podcasts and vidcasts of lectures are one avenue which may change the face of traditional notions of notetaking dramatically. These avenues could be encouraged and made universally accessible through subtitling and interpreting, diverting resources away from the add-on dependency model towards a more inclusive strategy.

Similarly, the use of electronic notetaking as a more general teaching tool giving the whole audience access would also be a shift towards inclusive practice. Indeed these more inclusive strategies may also help address the issues associated with economic imbalance that we discussed earlier as, according to Tinklin (2004), the focus would not be on the individual student needing access to an otherwise inaccessible main-stream activity but simply be a focus on making teaching more accessible for all students, the responsibility for resourcing the provision would then become the institutions and will need to be built in to existing budgets.

For some students, particularly those accessing courses by watching an interpreter, it may be more appropriate to move away from any form of notetaking service and instead provide the student with a method of recording the interpreter directly e.g. video. The main benefit of this system would be that subsequently deaf students could make their own notes directly from the recording enabling them to be more active in their learning whilst it would also reduce the impact of 'message decay' or 'mixed messages'.

On a more prosaic level, another method to reduce the impact of the disadvantages inherent in the decay model, would be to introduce a further human support mechanism in the form of a separately employed tutor who will be able to clarify and resolve contradictions in the material *already delivered*. Of course it will be necessary that any tutors engaged to undertake this activity are competent at explaining the subject specific elements of the confusion.

We have seen that notetaking as a means of reducing disadvantage for deaf students in Higher Education has become an automatic and accepted choice for students and services alike. However, we have also demonstrated the inherent failings of notetaking to provide equal access, and seen how the academic and technological environment, in which the notetaker is expected to operate, has developed. We believe, that focussing on and embracing the opportunities available through improvements in technology is likely to prove a more productive route towards accessibility, equality and inclusivity for deaf students, than simply attempting to improve the quality of the current model.

Key issues

1. Manual notetaking is not appropriately quality assured for use in the Higher Education context;

2. Should HE Support Services for deaf students be encouraging and supporting students to take limited notes of their own in teaching sessions?;

3. Research is needed into the impact of new technologies on the need for notetaking and the improvement of inclusive practices;

4. Whilst the employment of notetakers for deaf students is ongoing, the training and pre-requisite skills of workers needs to be reviewed;

5. The need for strategies that support deaf students and reduce the impact of the barriers created by the provision of notetakers should be understood and implemented more widely.

Further reading

Ahmad, W., Darr, A., Jones, L. & Nisar, G. 1998. *Deafness and ethnicity – services, policy and politics.* Cambridge: The Policy Press and The Joseph Rowntree Foundation.

Backroad Connections Pty Ltd. 2002 'What is the universal design and how can it be implemented?' *Australian flexible framework, quick guides series.* Australian National Training Authority.

Brien, D. 1992 *Dictionary of British Sign Language.* London: Faber and Faber

Byrnes, L.J., Sigafoos, J., Rickards, F.W. & Brown, P.M. 2002 'Inclusion of students who are deaf or hard of hearing in government schools in New South Wales' *Journal of Deaf Studies and Deaf Education* 7, 3: 244-57.

Di Vesta, F. J., and Gray, S. G. 1972 'Listening and notetaking' in *Journal of Educational Psychology* 63, 1: 8-14

Elliot, L., Foster, S. & Stinson, M. 2002 'Student study habits using notes from a Speech-to-Text Support Service' *Exceptional children.* 69: 25-40

Elliot, L., Stinson, M., McKee, B. & Everhart, V. 2001 'College students perceptions of the C-Print Speech-to-Text Transcription System' *Journal of Deaf Studies and Deaf Education.* Autumn 6, 4: 285-98.

Brazeau, G.A. 'Handouts in the classroom: is note taking a lost skill?' Available from: http://www.pubmedcentral.nih.gov/articlerender.fcgi?artid=1636926 [accessed May 07]

Green, C. & Nickerson, W. 1992. *The rise of the communicator.* Moonshine Books: England.

Hastings, D., Brecklein, K., Cermak, S., Reynolds, R., Rosen, H. & Wilson, J. 1997 'Report on note taking for deaf and hard of hearing students' in Stuckless, R. (Ed.), *National task force on quality of services in the postsecondary education of deaf and hard of hearing students.* NY: NETAC. [AN 1710].

Mole, J. and Peacock, D. 'Language issues for deaf students in higher education' in Adams, M. and Brown, S. (eds.) 2006 *Towards inclusive learning in Higher Education: developing curricula for disabled students.* London:Routledge

Kyle, J.G. & Woll, B. with G. Pullen, G. & Maddix, F. 1985 *Sign language: the study of deaf people and their language.* Cambridge University Press: Cambridge.

Lang, H.G. 2002 'Higher Education for deaf students: research priorities in the new millennium' *Journal of Deaf Studies and Deaf Education.* Autumn 7, 4: 267-80.

Marschark. M. 1997 *Raising and educating deaf children – a comprehensive guide to the choices, controversies and decisions faced by parents and educators.* Oxford University Press: Oxford.

McCall, R. 1992 *Hearing loss? A guide to self-help including: listening tactics, speechreading, social strategies, lip-reading, high frequency hearing loss.* Bury St Edmunds: St Edmundsbury Press Ltd.

Napier, J. & Barker, R. 2004 'Accessing university education: perceptions, preferences, and expectations for interpreting by deaf' *Journal of Deaf Studies and Deaf Education.* Spring 9, 2: 228-38.

Note-taker service guide. Produced by the Computer Centre for People with Disabilities at the University of Westminster in conjunction with The City Literary Institute for Deaf People funded by The Higher Education Funding Council for England Available at http://www.wmin.ac.uk/ccpd/ntguide/index.htm

Prospects – the UK's official graduate careers website. (Updated 2007). An overview of the graduate market - forecast of graduate salaries (How much can I earn?) Available from: http://www.prospects.ac.uk [last accessed May 07].

Sacks, O. 1989 *Seeing voices.* San Diego: University of California Press.

CHAPTER SEVEN

Investigating literacy support for deaf students in UK Higher Education: Learning from a New Literacy Studies approach

Professor Graham H. Turner

Introduction

This paper draws upon the academic disciplines of education studies, anthropology and applied linguistics to unpack an aspect of current educational practice within UK Higher Education. The aim is to investigate the service provided by Language Support Tutors (LSTs) to Deaf students, with a direct interest in the possible applications of knowledge deriving from this work. These are seen as being applications with respect to the development of all parties' understanding of the process and its implications, and the generation of relevant institutional policy. The analysis begins by reflecting briefly upon a number of crucial contextual factors which relate primarily to Deaf people's experiences in education generally and in relation to the English language, with particular reference to the use of literacy skills. The focus is then upon particular aspects of support available to Deaf students in relation to the production of written work. An outline is presented of a theoretical framework (drawing upon New Literacy Studies) which is then applied to this context, exploring in some depth a particular, detailed example.

The chapter concludes with a reflection upon this example and some key points for service provision are drawn out.[15]

Deaf people entering Higher Education (HE) bring with them participation in a history which has a profound impact upon how effectively, as students, they negotiate the demands of the academic environment. The view taken in the chapter is that it is not enough simply to regard them as disabled students, to be aided and supported by whatever technical gadgetry is available – in fact, this view is inadequate and inappropriate. Deaf students are different: physically, in that they do not hear lectures as students are expected to; linguistically, in that they use forms of communication which differ radically from the spoken/written norms of the majority; and culturally, having recourse to experiences relating to their engagement with Deaf culture (Higgins 1980, Padden & Humphries 1988, Wilcox 1989, Rutherford 1992, Lane et al 1996). All of this may be reflected in their attitude to education. These issues have been highlighted in the UK in recent years, as a result of the rapid increase in the numbers of Deaf students entering HE since 1990. Historically, Deaf students have simply not been greatly in evidence within such academic contexts (Daniels & Corlett 1990, Olohan et al 1995). This picture has changed, but inevitably the presence of Deaf students has given rise to new and sometimes unforeseen challenges (Barnes 1996).

The collective experience of Deaf education has been a troubled one. The prime position of oralism - the approach laying exclusive stress on teaching children and young people to speak and lip-read - which had dominated the education of deaf children in the UK for a century, was loosened in the UK after damning reports of its failure (Conrad, 1979). Virtual institutionalisation in 'special schools' decreased during the 1980s and deaf children began to enter mainstream schools, subject to a bewilderment of new methods and the revision of some old ones (Lane 1992). In the midst of this confusion, the last major review suggests that there has been no subsequent significant overall improvement in the education of deaf children (Gregory, Powers & Thoutenhoofd 1998),

---

[15] This paper owes its origins to a collaborative effort between the author and an experienced Language Support Tutor, Crissie Laugesen, who were for several years colleagues at the University of Central Lancashire. Crissie, with a background in language studies, has worked for some 25 years as an English-language tutor, scribe and translator with Deaf people. It is also appropriate to acknowledge the contributions of our colleagues, former colleagues and students – especially Lynne Barnes, Asif Iqbal and Tracy Gibson – to the work behind this paper. Responsibility for the paper's contents nevertheless remains with the author.

despite identifiable pockets of good practice (eg Knight & Swanwick 2002).

English in the education of deaf children

It is not intended to address here all of the issues raised by the uneven educational foundations available to Deaf people (Gregory et al 1998, offer a *fin de siècle* overview of the issues from a predominantly UK perspective), but to focus on one particular element of concern, namely the production of written texts. However, in order to understand why so many Deaf students have difficulties with the kind of literacy HE typically demands of them, and to appreciate Deaf people's prevailing mixed feelings about the English language, it is necessary to look back at their common educational experiences.

Years of oralist schooling have left many Deaf people with an accumulation of negative associations with the English language. For many Deaf people, English is not a language, a form of communication, but a subject they remember from school, and link with unpleasant experiences of being encouraged, cajoled, trained, forced to speak. For many Deaf people, 'English is not us, it is them, and they are oppressors'. It is the language of bureaucracy and authority, and is always a reminder of Deaf people's status as outsiders. Memories of school experiences of learning English are so significant and formative that they are literally commemorated by Deaf poets and artists, committed to the collective memory and woven into the fabric of the community's heritage. The British Deaf poet John Wilson captures this feeling succinctly in his signed poem *From the Depths,* in which he tells us that 'every Deaf person is taught to remember' the oppression of signed language perpetrated within predominantly oralist educational systems. Despite this strong sense of having been collectively wronged, many Deaf people remain profoundly ambivalent about their language choices. Although signing may be preferred, there is an ingrained sense that it must somehow be inferior because everyone says so; in this respect it is reminiscent of other linguistic minority situations (Edwards & Ladd 1983).

The disempowerment of Deaf people is not only, in this context, caused by the oppression of sign, but is also a result of the imposition of a language upon people unable to use or understand it fully. Learning to speak English perfectly is not just difficult, it is in practice physically impossible for very many profoundly deaf children. Deaf people are physically different. It is not that they just cannot or do not hear, but that a life that centres upon engaging with 'the hearing world' on its own terms is not considered a possible life for themselves by many Deaf people. As Carol Padden and Tom Humphries (1988:110) have most clearly articulated:

'the deep fear of Deaf people [is] that they may be forced to use a language intended for people with different biological characteristics.'

John Albertini and Nora Shannon have noted that it appears that Deaf writers':

'self-consciousness about writing... may result from an intense focus on grammar and mechanics in many writing classes for deaf students' (Albertini & Shannon 1996: 73).

It does not have to be like this, as more communicative approaches to writing – treating it as a social, purposeful activity – clearly outline (see, for example, Knight & Swanwick 2002). In the UK throughout the twentieth century, when it came to writing, teachers too often expected that deaf children would be unable to achieve, and concentrated on efforts to make the children's speech intelligible, at the expense of their literacy, self-expression and general education. As with any self-fulfilling prophecy worth its salt, the children's achievements were indeed limited, and as Deaf adults many now struggle with basic literacy.

Deaf people's literacy skills in Higher Education

The preceding discussion has attempted to set a scene for a more particular focus hereafter on Deaf writers. As Connie Mayer has observed (1999), literacy research in the education of Deaf people has tended to focus on reading rather than writing. As specialist tutors working with Deaf students are well aware, students entering universities now, in the changing climate of education for deaf children in the UK, have had fewer and fewer experiences of the kind outlined in the above account. The important point of this history, though, is that it tacitly underpins the experience of writing for many Deaf people, providing a massive cultural hurdle for the aspiring writer to surmount.

As was noted above, the review of deaf children's school achievements undertaken by Gregory, Powers and Thoutenhoofd (1998) indicates strongly that – despite any changes in school practices in the last two decades and more – we must expect Deaf students arriving at university to need the support of expert tutors to help them make sense of the intricacies of academic English, and to enable them to put their own often very lucid thoughts into acceptable, standard English for the written assignments which the university considers a necessary factor in the 'graduateness' of its degree-holders. They must be seen to meet certain standards – even when their previous education has failed to meet their own needs.

Even at this stage in their educational careers, English for many Deaf students remains an overwhelming obstacle. Yet Deaf students who complain 'I can't write!' or 'That's not what I mean!' are not always bemoaning their own failure to succeed (on the institution's terms) with written English. Comparisons for many with their control of their first (sign) language are often implicit in their remarks; English is considered comparatively inadequate to express their ideas in the way that they wish. Able to express themselves in their own language, they struggle to convey the same meaning in English and locate the weakness in the written language itself: it acts like a filter which disables the meaning and impact of what they want to say, and thus is not to be trusted. English, in these terms, is not a friend but an enemy; it is a language symbolic not of familiarity but of formality and of having to achieve on other people's terms.

Negative reactions to their educational experiences, from boredom through to fear and anger, have left many Deaf people convinced that reading and writing have little desirable part to play in their lives. Reading is a task resorted to out of necessity and is purely functional; writing is avoided wherever possible, or done in a desultory or reticent manner. Part of what be called a 'culture of aliteracy' that has evolved is the development of a variety of evasion techniques, avoidance strategies, corner-cutting tactics and the like. Tutors working with Deaf students often find that their priority when dealing with text is simply to get rid of it as quickly as possible. Text here is seen as 'alien', even to the extent that the students' own writing is seen less as an expression of their own thinking than as something which is automatically for and only of interest to hearing people. If the hearing reader has any difficulty in understanding texts the writer creates, then these are tacitly considered to be 'their problems' and of no concern to the writer - 'you wanted it, you read it' is the sense that is often given from talking with Deaf students.

Interestingly, modern technology has created new ways for Deaf people to engage in writing (Albertini & Shannon 1996). Electronic mail (e-mail) is now widespread and Deaf people have been identified as some of the most enthusiastic users of digital text messaging:

'Around 1997-98 when the text messages SMS became a standard on these mobile devices – they became deaf tools immediately. In a Norwegian survey from 1999 among people around 15-16 years old – it was discovered that the group that utilized the mobile phones/SMS the most was deaf youngsters' (Breivik, no date).

In these media, Deaf writers seem much less self-conscious and -critical. This may, one might speculate, have much to do with the perception of informality surrounding such interaction, as opposed to the formal, 'observed' nature of writing produced for an educational audience which is inevitably bound to adopt a critical stance.

Like others writing in an academic context, Deaf people of course vary greatly. Our experience of the most strongly self-critical writers includes the characteristic sense of frustration with the medium felt by writers who may refuse to write at all or who produce the bare minimum of a few lines. Some will produce a couple of paragraphs that are so small and cramped (using tiny type sizes) that they are impossible to read, almost as though the author wants to hide or lose the writing, anything to make it go away. Some students produce writing with anomalies which, while prescriptively 'wrong', reveal a startlingly effective capacity for self-expression, creativity and conceptual competence (Marschark 1997). Despite this, such 'errors' are seen as evidence of failure by the writers themselves.

There is much evidence of particular patterns of strengths and weaknesses. Among these is the common experience of receiving texts in which the Deaf writer with greater exposure to English demonstrates a rich written vocabulary (sometimes heavy on the technical style of a particular occupational or academic field). This may appear discordant with the surrounding non-standard grammar. In an academic context, feedback to the student may cast the result in a poor light, insofar as the inexperienced tutor may feel that the text has simply been strewn with as many 'big words' as the student can muster.

Re-contextualising writing

Thus far the focus has been on the educational (and specifically literacy) background characteristic of Deaf university students. At this point, it is necessary to step back from 'the coalface' and locate the discussion to follow within a broader theoretical framework of applied linguistics.

Scholarly work on literacy in the 1970s largely focused on the supposed cognitive consequences of literacy acquisition (we might locate this period chronologically as having lasted for at least the 'long decade' between the publication in 1969 of Goody's collection *Literacy in Traditional Societies* and in 1982 of Ong's *Literacy and Orality*). On the one hand, those who were deemed 'literate' were said therefore to become more capable as thinkers; on the other, students who were not seen as successful in literacy skills were described as having learning 'problems' requiring 'remediation'. The fact that this terminology has not become unfamiliar in such contexts suggests that this perspective retains a strong purchase within the field.

Yet recent decades have seen a shift or a realignment, away from an overriding concern for the products created by writers as quasi-independent artefacts – what Lea & Street (1999: 80) call 'the autonomous model of literacy' in which any inability to conform to received standard practices is seen as a 'deficit', a view highly contested in the literature (Kress 1997, Street 1997) – to the study of literacy as a social practice. Initially the insights derived from the growth in the field of sociolinguistics generated relatively little early interest in how literacy was made manifest: the sociolinguistic spin at first extended only as far as curiosity resulting from variation in the presentation of texts, including conventions of orthography (cf Stubbs 1980). However, the following decade saw the introduction of an alternative focus not on the products of literacy (most especially the analysis of 'errors') but on the ways in which processes, practices and events shape literacy (Heath 1983, Street 1984) and a renewed focus upon description rather than prescription.

Within the current decade, we have therefore seen continuing exploration of the growing field of literacy studies (for an introductory summary, see Barton 1994). The focus on literacy practices has become increasingly sharp, signalling the developing recognition that literacy is embedded in social contexts, and theoretical frameworks built around such insights have been constructed (Baynham 1995, Candlin & Hyland 1999). The field is now sufficiently mature that it has begun to re-explore on its own terms some of the questions upon which it once turned its back, for instance in the renewed interest in 'vernacular literacy' (Le Page 1997). The study presented here falls within what Brian Street and associates (1993a, 1993b, 1995, 2005) have dubbed the *New Literacy Studies* paradigm. In looking at Deaf students writing with the assistance of LSTs, particular inspiration is drawn on the one hand from Mike Baynham's initial exploration of the role of 'mediators of literacy' (Baynham 1993) and on the other from studies of literacy in academic contexts (eg Myers 1990, Lea & Street 1997, Ivanic 1998) in order to investigate at close quarters the nature of a particular set of mediated academic writing practices within HE programmes. Even within the new paradigm, relatively little close attention – especially when compared with the development of ideas about co-participation and co-construction in spoken interaction (Goodwin & Harness Goodwin, 1992) – has yet been paid to exactly how co-writers create texts (though cf. Witte 1992, Duin & Hansen 1996, Gollin 1999, Mace 2003) and even less to how this might articulate with the notion of students as academic novitiates serving an 'apprenticeship' before joining a discourse community (Brown et al 1989, Swales 1990, Lave & Wenger 1991, Lillis 2001).

Frameworking

The aim of this study is to adopt the theoretical construct of the 'literacy event'. A literacy event might be any sequence, involving one or more person, in which the production and/or comprehension of print plays a role. In coining the term, Heath (1982:53) says that a literacy event is 'any occasion in which a piece of writing is integral to the nature of the participants' interactions and their interpretative processes'. Crucially, in focusing on literacy events, the interest lies not just in the written product but more particularly in the context within which, and the process by which, it is created. In doing so, the aim of this chapter is to contribute to a vaunted shift in Deaf Studies research. The field has seen an extremely strong tendency, at the very mention of Deaf literacy, for the discourse to be shaped by a concentration on 'low levels of achievement', 'error analysis' and the like (eg Paul 1998a, does so in introducing a journal special issue on the topic). However, there is also evidence of a degree of frustration with the limitations of this approach and a proclaimed desire to see what Peter Paul calls *social-constructivist* approaches to the issue, emphasising that 'meaning-making is a social process' (Paul 1998b: 260), being more fully explored in research. In this spirit, then, this discussion has already demonstrated some significant features of the context within which the Deaf student may undertake mediated writing; below, we begin to explore the process, focusing on a particular literacy event in which a Deaf student interacts with an LST. Before this can be done, it is necessary to sketch the theoretical framework.

The New Literacy Studies field is interested in specific cultural meanings and practices which are embedded in power relations and are multiple and non-essentialist in character. (The latter point is frequently implicitly acknowledged by the use of the term 'literacies' in recognition of the range of alternative practices in which readers and writers may, from time to time, engage.). By placing texts authored by deaf people in an explicit social context, the intention is to illuminate both the interactional behaviours of participants in the data which follow, and also the social and cultural conceptualisations that give meaning to the uses of writing for those involved. This paper thus aligns with studies which look to conceptualise writing as a process, moving away from some well-rooted ideas about the nature of language and of literacy. There is an extensive literature using the 'deficit' model to consider the products of deaf children's writing in precisely these terms (see Meadow 1980 for an early overview; Musselman & Szanto, which whilst still replicating 'the conventional finding that deaf students have generally low written language skills' (1998: 253), exemplify a contemporary shift towards more holistic pedagogical responses to the problem) – and towards an understanding of literacy practices in a particular 'real' social context.

Literacy events are more than just words. Learning to write – in this case, to write 'through' a mediator – entails learning, negotiating and contesting ways of conducting a particular social relationship. Literacy events are not random or arbitrary, but are rule governed and structured. Although it may seem spontaneous, the mediated literacy event follows identifiable protocols and patterns: some topics and kinds of language are acceptable, particular social roles and relationships are called into play. For both student and tutor, therefore, learning how to participate in co-writing requires learning/ developing a set of rules that govern who can nominate which topics, how to get the floor, who can interrupt whom, who has the final word, where slang and swearing might be appropriate and so forth (Luke 1993).

Communication, being dependent on social relations, is inseparable from producing, reproducing and maintaining arrangements of institutionally structured power which are unequal (Lankshear 1997). Crucial to our understanding of the interaction between Deaf student and LST must be the recognition of their starkly differential status within this university setting. One is a student and one a member of staff; while the former is almost invariably the younger of the two, the latter has had the educational advantages. The LST is more familiar with the norms and expectations of the institution and the text which should be the output of their interaction must be created in a language with which the LST is most comfortable. On the other hand, however, the student is, in effect, the employer, typically being enabled to pay for the LST's services by a substantial, centrally-resourced Disabled Students' Allowances. In addition, the interaction that will occur between them takes place in the student's preferred language. Finally, the student in all cases would identify her/himself as Deaf, whereas the LST in most cases (and certainly in the case cited, despite her mild hearing loss) would self-identify as hearing. It would be naive to seek to 'read off' anything categorical about power from such a sketch: it would be more naive to assume these factors to be irrelevant to the interaction that takes place and thus to the resulting text.

A major element of what we seek to recognise here is the extent to which LSTs' working practices can function as an instrument of empowerment or disempowerment for the Deaf student. The baseline assumption here must be that the weight of history and culture suggests that Deaf students will be up against institutionalised norms liable to work against them. Ultimately, to complete their 'apprenticeship' into academia, Deaf students must cross divides of language and modality, culture and discourse. The LST is in a position to be either part of the solution or part of the problem: to explore the social context of language practices, writes Pam Gilbert (1993:325), is to explore:

> 'networks of power that are sustained and brought into existence by such practices. It is to explore how language practices are used in powerful institutions ... and how these practices contribute to the maintenance of inequalities and injustices.'

The sense negotiation process

The following data represent one small example of the process in which the Deaf student and LST jointly engage in order to create a submissable piece of work for assessment on behalf of the student. The data are in three parts: firstly, the text in draft form as presented to the LST following the student's initial independent work; secondly, translated from the original signed exchange, a short section of a one-hour language support supervisory session involving a second-year undergraduate Deaf student and an LST (the interaction was videotaped and is here reproduced with the kind permission of both participants); thirdly, the agreed revised version of the text (here the LST's changes are incorporated, in italics, without alteration into the text; as in the version produced at the time, some words or morphemes have been struck out).

First draft (FD)

1. They sent her to a primary school where Welsh was the parents decided that
2. they should learn some Welsh themselves, to understand more of the culture and
3. community in which they were living, so they went to evening class in the area.
4. What uses does the person have two languages and how well does he know

5. each: Children may development both languages at the same time, or learn one
6. language first and then the second.

Interactional transcript (IT)

LST:	'Go to school where Welsh was', what? (*points to page*)
Student:	(*checks page*) Their first language is Welsh. Spoken Welsh is their first language. Their parents learn Welsh.
LST:	(*writes: looks up*)
S:	Because... Because they are more relaxed using their first language.
LST:	Do you want me to add that?
S:	Yes. It is easier for them to understand. If the teacher uses English to teach the children it can become very complicated, but they understand the information better when it's given in Welsh and then they could translate it into English. They access both.
LST:	Shall I add that?
S:	(*nods*)
LST:	(*writes*) 'They go to school where Welsh is the first language.' Full stop. 'The parents realise they have to learn to speak Welsh themselves.' (*writes*) Where's my rubber? I've made a mistake. (*searches in bag: writes*) What did you say before about them being'confused'?
S:	If they are taught in English it can be very confusing for the children. They should learn in basic Welsh, their first language.
LST:	Right.
S:	They are more relaxed learning their first language.
LST:	Right, so they learn Welsh because they don't want their children to become confused when they go to school. (*long pause: writes*) Okay?
S:	(*checks work*) Yes, okay.

LST: Is that okay?

S: Yes, fine.

LST: (*reads on: writes - looks up*)

S: (*nods*)

LST: (*smiles: reads on*) Question mark needed there.

Revised version (RV)

1. They sent her to a primary school where Welsh was *the first language.* ~~*and*~~
2. The parents decided that they should learn some Welsh themselves, *and* to
3. understand more of the culture and community in which they were living, *and to*
4. ~~*feel*~~ *help their daughter feel less confused,* so they went to evening class in the
5. area.
6. What uses does the person have *for* two languages, and how well does he
7. know each*?* Children may develop~~ment~~ both languages at the same time, or learn
8. one language first and then the second.

Discussion

It is recognised that this paper cannot explore fully all of the issues raised by even this very small excerpt from the available data. It is intended simply to identify what is considered to be the major area of dilemma, with reference to personal observations. The connecting factor here is that all of the points raised link back to fundamental questions about the role of the LST - how decisions about what will go into the student's written final written submission have been made - and therefore to the matter of intellectual ownership of the finished product.

- Easily overlooked in the search for notable features of this data is the fact that a very large proportion of the draft text passes without any comment from the LST. What message does this send to the student? That this work cannot be improved by the LST's intervention? Or that it 'will do' – and does that mean it is average or that it will just achieve the pass mark?;

- In fact, there are aspects of the text other than those the LST raises that might be considered for improvement. For instance, no stylistic comments are made despite some rather pedestrian turns of phrase (as in 'both languages at the same time, or learn one language first and then the second' – RV lines 7-8) and gender discrimination (the use of 'he' for an unidentified subject – RV line 6). What does this tell the student about the value of elegance of expression and non-discriminatory practices in academic writing, or about the extent to which Deaf writers need concern themselves with matters of style?;

- In addition to the 'unmade comments', there is also an instance – the insertion of and in RV line 2 – where a problem has been created out of nowhere by the LST;.

- It is also clear from the transcript that the Student has made comments that are not reflected in the RV – for instance, 'They are more relaxed learning their first language' (IT line 21);

- The LST is seen, without explanation, signing things ('The parents realise...', IT line 14) which, to a fluent bilingual, are not consistent with the final text ('The parents decided...', RV line 2). Should the Student, who is not entirely bilingual, in fact conclude that the written word accurately translates the sign?;

- The LST notes (IT line 15) that she has made a mistake, but does not discuss with the Student the nature of that mistake. It may be trivial, but it was certainly a learning opportunity. Crucially, it also served to reinforce that, without reference to the Student's views, the LST is apparently the person who will decide where the mistakes are in this text;

- Changes are made (eg the insertion of for in RV line 6) which the LST does not actively negotiate with or explain to the Student. It is a common experience for the LST to find that students present what they admit is a fairly casual, underdeveloped text in full confidence that the LST will simply remodel it for them. There is thus some evidence here of the LST in effect colluding with this practice.

- By looking at data in this form, it can be seen that the process of negotiation which takes a written text in English, discusses it in British Sign Language and then reconverts the output of this discussion to written English is a complex one. One instance in which this shows clearly begins in IT line 7: 'If the teacher uses English to teach the children it can become very complicated, but they understand the information better when it's given in Welsh'. Here the student uses a sign which can be translated as either 'complicated' or, less frequently, 'confused', but does so with a lip-pattern which clearly indicates 'complicated'. Soon after the LST is distracted by the search for her eraser and has to check, asking: 'What did you say before about them being 'confused'?' (IT lines 16-17) At this stage, she has unwittingly introduced a shift in the meaning, using the same sign but producing the lip-pattern 'confused'. The Student moves with the shift, responding: 'If they are taught in English it can be very confusing for the children' (IT line 18). If this is an agreed change, then the negotiation of that agreement must have been extremely subtle;

- The student is sometimes asked within the interaction whether he agrees to the changes the LST is making. This must be recognised as a deeply problematic element of the educational practice. If the student knew the best way to express his thoughts on paper, he would surely have done so in the first instance. Both participants know that the LST is the English-language 'expert'. So to what extent is the student properly equipped to challenge what the LST produces? In IT line 23, the LST asks: 'Okay?' The student looks at the work and replies: 'Yes, okay.' It is clear from her next turn at talk that the LST has some uncertainty about what they have achieved here, since she comes back with: 'Is that okay?' (line 25). Again the student replies: 'Yes, fine'. Presumably it is accepted that the student has given his assent to something – and does so again in IT line 28 when he nods in response to the LST's prior look. When the student submits this work for assessment, he will accompany it with a standard cover sheet, required of all students, asserting his ownership of the work. That such ownership should be constituted in part out of such nods, glances and remarks seems to us a matter warranting further consideration;

- Finally, in IT line 29, the LST is seen returning abruptly to a didactic role – she simply asserts: 'Question mark needed there' –

after her apparent subservience and approval-seeking in the preceding exchange.

Issues arising

This brief discussion at least indicates that the role of the LST with Deaf students in HE is more complex than might at first meet the eye and that the insights and approach of the New Literacy Studies enable us to reconsider these particular literacy events through a usefully different lens. It becomes clear, in particular, that the relationship between the two parties is not a mere matter of coldly linguistic finesse, ie focusing exclusively on an external object and adjusting a text 'out there' by applying a little fine-tuning to words on a printed page. On the contrary, the relationship is a profoundly social one with hidden nuances of power and interpersonal alignment which is almost entirely unexamined by the individuals concerned, the institutions in which the literacy events occur, or any other interested parties. A great deal simply passes on trust between the LST and the student: and, having done so, of course, it also faces scrutiny elsewhere in the system in the same way. For instance, when the subject lecturer receives the Deaf student's work for assessment, he/she is expected similarly to take it on trust that the student's declaration of ownership is a true and unproblematic one.

Salient questions remain to be examined in relation to this whole process. In particular, what role specification should LSTs have? Is there a commonly understood set of norms for the role? It is felt that the sector still needs to keep under review the policy (common among institutions of HE in the UK) of insisting that Deaf students must submit written work for assessment. If it is to be retained, then more serious consideration might be given to models of assessment of student readiness for this aspect of HE study (as discussed, for example, in Albertini et al 1997). A more preferable argument is that there is a real and logical case – having come so far in acceding to the principle that the student should not be made to bear the weight of the failure of the system – for permitting Deaf students record work directly in BSL, even if the institution should subsequently choose or need to assess a translation of the work undertaken by a suitably qualified and regulated service provider. The same kind of translation service could usefully be provided to students requiring the supply of reading materials in a signed format. If these alternative practices and supplementary roles were finely developed, LSTs could look forward to being able to concentrate on actual language tutoring to enhance the literacy skills of Deaf students as part of their academic course.

Questions remain about other indirect participants in the process. These literacy events always have the goal of creating texts for consumption by third parties. Do other participants, e.g. subject lecturers, understand the process and do they trust it? What expectations do they have about the language tutor's role? They, too, need to be more critically aware of what is behind the submitted assignment. Finally, the LSTs' training needs and the necessity of developing subject lecturers' awareness of the process has been mentioned.[16] It must also be appropriate to enquire into the training needs of the students and what it is that will most effectively enable them to use the relevant services. Students will not be empowered by the mere presence of a language tutor – they need to learn how to make the most of the opportunities afforded to them.

This chapter has attempted to explore, via the key source of a case study exemplifying interaction between a Deaf student writer and a Language Support Tutor, issues arising in the co-construction of academic texts in the context of HE learning. In doing so, it is hoped this discussion can contribute to the challenge articulated by Barbara Schirmer (2001) to renew a set of connections between research and literacy practice in the field of Deaf education.

Key questions arising from this discussion

1. Student perspective
   What are the responsibilities of the Deaf student in order to make the working relationship with a Language Support Tutor as effective as possible, ensuring the integrity of the student's work?

2. Practitioner perspective
   How can a theoretically-informed awareness of the co-constructed nature of the target text assist the practitioner in identifying the boundaries of her role?

3. Trainer perspective
   In the light of this account and discussions elsewhere in this volume, what skills do Language Support Tutors actually need and how best should we ensure that these can be acquired?

4. Pedagogical perspective

---

[16] See also Chapters Eight and Nine of this publication

When all is said and done, does language support of this kind achieve all that it sets out to do?

5. Employer perspective
   If the accounts given in this volume set out an accurate picture of the Language Support Tutor's work, what kind of people should we be looking for to undertake this work?

6. Educational policy perspective
   What could be done to make the work of the Language Support Tutor unnecessary in the future?

7. Research perspective
   Is the picture painted in this article typical and what research is required to enrich our understanding of current practices?

8. Theoretical perspective
   What do we learn about New Literacy Studies by exploring this kind of situation?

Further reading

Albertini, J., Bochner, J., Dowaliby, F. & Henderson, J. 1997 'Valid assessment of writing and access to academic discourse' *Journal of Deaf Studies and Deaf Education*, 2, 71-77.

Albertini, J. & Shannon, N. 1996 'Kitchen notes, "the grapevine", and other writing in childhood' *Journal of Deaf Studies and Deaf Education*, 1, 64-74.

Barnes, L. 1996 'Mass Higher Education and the deaf student: widening access or limiting participation?' Paper presented at *The Dilemmas of Mass Higher Education Conference*, Staffordshire University, UK.

Barton, D. 1994 *Literacy: An introduction to the ecology of written language*. Oxford, Blackwell.

Baynham, M. 1993 'Code switching and mode switching: community interpreters and mediators of literacy' in Street, B. Ed. *Cross-cultural approaches to literacy*. Cambridge, Cambridge University Press.

Baynham, M. 1995 *Literacy practices: investigating literacy in social contexts*. London, Longman.

Breivik, J-K. (no date) 'Global connections in Deaf Worlds through technology.'
http://sell.hil.no/konferanser/funksjonshem04/papers/1b-breivik.doc. Accessed 21 June 2007.

Brown, J., Collins, A. & Duguid, P. 1989 'Situated cognition and the culture of learning' *Educational Researcher*, 18: 32-42.

Candlin, C. & Hyland, K. Eds. 1999 *Writing: texts, processes and practices*. London, Longman.

Conrad, R. 1979 *The deaf school child: language and cognitive function*. London, Harper & Row.

Daniels, S. and Corlett, S. 1990 'Deaf students in Higher Education'. *RNID Research Report 9*. London, Royal National Institute for Deaf People.

Duin, A. & Hansen, C. Eds. 1996 *Non-academic writing: social theory and technology*. Mahwah, NJ, Lawrence Erlbaum.

Edwards, V. & Ladd, P. 1983 'British Sign Language and West Indian Creole' in Kyle, J. & Woll, B. Eds. *Language in sign: An international perspective*: 56-74. London, Croom Helm.

Gilbert, P. 1993 '(Sub)versions: using sexist language practices to explore critical literacy' *Australian Journal of Language and Literacy*, 16, 4: 323-332.

Gollin, S. 1999 '"Why? I thought we'd talked about it before": collaborative writing in a professional workplace setting' in Candlin, C. & Hyland, K. Eds. *Writing: Texts, processes and practices*: 267-290. London, Longman.

Goody, J. ed. 1969 *Literacy in traditional societies*. Cambridge, Cambridge University Press.

Goodwin, C. & Harness Goodwin, M. 1992 'Assessments and the construction of context' in Goodwin, C. & Duranti, A. Eds. *Rethinking context: language as an interactive phenomenon*:147-189. Cambridge, Cambridge University Press.

Gregory, S., Powers, S. & Thoutenhoofd, E. 1998 *The educational achievements of deaf children*. London, Department for Education & Employment.

Gregory, S., Knight, P., McCracken, W., Powers, S. & Watson, L. Eds. 1998 *Issues in deaf education*. London, David Fulton Publishers.

Heath, S. B. 1982 'What no bedtime story means: narrative skills at home and at school' *Language in Society* 11: 49-76.

Heath, S. B. 1983 *Ways with words.* Cambridge, Cambridge University Press.

Higgins, P. 1980 *Outsiders in a hearing world.* London, Sage.

Ivanic, R. 1998 *Writing and identity: The discoursal construction of identity in academic writing.* Amsterdam, John Benjamins.

Knight, P. & Swanwick, R. 2002 *Working with deaf pupils: sign bilingual policy into practice.* London, David Fulton Publishers.

Kress, G. 1997 *Before writing: rethinking the paths to literacy.* London, Routledge.

Lane, H. 1992 *The mask of benevolence: disabling the deaf community.* New York, Alfred A. Knopf.

Lane, H., Hoffmeister, R. & Bahan, B. 1996 *A journey into the DEAF-WORLD.* San Diego, CA, Dawn Sign Press.

Lankshear, C. 1997 *Changing literacies.* Buckingham, Open University Press.

Lave, J. & Wenger, E. 1991 *Situated learning: legitimate peripheral participation.* Cambridge, Cambridge University Press.

Lea, M. & Street, B. 1997 *Perspectives on academic literacies: An institutional approach.* Swindon, Economic and Social Research Council.

Lea, M. & Street, B. 1999 'Writing as academic literacies: understanding textual practices in Higher Education' in Candlin, C. & Hyland, K. Eds. *Writing: texts, processes and practices* : 62-81. London, Longman.

Le Page, R. B. 1997 'Introduction' in Tabouret-Keller, A. et al (eds.) *Vernacular literacy: a re-evaluation* :1-19. Oxford, Clarendon Press.

Lillis, T. 2001 *Student writing: access, regulation, desire.* London, Routledge.

Luke, A. 1993 *The social construction of literacy in the primary school.* Melbourne, Macmillan Education Australia.

Mace, J. 2003 *The give and take of writing: scribes, literacies and everyday life.* London, NIACE.

Marschark, M. 1997 *Raising and educating a deaf child.* Oxford, Oxford University Press.

Mayer, C. 1999 'Shaping At the point of utterance: an investigation of the composing process of the deaf student writer' *Journal of Deaf Studies and Deaf Education*, 4: 37-49.

Meadow, K. 1980 *Deafness and child development.* London, Edward Arnold.

Musselman, C. & Szanto, G. 1998 'The written language of deaf adolescents: patterns of performance' *Journal of Deaf Studies and Deaf Education*, 3: 245-257.

Myers, G. 1990 *Writing biology: texts in the social construction of scientific knowledge.* Madison, University of Wisconsin Press.

Olohan, S. et al Eds. 1995 *Access and communication support for deaf and hearing impaired students in Higher Education.* Nottingham, Nottingham Trent University.

Ong, W. 1982 *Literacy and orality: the technologizing of the word.* London, Methuen.

Padden, C. & Humphries, T. 1988 *Deaf in America: voices from a culture.* Cambridge, MA, Harvard University Press.

Paul, P. 1998a 'Introduction to the special issue on literacy' *Journal of Deaf Studies and Deaf Education*, 3: 177-178.

Paul, P. 1998b 'A perspective on the special issue on literacy' *Journal of Deaf Studies and Deaf Education*, 3: 258-263.

Rutherford, S. 1992 'The culture of American deaf people' in Wilcox, S. (ed.) *Academic acceptance of American Sign Language* : 21-42. Silver Spring, MD, Linstok Press.

Schirmer, B. 2001 'Using research to improve literacy practice and practice to improve literacy research' *Journal of Deaf Studies and Deaf Education*, 6: 83-91.

Street, B. 1984 *Literacy in theory and practice.* Cambridge, Cambridge University Press.

Street, B. 1993a *Cross-cultural approaches to literacy.* Cambridge, Cambridge University Press.

Street, B. 1993b 'The new literacy studies' *Journal of research in reading*, 16, 2: 81-97.

Street, B. 1995 *Social literacies.* London, Longman.

Street, B. 1997 'The implications of the new literacy studies for literacy education' *English in Education*, 31,3: 26-39.

Street, B. ed. 2005 *Literacies across educational contexts; mediating, learning and teaching.* Philadephia, Caslon Press.

Stubbs, M. 1980 *Language and literacy: the sociolinguistics of reading and writing.* London, Routledge.

Swales, J. 1990 *Genre analysis: English in academic and research settings.* Cambridge, Cambridge University Press.

Wilcox, S. Ed. 1989 *American deaf culture.* Silver Spring, MD, Linstok Press.

Witte, S. 1992 'Context, text, intertext: towards a constructivist semiotic of writing' *Written Communication,* 9: 237-308.

Woodward, J. 1972 'Implications for sociolinguistic research among the Deaf' *Sign Language Studies*, 1: 1-7.

CHAPTER EIGHT

Language Tutors under the microscope

Lynne Barnes and Laura Doe

Introduction

The last decade or so has seen increasing numbers of deaf students entering Higher Education, encouraged by the emergence of government policies to widen participation, new legislative and economic frameworks, new academic infrastructures and higher expectations for flexibility (Mole and Peacock, 2006:119). Furthermore, improvements in both the quality and quantity of support services offered to deaf people have led to more Deaf British Sign Language (BSL) users entering Higher Education, than ever before. In our own institution the numbers of BSL users rose from zero in 1992/3 to forty-five in 2001/2. Since this time, the number of BSL users within our institution has declined slightly, but the overall picture, reflected nationally, is one of steady increase. *(See HESA statistics, available online at: http://www.hesa.ac.uk).*

Deaf students now form a minute, but 'measurable group' (Mole and Peacock, 2006:119) of students within an increasing number of universities across the UK. Supported and safeguarded by a range of legislative and educational initiatives (for example Disability Discrimination Act, Part 4, 2001; DDA, 2005), deaf students are experiencing far greater access to the curriculum and university-wide services. Nevertheless, it is also evident that many deaf students still face linguistic barriers which impact upon their opportunities for success in HE. According to Quigley and Paul (1984):

> 'in spite of almost 200 years of effort in the United States and more than 300 in Europe, only limited success has been achieved in developing language in deaf children to the extent where it serves as an adequate vehicle for educational development.' (Quigley and Paul, 1984:21)

In order to address some of these difficulties, Language Tutors (LTs) are often employed in HE institutions to support individual deaf students. Language tutors clearly play a crucial part in the academic success of deaf students and yet very little has been written about defining the precise role of these tutors, and what actually constitutes language tuition. In the absence of a national qualifications framework for this type of work, questions are also raised as to how equity and parity are achieved across institutions and the wider sector.

Following on from Turner's theoretical framework,[17] this chapter seeks to explore the working practices of LTs and to consider some of the key features of this role, namely English teaching, 'scaffolding' and translation. Through analysing the support provided by LTs, the authors make suggestions as to how the language tuition role could be further developed and improved. The notion of introducing a minimal English skills level for deaf students entering HE will be discussed, along with the role of translation skills and the possibility of dividing the complex LT role. The need for LTs to have appropriate qualifications and training will also be examined and suitable courses or qualification routes will be suggested.

Deaf students

Language is acquired through plentiful exposure to meaningful linguistic interaction in early childhood. For severely and profoundly deaf people, acquiring language is clearly a different process from the ways in which hearing people develop language. While deaf children have the same potential to develop language as other children (and at the same age and rate of development), unfortunately relatively few do so (Brennan, 1999: 4). Arguably, one reason for this is that most deaf children are not given early access to a sign language and their limited access to English typically makes the development of a first language a slow and difficult process.

Without access to a first language, severe deafness drastically reduces both the quantity and the quality of linguistic input available and

---

[17] Chapter Seven of this publication

accessible to the deaf person. Therefore, it is common for many deaf children to start school with a language deficit, when compared with hearing peers (Mole and Peacock, 2006:120). This deficit is exacerbated by an education system where many deaf children are placed in mainstream schools and expected to access the curriculum directly through spoken English alone or through a mixture of languages and language systems, including spoken English, Sign Supported English, BSL and written English:

> 'The mixing of languages and communication modes can be confusing to children who are already disadvantaged in their language acquisition methods and stages.' (Mole and Peacock, 2006:121)

Consequently many deaf children miss a great deal of information which can hamper understanding of English grammar and result in a limited vocabulary and more restricted literacy skills than hearing peers.

Studying at HE level requires all students to understand and use academic language and literacies. They need to be 'fluent and confident using the spoken and written language conventions of their academic discipline' (Mole and Peacock 2006:122). Deaf students entering universities under-prepared in terms of their literacy and their ability to access and produce written English at HE level struggle to access this academic discourse (Walker et al, 1996).[18] Information gaps between academic staff expectations and student interpretations of what is involved in student writing (Cohen, 1993, Lea, 1994, Lea and Street, 1997 cited in Lea and Stierer, 2000) become more complex when one considers that the deaf student is often involved in mediated learning via a third party. These third parties (i.e. interpreters or notetakers) may themselves have minimal knowledge of either the subject or the language of Higher Education (Robbins 1996; Harrington 2001; Winston 2004 all cited in Mole and Peacock, 2006:124):

> 'It is inevitable that inaccuracies and misunderstandings occur and that Deaf Students often struggle to fully achieve their academic potential or become fully integrated into the community of learners.' (Harrington, 2000, cited in Mole and Peacock, 2006:124)

---

[18] See also Barnes, Chapter Nine of this volume

The role of Language Tutors

In order to address the language barriers identified above, many deaf students in HE are supported individually by language tutors or other support/learning tutors. The purpose of an LT is to bridge the language and information gaps within academic discourse, and to create a learning environment where by deaf students are provided with access to their course materials and assignments and supported in their production of written English.

Seeking to understand the LT role is in itself a difficult task. The activities undertaken by LTs vary 'depending on the students themselves and the institution within which the LT is working' (Dodds et al 2005). In addition, the LT's own skills and qualifications can influence their style and approach to language support.

Furthermore, there is currently a lack of national standard qualifications[19], formal training and standard working practices for LTs working within Higher Education. This complicates the language tuition role and raises questions about the quality and parity of language support being provided to deaf students.

Despite the complexity of the role, there are several common activities which appear to be undertaken by LTs: helping students prepare for assignments, assisting with planning and organisation of projects, advising students about the presentation of written work, and modifying the language of course materials, examinations and assignment briefs where appropriate (Barnes, 2006: 108). Other language support tasks include clarifying English texts, translating material from British Sign Language to English and vice versa, and the teaching of study skills and English grammar. For the purpose of analysing the role of LTs, these activities can be separated into three main areas of language tuition: English Teaching, 'Scaffolding' and Translation.

English teaching

As might be expected, a significant part of the LT role involves the teaching of English. Research has shown that when asked *what* their work entails, LTs typically identify the following activities: correcting common mistakes (including grammar, spellings and tenses); teaching the meaning of idioms; explaining questions and restructuring sentences (Barnes, 2005).

---

[19] Some institutions, such as City Lit in London, offer courses which train people to teach English to deaf learners in Further Education. Whilst these courses are relevant to the LT role, there are still no national standard qualifications or compulsory training for tutors in HE.

According to LTs, the weaknesses evident in deaf students' work are typically due to a lack of proficiency in English grammar and the inability to read and write at an appropriate academic level (Barnes, 2005:37). Deaf students are also aware of their own limitations with English and consider their main weaknesses to be grammar, vocabulary, spelling, organisation and the structure of work (Barnes, 2005:38).

Some LT sessions are used solely as English teaching tutorials, with every grammar mistake being highlighted, explained and amended. Whilst a necessary activity, this is very time consuming for both the LT and student, particularly as the student has a limited amount of time to prepare for assignments and to meet with their tutor. On other occasions, the English teaching appears to be much more subtle:

> 'I teach English – but not specifically. It's always there beneath the surface' (Tutor quoted in Barnes, 2005:68);
>
> 'I wouldn't inflict grammar or vocabulary exercises on a student without linking that to their work – in fact I draw it all from their work and create it ad hoc or custom made' (Tutor quoted in Barnes, 2005:68).

The teaching of English is particularly important for those deaf students for whom English is a second language; they need the additional support to develop their skills and confidence:

> 'If I wrote in English, my second language, and handed that work in, I know I would fail. They may just give me a bare pass at 40%, but I don't want that. I want a good grade' (Student quoted in Barnes, 2005:41).

Without a doubt, some of the English teaching also falls into a proof-reading category. Time constraints often dictate that a tutor is left checking spellings and grammar at the last minute before an assignment is handed in. Ideally, time-management and forward planning would render this unnecessary, but the reality is sometimes different. Nonetheless, for language tuition to work effectively, and for the student to benefit from English tuition, they should be present and understand why the tutor is correcting their English. Language tuition involves much more than just proof-reading; LTs identify the English mistakes and then explain, and negotiate, the appropriate corrections. In this way, students learn how to correct their own work, and in time, rely less on their language tutor for support. As Karlin (2005) states:

> 'The LT doesn't work so much as a ghost writer or editor as a collaborator. The LT goes through student work side-by-side with the student and suggests more standard forms of written English. This kind of collaboration can be very liberating for a deaf student, building the knowledge and confidence to be more expressive in English than she would otherwise have. This is a good example of supportive empowerment.' (Karlin, 2005)

Scaffolding

Besides English teaching, there are several other activities which typically occur during language tuition sessions; students sound out ideas to their LTs, tutors offer practical examples, vocabulary is extended and explained, and quotations are discussed in depth. Students use their LT as 'a sounding board; learning from the interaction, discussing ideas, creating plans and confirming that they are on the right track.' (Barnes, 2006:120).

It can be argued that these activities are a form of 'scaffolding' where the deaf student interacts with their LT as a means of developing their ideas and understanding of the literature or assignment.

Several researchers have identified scaffolding as a kind of talk which helps learners to complete a task they could not have managed on their own (Martin, 2005). The tutor is aware of the learner's level of understanding and builds on this to help the learner achieve the next step. In this way, the tutor makes the task more manageable; at the same time, the learner internalises these ways of tackling the task, and should be able to do it more independently next time:

> 'With "scaffolding", learners do not just learn facts or information – they also learn ways of thinking and strategies to help them in the future.' (Mercer, 2000 cited in Martin, 2005)

In addition to learning from tutors, students can also learn from each other. This is another form of scaffolding where students interact and share their ideas in order to develop their knowledge and skills. Discussions about the meaning and vagaries of assignment questions; initial perceptions of tasks, picking apart theoretical concepts, of discipline-specific terminology, sharing of good quotes and sources all make for a strong academic community, which is necessary for acquiring academic literacy.

As many deaf students access HE through a third party, it can be argued that deaf students have limited access to the scaffolding and learning conversations which take place in and out of the classroom. Therefore, deaf students may use their LTs as a sounding board in order to compensate for the lack of, or limited access to, a peer group. Scaffolding is an important way for deaf students to discuss their ideas and develop confidence in their ability and knowledge. It can be argued that this activity also has a social function:

> '... sometimes I feel there's an element of other responsibilities as well...if the student I'm working with is the only deaf student in the class, they can't take advantage of any subject-specific peer support in the same way that hearing students would. There's a risk they might feel isolated or excluded from that network, so maybe I see it as part of my role to fill that social gap...' (Dodds et al, 2005)

Translation

A key activity that takes place during language tuition sessions is the translation of information from BSL to English and vice versa. Translation has many guises: straight translation of books, chapters or articles into BSL; translation of smaller items such as paragraphs, quotes or even singular vocabulary; translation from BSL to English – to clarify what has been written by the student; translation from English to BSL (back translation) to check whether the written extract accurately reflects what the student intended (Barnes 2006:116).

Some students simply need access to materials via straight literal translation. For other students, particularly those whose first language is sign language and for whom English is a fairly weak second language, tutors are involved in some kind of *enhanced* translational activity – a sort of translation with the key concepts clearly explicated and where the client makes informed linguistic choices (Dodds et al, 2005).

For students whose first language is BSL, enhanced translation is an integral part of language tuition as the students quite simply cannot begin their work without firstly gaining knowledge of the written material. In many of these cases, LTs are involved in a 'judgement call' where they have the responsibility of deciding which sections are important enough to translate. If the student has no access to the literature, they are reliant upon the judgement of the tutor:

> '... If there's not enough time [...] I skim read the text and summarise what it is saying. But that gives me the power to decide what I tell them, what is important and what is not worth translating – and I don't like that. You are judging what the student needs.' (Tutor quoted in Barnes 2006:117)

This raises questions about the role of LTs - should they be making these types of decisions? Are LTs inadvertently influencing the student's work by making these judgment calls?

Translation is mainly used in language tuition sessions to clarify meaning and check understanding. In particular, those tutors who work bilingually tend to ask for clarification of the students' written English via BSL:

> 'She asks me what it means. I'll sign what I think it should say. She'll understand – and then start to amend my English so that it does say what I want it to say. She'll ask me to read it again. I ask her to sign it. She signs it and I'll agree that's what I meant; and so it goes on.' (Student quoted in Barnes, 2005:51);

> 'Normally, I type, my tutor reads. Then she asks me to sign bits, to clarify what I mean. I sign, my tutor understands and amends the English to reflect what I have signed.' (Student quoted in Barnes 2005: 60)

It is clear that the language tuition process involves a significant amount of translation and back translation. This indicates 'code-switching' and 'mode-switching' (Baynham, 1995) where LTs and their students regularly switch between languages and modalities. In addition, it appears that language tuition sessions involve 'double-mode shifts' as the LTs and students shift from sign (via speech) to text (Barnes 2006:113). The translation process also involves a considerable amount of negotiation between LTs and their students. In particular, Barnes (2005) found that LTs regularly translate and negotiate suitable quotes with their students:

> 'She will translate the quotes [I've used]. I often think they mean the opposite of what they actually mean. My LT explains the meaning and that it's wrong for my argument. So, I'll have to go off and find another source to support my view. I'll get another book and show her the quote. It will still be wrong – so she will look through the book and find a more appropriate quote. She

> signs it to me, and I say, 'Fancy that! That's what I wanted to say' and then I'll use that quote instead' (Student quoted in Barnes 2005:65).

Translation clearly benefits deaf students in several ways – not only do they access the course material in their own language, but the translation process enables deaf students to gain a pride in their own work. Deaf students do not always have the appropriate language skills to check their own written work and therefore, back translation plays an important role in helping students to develop confidence in their writing ability:

> 'When I worked with my LT and she translated for me – it really hit me! It proves deaf people can do it. Some people say deaf people can't do it, but with LT support and translation, they can!' (Student quoted in Barnes, 2005: 43)

Blurring of boundaries

Having identified three of the main activities which take place during language tuition sessions, it is appropriate to briefly consider some of the 'grey areas' of language support. The break down of language tutorials can easily occur when roles become blurred, or when the struggle for power and control is unequal. For example: during the scaffolding process, or when LTs make judgement calls about the translation of information.

Barnes (2005) identified occasions when tutors have exercised too much power by making editing decisions, deciding on content, drawing up essay plans and choosing quotes. In particular, LTs highlighted 'brainstorming' at the start of assignments as one example of how they might influence the deaf student's work (Barnes, 2006:118). There would seem to be a fine line between scaffolding and the sharing of ideas and over-directing the student work.

Whilst many LTs undoubtedly provide appropriate support and are aware of the boundaries, it seems some tutors can be over helpful and controlling. When this happens, the ownership of work can also become an issue between LTs and their students. Many of these 'grey areas' could potentially be addressed if there was standard professional training and a national code of practice for LTs.

Re-evaluating the role of the Language Tutor

As previously highlighted, the LT role is complex, varied and can be difficult to define. It is evident that LTs are, and should be, flexible in their approach to working with deaf students; adapting their role according to the students' linguistic requirements. Whilst the language tuition sessions are primarily led by the student, LTs are involved in the translation of information, take responsibility for the teaching of English and have significant input regarding the 'scaffolding' process. However, if one considers that each student usually has only one or two LT sessions per week, one can question where the time is found to complete all of these activities. If language tutors are going to work effectively with students they need time to teach English, engage in scaffolding and bridging information gaps and/or translate text in order to empower students towards independent learning. This suggests a need to be more realistic about what LTs can actually achieve in the time available. This could be done by:

- introducing a minimum level of English requirement for all Deaf students entering HE;
- dividing the current LT role into three separate roles;
- introducing standard qualifications and training for LTs working in HE institutions.

Minimum level of English for deaf students

In order to reduce the amount of time LTs spend teaching English to their students, a minimum level of English could be introduced as a requirement for all deaf students entering HE. This happens in some universities already, namely those institutions that ask for a pre-requisite qualification in English before entry onto degree courses. This is also the case in the United States, where there appears to be no language tutor role within HE institutions (see SDP3, 2005). Alternatively, some universities offer 'access courses' for deaf students prior to starting university; these courses enable deaf students to develop their English, academic and study skills in preparation for their degree course.[20] However, this is only possible for institutions that have a large number of deaf students, or who are able and/or willing to become a 'centre of

---

[20] See Nunn and Quinn, Chapter 4 of this book

excellence' for deaf students – thus arguably, limiting individual university and course choice.

Requiring deaf students to have a minimum standard of English would be problematic, as there is no clear basis for determining at what level this would be set. One argument might be to require deaf students to have a similar standard as international students coming to England to study (Dodds et al 2005). However, international students can achieve sufficient levels of literacy through full immersion in the majority language around them; deaf students do not have this option. It can also be argued that the current International English Language Testing System (IELTS) exams are based on standards for hearing international students who learn a second language aurally. In many cases, deaf students do not have a strong first language on which to build their second, neither do they have access to the language of discourse around them.

There are several other concerns with the introduction of a minimum level of English for deaf students prior to entering university. It could be argued that one is discriminating against those students who, through no fault of their own, have underachieved because of failings within their education system. Also, as students progress through their course and the work becomes progressively more difficult it is impossible to forecast that a deaf student who has an acceptable level of English on entry will succeed in Year Three of their degree course:

> 'Language level at the beginning of a period of study is not a good predictor of final success. Language plays a role but not a dominant role in academic success once the minimum threshold of adequate proficiency has been reached. Thereafter it is individual, non-linguistic characteristics both cognitive and affective that determine success' (Criper and Davies cited in Mawer, 1999).

However, whilst accepting that there are considerable risks in setting minimum English skills levels for deaf students on entry to university, the fact does remain that with no assessment of this skill, universities may be setting some students up to fail. If students cannot access the literature sufficiently to understand knowledge of course materials and concepts, and demonstrate (even via BSL) the achievement of learning outcomes, then ultimately, they cannot succeed.

In addition to assessing a deaf student's level of English, one could argue that their level of BSL should also be assessed prior to entering HE. Deaf people have a much wider variety of language learning experience than other groups of people. It is not enough to assume that because a deaf person signs, that they have a high enough level of BSL to access the Higher Education academic environment. For example, some deaf people may have either BSL, or English, as their first language; alternatively, they may be fully bilingual; they may use a different home language (not English or BSL); or they may have had very limited exposure to any language at all. This has an impact on how they access the academic curriculum. According to Winston (2004):

> 'More familiar…is the placement of deaf students into interpreted educations without any sense of their language abilities. Or rather, the sense is often that they have few language abilities, either in signing or in English.' (Winston 2004)

Separating roles

The second suggestion involves separating the current LT role into three distinct job roles: translation services, English classes and language tuition (Dodds et al, 2005).

A stand-alone translation service could be provided for those students who have high fluency in BSL; this service would be responsible for translating academic literature from English into BSL and signed assignments (exams and coursework) into written English. For some deaf students, this would be the only support necessary.

The second role would involve teaching core English skills in separate English classes for those deaf students who required it. The content of these English classes would include, for example, how to structure presentations and essays, teaching grammar, vocabulary and spelling:

> 'Ideally, these English classes would be taught by bilingual deaf tutors, drawing on their inherent strengths: culture, empathy, signing skills and so forth' (Barnes, 2006:122).

These classes would also create a peer group for deaf students, giving them the opportunity to scaffold their ideas and knowledge.[21]

Finally, after separating out translation services and the teaching of English skills, the activities which remain constitute language tuition (Dodds et al, 2005). LTs could then focus primarily on academic socialisation, academic literacies (See Lea and Street in Lea and Stierer,

---

[21] See Nunn & Quinn, Chapter Four of this publication for further discussion.

2000) and literacy skills, through activities such as scaffolding and enhanced translation (Barnes 2006).

However, the separation of roles is not as straightforward as it might initially appear. The separate English skills classes might be appropriate for universities where there are several deaf students, but for institutions where there is only one or two deaf students, putting on additional English classes could be problematic (Dodds et al 2005). Time and financial constraints also need to be considered. Separation of these activities necessarily constitutes extra tutorial sessions and additional funding requirements, which may or may not be feasible. Finally, the question still remains as to what are appropriate qualifications and training for these roles.

Standard qualifications and training for LTs

There is currently no national qualifications framework for LTs working with deaf students in HE, which raises questions about the quality of language support being provided nationally and suggests that the service deaf students receive may vary greatly according to the skills and experiences of their LT. It could be argued, for example, that a student working with a highly skilled BSL/English translator may have much better access to their course than the student working with an LT who has limited BSL skills (Barnes 2006:108). If this is true, then some deaf students may be being disadvantaged. In order to ensure deaf students receive an equal standard of language support, it is crucial that the tutors are appropriately trained and qualified.

Suggested skills necessary for LTs working with deaf students include; signing skills, English skills, an HE degree, translation skills, knowledge of deaf culture and 'deafisms' (Dodds et al 2005). In addition, tutors need some sort of teaching qualification. The identity of an appropriate teaching qualification is more problematic. For example, one can question whether a generic Postgraduate Certificate in Education (PGCE) teaching qualification is appropriate. Other more relevant qualifications might be Teaching English as a Foreign Language (TEFL) certificates or some of the Level 4 Subject Specifications for Teachers of English for Speakers of Other Languages (ESOL) (Department for Education and Skills and the Further Education National Training Organisation, 2002). However, none of these qualifications on their own would prepare a tutor for teaching English or working bilingually with deaf students.

Language tutors in particular offer a specialist learning support role, which differs considerably from that of a lecturer or classroom teacher.

Yet, a qualifications framework for those in a learning support role does not currently exist. This has recently been recognised within the FE sector; from September 2007, all new entrants to teaching or tutoring will be required to complete a new award which will prepare them to teach. The Skills for Life team at Lifelong Learning UK (LLUK) is currently developing proposals for a qualifications framework for learning support in England, based on the Qualifications and Credit Framework (QCF) model. These qualifications will be:

> 'credit based with core and optional units at different levels, so that qualifications can be built flexibly and in a way that can meet the range of needs in the sector.' *(http://www.lifelonglearninguk.org/)*

Whilst this development is aimed at the FE sector, such a qualifications framework could easily be adapted for tutors in Higher Education. More specifically, flexibility should allow for a modular mix and match. Core tutoring modules could be undertaken alongside more specific and specialist modules for working with deaf learners. What emerges is a specialist qualification for language tutors working with deaf students, which:

> 'qualifies tutors to teach within the sector within this defined role and will lead to Qualified Teacher Learning and Skills (QTLS) status after registration with the Institute for Learning (IfL) and a defined period of Continued Professional Development (CPD) have been achieved' (CTLLS Handbook, 2007).[22]

Combining this teaching qualification with specialist modules for teaching deaf learners and pre-requisite BSL skills, LTs achieve a professional qualification at Diploma in Higher Education level, which would ensure high level tutoring skills and national standards recognised by the sector and the Qualifications and Curriculum Authority (QCA). An example of what the specialist qualification could look like has been included below.

---

[22] The full citation for this source is 'Certificate in Teaching in the Lifelong Learning Sector (Associate Lecturer Award) Handbook, 2007'

Table 1: Associate Lecturer:
Language Tutor for Deaf students in HE (Graduate Diploma)

Module 1: Preparing to teach in the Lifelong Learning Sector (or equivalent) **Module 2:** **Tutoring deaf learners** • Deafness, deaf students and literacy • Deaf awareness/deaf culture • Scaffolding • Academic literacies • Teaching the 'Deaf Way'	**Module 3:** **Professional practice** • Teaching and reflecting on practice • Professional issues • Roles • Boundaries • Codes of practice **Module 4:** Translation theory **Modules 5 & 6:** NVQ Level 3 BSL
Modules 1, and 3 are equivalent to the Certificate in Teaching in the Lifelong Learning Sector (Associate Lecturer)	Modules 1 to 6 are equivalent to the Dip HE Teaching in the Lifelong Learning Sector (Associate Lecturer)
NB: Entry requirements are a degree and BSL Post-Stage Two	

NB: Modules 1, 2 & 3 = Certificate in Teaching in the Lifelong Learning Sector (Associate Lecturer)
Modules 1-6 = Dip HE in Teaching in the Lifelong Learning Sector (Associate Lecturer)

Furthermore, if the LT role was to be separated out as previously detailed, then what emerges is a BSL/English continuum, overlapped with this continuum of skills and qualifications (see figure 2). For students requiring straight BSL translation, fully qualified interpreters trained in translation theory would provide this service. Tutors teaching English to classes of BSL users would need to be bilingual and bicultural, hold a degree in English and a teaching qualification. Language tutors working with BSL users would undertake the Associate Lecturer: Language Tutors for Deaf Students in HE Award. Tutors working monolingually with non-BSL deaf students would not require the BSL signing skills and thus would exit with a Certificate rather than a Graduate Diploma qualification.

Table 2: A Proposed Framework of Skills, Qualifications and Attributes for Language Tutors (after Barnes 2005)

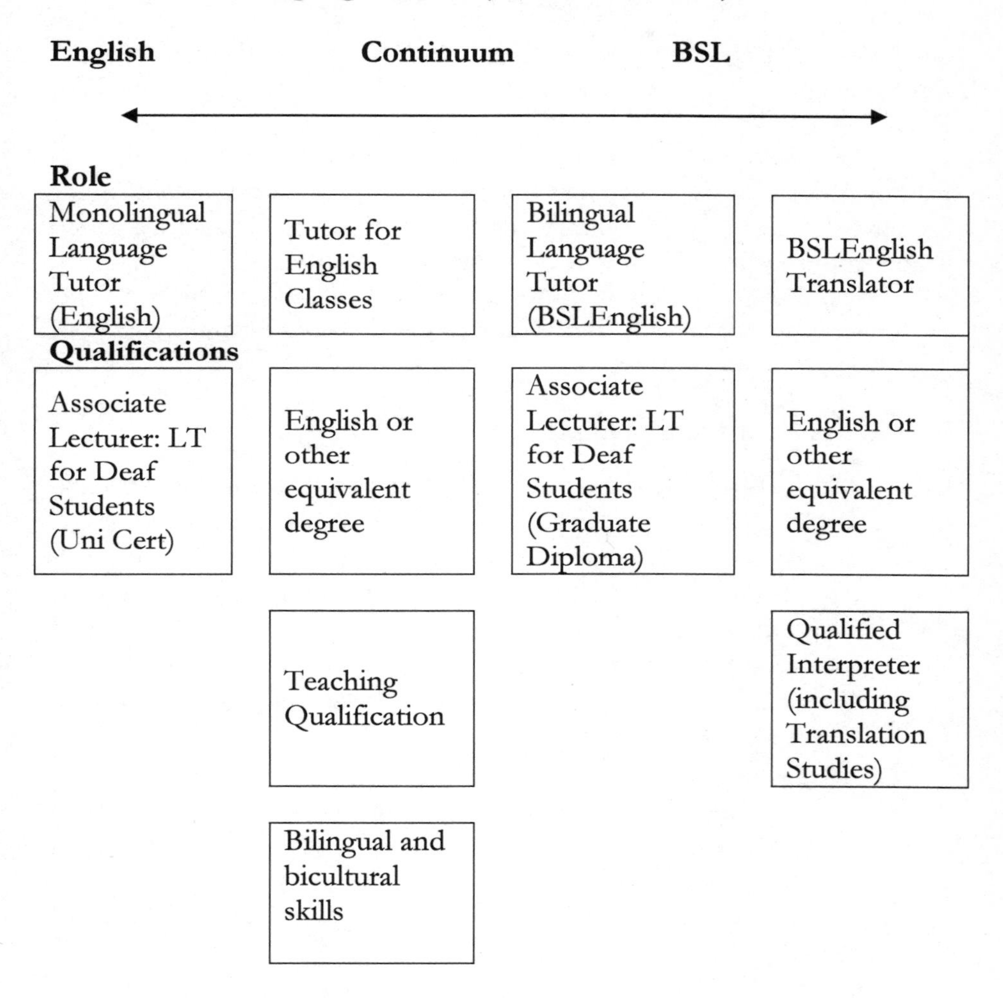

English ⟵ **Continuum** ⟶ **BSL**

Role			
Monolingual Language Tutor (English)	Tutor for English Classes	Bilingual Language Tutor (BSLEnglish)	BSLEnglish Translator
Qualifications			
Associate Lecturer: LT for Deaf Students (Uni Cert)	English or other equivalent degree	Associate Lecturer: LT for Deaf Students (Graduate Diploma)	English or other equivalent degree
	Teaching Qualification		Qualified Interpreter (including Translation Studies)
	Bilingual and bicultural skills		

Conclusion

This chapter has considered the role and working practices of LTs within HE. It is clear that LTs play an important role within HE institutions by supporting deaf students in overcoming language barriers to their learning. In particular, English teaching, scaffolding and translation have been identified as key features of language tuition sessions.

As more deaf students continue to study at university level, it seems likely that the demand for LTs will also increase. Therefore, to ensure equality of access and provision, it is crucial that LTs are meeting the needs of their deaf students. In order to address some of the complexities of the LT role, three suggestions are put forward: a minimum level of English (and BSL) could be introduced for deaf students, the LT role could be separated into more appropriate, manageable and distinct functions and formal qualifications and training could be developed for LTs.

In the absence of appropriate qualifications for tutors working in Higher Education, it has been suggested that the new qualifications framework for learning support tutors in the FE sector could be adapted to incorporate specialist modules for tutors of deaf learners. In this way, tutors will be accredited with a national qualification which reflects professional practice and status and students are ensured parity of provision across the sector.

Key points for further discussion:

- Do LTs need to have standard teaching or tutoring qualifications?;
- Would LTs be prepared to undertake qualifications of this kind? The relatively small numbers of people undertaking this role mean that it is unlikely that courses can be run locally. Would a national course attract students?;
- Would LTs already in work and under demand, feel the need to undertake more training?;
- Who would deliver and teach this qualification?;
- Is it appropriate to set a standard minimum level of English entry requirement for deaf students, or should it vary depending upon the course/university?;
- What are appropriate minimum skill levels of English and BSL? What assessment tools would be used? Who would assess the candidates and when would this assessment take place?;
- Does the above discriminate deaf students, if non-deaf students are not required to undertake this type of assessment?;
- If institutions are to provide a translation service, who would supply this service, given the current shortage of qualified interpreters currently employed in universities?;

- How would universities with only very few deaf students provide these services? Would the development of regional English classes be possible?;
- Given current funding levels and the fact that deaf students often exceed the maximum Disabled Students Allowance awards, are services of this kind feasible?

Further reading

Adams, M. & Brown S. (Eds.) 2006 *Towards inclusive learning in HE: developing curricula for disabled students* London, Routledge

Barnes, L. 2005 *Assessment of deaf students: an investigation into the working practices of language tutors* Unpublished MA dissertation

Barnes, L. 2006 'Formal qualifications for language tutors: a case for discussion' in *Deafness and Education International* 8, 3:106-124

Baynham, M. 1995 *Literacy practices. investigating literacy in social contexts.* London: Longman

Brennan, M. 1999 'Challenging linguistic exclusion in deaf education' in *Deaf Worlds* 15, 1:2-10

Dodds, J., Barnes, L., Haddon, C. Mowe, K and Pollitt, K. 'Around the language table: a discussion about the working practices of language tutors with deaf students'. *Supporting Deaf People (SDP3) on-line conference* 10-15th March 2005.

Direct Learn Services (http://www.online-conference.co.uk/WebX?14@43.uQVmaG8daGw.39364@ee8424 – accessed 10-15.03.05)

Harrington, F and Turner G. (eds) 2001 *Interpreting interpreting.* Coleford: Douglas McLean.

Higher Education Statistics Agency (HESA) http://www.hesa.ac.uk/holisdocs/pubinfo/stud.htm Accessed 1.5.07

Karlin, B. 2005 *Supporting Deaf People (SDP3) on-line conference* 10-15th March 2005. Direct Learn Services (http:// www.online- conference.co.uk/WebX?14@43.uQVmaG8daGw.39364@ee8424 – accessed 10.03.05 -15.03.05)

Lea, M.R. and Stierer, B. 2000 *Student writing in Higher Education: new contexts.* Buckingham: SRHE and Open University Press.

Martin, W 2005 'Education as dialogue: some implications for deaf learners'. *Supporting Deaf People (SDP3) on-line conference.* 2005. Direct Learn Services Ltd. (http://www.online-conference.co.uk/WebX?14@43.uQVmaG8daGw.39364@ee8424 – accessed 10.03.05)

Mawer, G. 1999 *Language and literacy in workplace education*. Singapore: Addison Wesley Longman

Mercer, N. 2000 *Words and minds: how we use language to think together.* London: Routledge.

Mole, J. and Peacock, D. 'Language issues for deaf students in Higher Education' in Adams, M. & Brown S. (Eds.) 2006 *Towards inclusive learning in HE: developing curricula for disabled students* London, Routledge

O'Neill, R. 2005 'Why moderate language?' *Supporting Deaf People (SDP3) on-line conference* 10-15th March 2005. Direct Learn Services (http://www.online-conference.co.uk/WebX?14@43.uQVmaG8daGw.39364@ee8424 – accessed 10.03.05)

Paul, P 1998 *Literacy and deafness: the development of reading, writing and literate thought* Needham Heights, Allyn and Bacon
Quigley, S and Paul, P 1984 *Language and deafness* San Diego, College-Hill

Rodda, M. and Eleweke, J. 2000 'Theories of literacy development in deaf people with limited english proficiency' *Deafness and Education International* 2, 2: 101-113

SDP 3: Supporting Deaf People on-line conference 10-15th March 2005. Direct Learn Services (http://www.online-conference.co.uk/ WebX?14@43.uQVmaG8daGw.39364@ee8424 – accessed 10.03.05 -15.03.05)

Turner, G. & Laugesen, C. 1998 'Write ways and wrong ways: literacy support for deaf students in higher education'. Paper presented at the *3rd International Conference on Higher Education and Disability*, Innsbruck, July 21-25, 1998

Walker, L., Adams, L, Coverdale, R., McCracken, M., & Murfitt, K. 1996 'Assessment issues in Higher Educational settings for deaf students' http://www.tcd.ie/disability/docs/DNA/deafassess.pdf - accessed 9.04.05)

Winston, B 2004 'Language myths of an interpreted education'. *Supporting Deaf People (SDP2) on-line conference* 2004. Direct Learn Services Ltd. (http:// www.online-conference.co.uk/ WebX?14@43.uQVmaG8daGw.39364@ee8424 – accessed 11.3.05)

CHAPTER NINE

We have started but can we finish?: towards accessible assessments for deaf students

Lynne Barnes

> 'Assessment and examination policies, practices and procedures should provide disabled students with the same opportunity as their peers to demonstrate the achievement of learning outcomes.' (Quality Assurance Agency for Higher Education (QAA) Code of Practice, 2000, Precept 13)

It has long been common practice for institutions of Higher Education in the UK to permit alternative forms of assessment for disabled students. This has been concurrent with 'equal opportunities' policies and widening participation initiatives which have encouraged many institutions to open their doors to non-traditional students. The significant rise in the numbers of disabled students entering Higher Education over the last decade, has resulted in escalating numbers receiving special examination arrangements. However, historically, the development of special examination arrangements has not been based on rigorous research, but has been expedient as a 'bolt on' solution to existing practice (Waterfield & West, 2002). Subsequently this has led to confusion about the purpose of assessment, and fears that this widely used practice of special assessment arrangements has violated the principles of assessment and undermined the validity of assessment in Higher Education (Sharp and Earle, 2000:191).

More recently, further drivers for change have focussed attention on the validity of current assessment practice and have required Higher

Education institutions to 'take a more inclusive approach to the teaching, learning and assessment of disabled students' (Waterfield et al, 2006:80). These drivers include disability and equality legislation, Quality Assurance Agency for Higher Education (QAA) periodic subject reviews, the importance of student retention to university finances and the increasing cost of high numbers of special examination arrangements for disabled students (SPACE Project, 2007).

Disability-specific legislation is of particular importance. In 1995, the Disability Discrimination Act (DDA) brought in measures to prevent discrimination against people with disabilities. The provisions of the Act have since been widened via the DDA Part 4 (Special Educational Needs and Disability Act [SENDA] , 2001) to include education, training and awarding bodies. This means that universities (amongst others) are now obliged to review their current policies and practices with regards to discrimination against disabled students, and to make 'reasonable adjustments' wherever possible. Whilst the precise meaning of 'reasonable adjustments' is not clearly defined, it is stated that:

> 'if any arrangements at the institution place a disabled person at a 'substantial disadvantage', the institution is required to take such steps as are reasonable to prevent that disadvantage.' (JISC Technology for Disabilities Service cited in McCarthy and Hurst, 2001:6).

This includes making adjustments to assessment arrangements which would otherwise place disabled students at a substantial disadvantage in comparison to students who are not disabled (Federation of Awarding Bodies [FAB], 2005:5).

The need to consider change and eliminate the barriers to developing more inclusive practice is made more timely still by the advent of what are commonly referred to as 'the Positive Duties' set down by the DDA 2005, which amends the DDA 1995 (SPACE Project, 2007). This Disability Equality Duty necessitates a new approach for Higher Education institutions, as it shifts emphasis from retrospective individual action to tackle discrimination towards an anticipatory and proactive problem-solving approach. The new duties demand a cultural shift in thinking; for example:

> 'institutions [now] have the opportunity to move from assimilation of disabled students into a largely unchanged course assess-

> ment regime, to the transformation of the entire assessment culture ' (SPACE Project, 2007)

This chapter discusses the implications of alternative assessment strategies for deaf students and provides examples of good practice which illustrate fair assessment methods. These inclusive assessment strategies allow students to demonstrate their acquisition of course learning outcomes without compromising the validity of the assessment process. Issues regarding these assessment arrangements will also be highlighted. In order to do this, it is necessary to consider the wider picture of current assessment policies and academic practice within the framework of increased diversity amongst the whole student population and the need for more inclusive learning.

Principles of assessment in Higher Education

The purpose of an assessment, whether it is formative or summative, is to determine a students' academic achievement and skills. Assessment provides the means by which students are graded, enables students to obtain feedback on their learning and enables staff to evaluate the effectiveness of their teaching. Furthermore, assessment determines students' progression through their programmes of study and enables them to demonstrate that they have achieved the intended learning outcomes:

> 'Ultimately, assessment provides the main basis for public recognition of achievement, through the awarding of qualifications or credit.' (QAA, 2000:4)

Given the above, the validity of assessment is its most important quality (Crookes et al cited in Maclellan 2004) and is of gravest concern to assessment designers within a Higher Education system which values meritocracy and rigour.

Clearly, academic requirements and standards cannot be compromised and should be applied to all students, regardless of whether or not they have a disability. Institutions of Higher Education have a public responsibility not merely to assess their students, but also to ensure that these assessments are valid and reliable indicators of the possession of some specified set of skills or body of knowledge (Sharp and Earle, 2000:192). In order for this to happen, examinations and assessments must meet rigorous standards so that all students are genuinely tested against an academic benchmark (Disability Rights Commission [DRC]

2002:4). Similarly, if assessments are to fulfil their purpose, they must also be flexible regarding the mode of measurement so that each student has an equal opportunity to demonstrate their achievement:

> 'In all cases it will mean being clear about precisely what is being assessed so that modifications can be made without compromising academic standards.' (DRC 2002:4).

1. Principles for making 'reasonable adjustments'

Whilst there are numerous publications which offer guidelines regarding the assessment of disabled students' work, the notion of making adjustments to examinations and assessments is not universally understood, nor welcomed.[23] The greatest concern is levelled at the validity and reliability of assessment which has been adjusted to meet the needs of the deaf or disabled student (See research by Walker et al, 1996). The idea of compensation is an area of concern for many academics, and one which leads to resistance from assessment designers. Sharp and Earle (2000) present the argument that the only permissible alternative forms of assessment are those which test identical knowledge and skills as those undertaken by non-disabled students.

Therefore, universities have a duty to ensure that their graduates possess the knowledge and skills which their qualifications purport to demonstrate. This leads to greater responsibility for those designing assessments to be aware of, and to be explicit about, the skills and knowledge their assessments are intended to test, and to ensure that their assessments genuinely test nothing more than the students' skills and knowledge.

2. Literacy development and deaf learners

In exploring 'reasonable adjustments' and alternative assessment strategies for deaf students in Higher Education it is useful to explore the reasons these might be necessary, namely the implications of deafness and both past and present education policies for deaf learners. Many academic tutors associate deafness with an inability to hear, and are often unaware of the linguistic difficulties facing deaf students. They

---

[23] See for example, Disability Rights Commission :The DDA Part 4: Examinations and Assessment Good Practice Guide; QAA for Higher Education (1999) Code of Practice (Section 3): Assurance of Academic Quality and Standards in Higher Education (p16); Federation of Awarding Bodies (FAB) (2005) Good Practice Guide: The Application of Reasonable Adjustments and Special Considerations in Vocational Qualifications

may not appreciate the extent to which assessment techniques, including written examinations in English, are a barrier for deaf students to academic success in Higher Education (Walker et al, 1996).

Research on language, literacy and deafness is common-place, as attention to the low attainment levels of deaf children in schools remains a high priority for educationalists in the field. In particular, Paul (1998a; 1998b) documents the difficulties deaf pupils have in acquiring English as a first language, and in particular text-based literacy skills (Barnes, 2005: 15).

Paul (1998b:6) makes a distinction between communicative and academic proficiency. Without BSL, or a native first language, he is doubtful whether deaf students can ever develop high-level English text-based literacy skills. This in turn has led some researchers to question whether text-based literacy is a realistic goal for the majority of students with severe to profound deafness (Paul, 1998a; O'Neill, 1999). This has direct relevance to the assessment of deaf students, particularly text-based assessment:

> 'It is often difficult for academic staff to realise the limited access deaf students have to spoken language and the fragmented data on which they base their understanding of the rules of English syntax. Deaf people characteristically have problems with written English that they can never fully eliminate.' (Walker et al, 1996:17)

3. Implications for assessment

Given the above, it can be argued that many deaf students may be being disadvantaged by current Higher Education assessment strategies which focus primarily on traditional unseen written examinations and tutor-marked written essays and dissertations. (SPACE Project, 2007)

Research by Walker et al (1996) found that deaf students lacked confidence in their ability to understand the English of the question or the instructions of the assignment task. Students felt ill prepared to respond to the question or assessment task because they either relied on the accuracy of the notes taken for them by someone else or on their incomplete understanding of the text they had studied. Many deaf students did not feel confident in their ability to write information in grammatically correct English. Furthermore, students mentioned an element of panic induced by this feeling of inadequacy which led to confused thinking (Walker et al 1996:65).

It is necessary to introduce alternative assessment procedures if such fears are to be alleviated and deaf students are to have the same opportunities to achieve as their hearing counterparts. Minimising the potential impact of impairment on a student's performance at assessment as a means of allowing students to demonstrate their abilities and skills seems a 'reasonable adjustment' to propose (FAB. 2005). Accepting such criteria, it appears reasonable, for example, to allow a student whose first or preferred language is British Sign Language, to sign exam responses or submit assessed coursework in British Sign Language.

Alternative approaches to assessment

National organisations of disability officers and assessment centres, e-discussion groups, national and international conferences, local education authorities and regional networks all bear witness to an increasing amount of good practice amongst Student Support Services. However, it is clear that within the sector there is also a wide range of discrepancy, both in the kinds of alternative assessments offered and the decision making processes involved in making such offers (Sharp and Earle, 2000:194).

Adopting the assessment framework outlined by Waterfield et al (2006) it is possible to categorise these 'special assessment arrangements' into three distinct categories; the contingent approach, the alternative approach and the inclusive approach. It is useful to discuss the implications of each approach for deaf students.

1. The contingent approach

Clearly, different types of assessment make different demands on the student and will influence whether 'reasonable adjustments' will be needed, and if so, the kind of reasonable adjustment which may be put into place. The adjustments that are appropriate for a particular assessment will depend upon specific assessment requirements, the type of assessment and the particular needs and circumstances of the individual student (Federation of Awarding Bodies, 2005, Section 6:11). In reality, however, the majority of 'reasonable adjustments' are not alternative or inclusive, but are made for individual disabled students and as such are contingent arrangements made to already existing assessment practices. By their very nature, these are compensatory arrangements, 'fitting people into what is already available' (Stuart cited in Waterfield et al, 2006:81).

Examples for deaf students include extra time, separate rooms, modification of English for written exam papers, signed exam questions, language tutorials and extensions to deadlines.

1a: Extra time

The allocation of extra time is the most prevalent 'special arrangement' (SPACE Project, 2007) for deaf (and disabled) students. This allocation is usually awarded for extra reading time and for the checking of grammar and spelling. However, issues do arise as to how this extra time is allocated. In the absence of research to support the efficacy or the appropriateness of extra time allocation, it is difficult to know whether the student is being advantaged or disadvantaged. Furthermore, the decision-making process, including who makes the decision, may appear arbitrary. Judgements can be made at initial stages of the course, with no dialogue with academic tutors as to the appropriateness of this (usually 25%) extra time allocation. Deaf students may need more than the usual amount of extra time if, for example, they are using a modified paper in conjunction with the original exam paper, if they are working across two languages, from BSL to English, or if they are using an amanuensis via an interpreter.

Consideration also has to be given to the time needed for the practical aspects of students signing assessments, such as translation, processing, editing/re-filming delays and the potential for technical problems. Further research is needed on this important aspect of assessment of deaf students to ensure a fair and equitable assessment process for all students.

Furthermore, whilst the provision of separate rooms for extra time in exams is widely accepted, this is problematic for the deployment of invigilators, the use of space and time-table restrictions. Single-occupancy rooms are a luxury, whilst sign language and hearing aid users working in rooms with other disabled students might easily be distracted or distract others. In addition, it is not always clear whose responsibility it is to book these rooms, causing conflicts between academic staff, departmental administrators and disability services which ultimately affect the student. Crucially, separate room provision is rarely available for the increasing number of in-class tests that are becoming the norm, especially in maths and science-based subjects. Research by Waterfield et al (2006) revealed a high degree of uncertainty surrounding in-class procedures. Some students had never been offered such an arrangement and therefore lacked an understanding of how to access it, reflecting a 'grey area of undischarged responsibility'. (SPACE Project, 2007) Similarly, students who are completing coursework assignments or in class-tests via computer-based or e-learning rarely receive extra time, and crucially, the language of these assessments is rarely, if ever, modified. This can pose a huge barrier to their success.

1b: Modified papers

Many institutions offer modified examination and assignment papers; papers which are rewritten in plain English, in a format more appropriate to the student's language requirements. Whilst this is largely common practice, many academics are still wary of language modification in exam situations, confusing modification with a compromise of academic standards (Walker, 1996:20).

Furthermore, issues arise concerning who should modify these papers. In some institutions, teachers of the deaf are employed to undertake this task; in other institutions, such personnel are simply not available. As a consequence, freelance tutors may be employed instead, who do not know the individual students' language level, nor the subject areas. This can lead to modified papers which do not reflect the original questions, or which confuse, alter or misinform the student.

Clearly, the most appropriate person to undertake this task is the subject tutor. It is evident that a modified paper would benefit all students; therefore, if tutors wrote the original paper in accessible English, there would be no need for modification at all (CACDP, 2005:11). Advisers working alongside module tutors and assessment designers can facilitate this process, thus eliminating questions as to who is responsible and/or qualified to undertake this modification process.

1c: Signed questions

For some students, modification of exam papers, on its own, may not be sufficient. For deaf students who access the curriculum via British Sign Language (BSL) it is reasonable to assess them in a manner which 'reflects the candidates normal way of working' (FAB, 2005:17). This means that students should have access to an interpreter, who can be called upon to translate any/all of the questions, as necessary, from English into BSL.

It can be argued, that for quality assurance, questions should be prepared in BSL, before the exam. No two interpretations are ever the same, so live interpretation of questions might give a different perception on the second or third interpretation. Students might lose their train of thought if presented with slightly different translations. One solution would be to film questions onto DVD, providing students with the same access as hearing students and allowing them to go back and forth to whichever questions they wish. This system would allow greater parity for multiple students doing the same exams. Preparation would include discussions with the tutor regarding the translation process, thus avoiding giving unfair advantage to the deaf student. Clearly, for this to happen, the interpreter must be familiar with the subject; preferably, they would be the regular classroom interpreter:

> 'The sign language used must be carefully selected to ensure that the validity and reliability of the assessment is not reduced, and the integrity or reliability of the qualification is not compromised.' (CACDP, 2005: 11)

1d: Coursework

The difficulties some deaf students have in presenting written English clearly affect the grades they receive for assessed coursework. Many deaf students have the ability to think and conceptualise in British Sign Language, but find it difficult to put their thoughts down on paper. Emphasis on written essays and reports create barriers for deaf students working in their second language. Tutors also experience difficulties grasping the content and the argument of deaf students' coursework because of the way it has been expressed:

> 'Lecturers have difficulty in separating the assessment of knowledge content of the course from the students' ability to communicate that knowledge in English, particularly written English' (Walker et al, 1996:44);

> 'If I wrote in English, my second language, and handed that work in, I know I would fail. They may just give me a bare pass at 40%, but I don't want that. I want a good grade' (Student quoted in Barnes, 2005:41).

For this reason, in many institutions, deaf students work on a regular basis with Language Tutors (LTs) or other support workers whose role includes helping them prepare for assignments; checking comprehension of the task and the understanding of written materials, assisting with the planning and organisation of projects, advising on essay structuring and about the presentation of written, signed or spoken work:

> 'Without language tuition, the lecturers would read my work and fail it. University is highly academic. My own English is not at the

same standard as required by the University system' (Student quoted in Barnes, 2005:41).[24]

The provision of language/specialist support for written course assessment can be viewed as a 'reasonable adjustment' for deaf students. Nevertheless, this is still a contingent approach if the nature of the assessment remains the same. In reality it means the deaf students have extra tutorials to organise, prepare for and attend, within time constraints laid down by often inflexible submission dates. Even if deadlines are extended, the burden does not disappear as the next assignment brings time constraints of its own.

Implementing Waterfield's framework (SPACE Project, 2007) it is possible to classify these 'reasonable adjustments' as compensatory in nature. The student is fitting into the already existing assessment system without discourse as to whether this is the most equitable and inclusive practice:

> 'Because there has not been a dialogue about the value of 'special arrangements' this approach has become the cultural norm, a form of hegemony which has precluded staff and disabled students contemplating different ways of doing things.' (SPACE Project, 2007)

2. An alternative approach

It has been argued above that assessing deaf students in the time honoured tradition of written examinations and long coursework essays is not the most appropriate method for many deaf students. Regardless, of contingent 'special arrangements', barriers to assessment still remain. For example, exam questions may be signed to deaf students, but for many, understanding the written exam questions is only half of the problem:

> 'Students who are deaf encounter particular disadvantages in current examination processes which require written English responses to questions or tasks.' (Walker, 1996:7)

As previously outlined, students may work with specialist language or support tutors who ensure that their coursework conforms to conven-

---

[24] See Chapters Seven and Eight of this publication for more discussion of the Language Tutor's role

tional academic style and is accessible to the subject tutors in terms of grammar, punctuation, spelling and so forth. However, this service is largely unavailable in exam situations. The subject tutors may not see the deaf students' unaided writing until an exam paper is submitted. Marking this work may prove difficult for the tutor, especially if they have no previous knowledge of deaf learners and are therefore unfamiliar with deaf English:

> 'The difficulties are two-sided. Not only do many deaf students have difficulty understanding what is required of them in a question, but the examiners often have difficulty interpreting the responses when standard forms of English syntax are not used.' (Walker et al, 1996:20);
>
> 'I have been seeing with my tutor to discuss about my exam why I am failed so he said to me I have found it he only looking for words which I am passed so I said to him make sure he is need understand what I am write about in the exam. [...] I know there is still problem with my English again in the exam paper.'
> (Personal communication with author, 4th July 2006).

This student passed four modules via continuous coursework at 2:1 level, but failed two examination papers.

For this reason, alternative assessments could be offered. For example, after a written examination, a viva voce could be offered to deaf students in their first or preferred language. Via BSL, the students could explain or expand upon their written answers, and the subject tutors be confident that the student has the requisite knowledge to answer the question. Clearly, there would need to be quality assurance measures in place; skilled and trained interpreters, familiar with the subject material; external examiners made aware of the implications of deafness on English language learning; training sessions for examiners and students. Discussions would also need to take place regarding the most appropriate timing for this event.

Another alternative would be to allow this examination to be produced in BSL.

2a: Assessment in BSL

Although there are plenty of examining and awarding bodies which recommend this alternative practice in post-SENDA education (see for example, QAA for Higher Education, 1999; CACDP, 2005; FAB, 2005;

Doyle, C & Robson, K. 2002:50),this is still a relatively new break-through in Higher Education – and warrants additional exploration and discussion. Furthermore recent e-discussion groups within the sector reflect both an increase in this practice, and the lack of guidelines for institutions wishing to implement this provision. The following is suggested as a practical framework.

There are two methods which can be used:

a: responses signed to video/DVD and translated later by interpreters;

b: a 'live' version, where the student signs his or her responses, an interpreter voices over and a notetaker or amanuensis writes down the answers in situ. Both of these methods will be discussed.

Ideally, the students should sign their responses to video. A separate room and an invigilator are required (and, of course, access to technical assistance, should problems occur during filming). Students watch the signed questions via DVD, if possible, or via an interpreter. They make notes and then sign their answers to camera. An appropriately skilled and qualified interpreter takes the video tapes/DVD and the student's notes, and prepares a translation. It may also be appropriate for the interpreter to prepare a 'translator's notes document' for the tutor, to explain the process and to highlight any key issues or specific translation decisions. A second interpreter is required to sample/moderate the translation. Finally, the translation, the student notes, and the translator's notes are passed to the tutor for marking.

For the 'live' interpretation, the student signs their answers in BSL; this is interpreted (by, preferably two interpreters) in situ and the voice-over written down/recorded by a notetaker or amanuensis. This exam should be filmed for quality assurance purposes. Whilst a more immediate practice, this method is far more open to abuse and may disadvantage the student. Live, simultaneous interpretation can never mirror a full consecutive translation; time-constraints cause significant anxieties and the number of people involved in this process is not only intimidating, but allows for another layer of filtering or decay as the message is passed from the student, through the interpreter, through the notetaker to paper:

> 'An issue […] for the (simultaneous) interpreter is the way in which they may be forced by circumstances to filter the message [...] Interpreters are constantly making choices about how they

carry out the translation of that message. The manner in which the message is translated, the lexical choices and grammatical decisions interpreters take and all lead to some nuances of the original message being altered.' (Harrington, 2001:81)

It can also be assumed that the notetaker who cannot physically record a verbatim translation, is also making choices and filtering the message.[25]

In a case study carried out by the author, this particular methodology produced evidence of disadvantage for the student. The 'live' exam took an inordinately long time; the whole situation made the student nervous, and he struggled to answer the questions. Subsequently, he began to use idiosyncratic sign or simply forgot the signs he needed to use. The interpreters needed to stop the student and check for clarification and accuracy. The voice-over whilst accurately reflecting the student's responses caused difficulties for the amanuensis, who also requested clarification. Consequently, the student was interrupted and questioned many times during the exam, so much so, that he lost confidence in his own BSL, and in the next examination insisted on writing in English.

Coursework may also be completed via BSL using similar methodology as for exams; differing only in that the student prepares their own recording before handing it to the interpreter/translator. In practice, if feasible, it is useful for the interpreter to be present at these recordings, in order to clarify any ambiguities. On completion of the translation, the interpreter should provide the student with a 'back translation', either in person, or on video/DVD, in order for the student to verify and authenticate their work. This is an important procedure within the process and should not be underestimated (FAB, 2005:28).[26]

On receiving their translation, following 'back translation', it is possible that the student will want to amend their work. For example, they may wish to meet with their Language Tutor for further advice on structure. In a recent case, a student undertaking his dissertation in BSL added references at this point, as it was felt to be too cumbersome and unwieldy to reference via sign language. The student then handed in their notes and the translator's notes, along with the final dissertation.

Of course, this is only one way in which a deaf student may submit their coursework. It is necessary to keep in mind the diversity of abilities amongst deaf students and the variety of courses with their own tacit requirements when discussing the alternative assessment procedures

---

[25] See Chapter Six of this publication for discussion of this process

[26] See also Barnes and Doe, Chapter Eight of this publication

which may be used with students (Walker et al, 1996: 65). Furthermore, it may not be appropriate for students to use BSL for every course assignment. Fitness to purpose needs to be considered. Also, because one student has negotiated an alternative assessment for a particular subject, at a particular year level in a particular course, it does not follow that other deaf students automatically have the right to a similar assessment procedure without going through relevant discussions with course tutors and academic/disability advisers. Nor does it follow that every student would wish to use BSL in exams.

In a recent survey, Barnes (2005) found that the majority of students indicated that although they experienced difficulty in writing their exam responses, they would prefer to be assessed in the same manner as their fellow students. Their reasons reflected the majority language perspective; citing the view that the world is hearing and upon leaving university they would be expected to use English:

> 'Even networking via e-mail requires English. Without this form of communication you are always relying on a third party to interpret….. We need more English to become independent.' (Student quoted in Barnes, 2005:47)

Some students recognised difficulties regarding the practicalities of producing work in BSL. Most students have not been trained to sign to video, and many felt unsure of how this would work:

> 'If you write, you can stop and think and go back and amend your work. If you sign, your mistakes can be recognised straight away. How would you support your views? How do you sign a bibliography?' (Student quoted in Barnes, 2005:47)

Interestingly, the students who did want to present their work in BSL differentiated between course work and exams. All felt comfortable working in English and with their LT on written assignments, but felt that exams were different, and more difficult for deaf learners:

> 'In exams there are always two tasks: a) thinking about writing in English clearly and accurately and b) the knowledge and skills that are being tested. It is very confusing and burdensome to have to consider both in an exam situation. Also you are nervous, so this adds a third dimension. It would be much better to just focus on the information and content.' (Student quoted in Barnes, 2005:48).

Clearly, there are many issues regarding the use of BSL in exams and coursework; not least the current traditionalist assessment culture within Higher Education. Other significant barriers include the availability of financing, appropriately qualified/trained interpreter resources and time constraints. In addition, students need to be trained in how to formulate, structure and present answers in BSL. They need clear guidance on referencing, producing bibliographies and meeting the academic standards required in the learning outcomes. Robust standardisation and quality assurance procedures must be put into place. Technical assistance is also needed. Furthermore, this method of assessment may not be fully accepted by some academics, who still associate written assessment with competency standards (Walker et al, 1996:65).

3. The inclusive approach

One response to this deep-seated traditionalism is to think inclusively when designing assessment instruments, so that alternatives are built in at course planning and validation stages. This would enable deaf and disabled students to have equivalent assessment experiences to their peers (Adams and Brown, 2006:187).

As the student population diversifies more varied approaches to learning, teaching and assessment are already being implemented across the sector. Lecturers are being encouraged to develop a more diverse range of innovative assessments to allow students to work in creative, non-written or partly written formats to demonstrate their achievement of learning outcomes. A recent government-funded teaching, learning and assessment website (www.creativeassessment.org.uk) recommends assessments such as interviews, presentations, portfolios, vivas, coaching, posters, videos, annotated albums and practical projects such as exhibitions or other live events. Many of these modes of assessment will benefit the deaf student.

An inclusive approach to assessment would mean giving all students a range of different types of assessment rather than relying on just one or two methods which disadvantage some learners. By creating an inclusive curriculum and assessment design, it can be argued that the diverse student population is being offered choices that align with their abilities (Adams and Brown, 2006:187) and that they are not being singled out for 'special' consideration.

Writing learning outcomes with flexible interpretations for assessment procedures, for example, the concept of being able to 'produce' a learning outcome, allows for the outcome to be tested orally, visually and/or in written form (Mon, cited in SPACE Project, 2007). This allows for the use of BSL and reduces the need for 'an alternative assessment that is only appropriate for a minority of disabled students' (SPACE Project, 2007). In this way, video portfolios, research projects and oral/signed presentations could replace or partly replace written essays, end-of-course exams and written reports. Interviews, poster presentations and practical projects offer deaf students an opportunity to meet learning outcomes in a more visual and non-threatening way, on a par with their non-deaf peers.

Visual and creative assessments which can be produced in BSL by deaf students, also benefit other students who learn in a more visual rather than a linear or lexical way. Clearly, work produced in BSL would have to be of the same academic standard as a written assignment; the only difference would be in the method of it being recorded (SPACE Project, 2007). This points to making sure that learning outcomes are clearly defined and the purpose of key competencies evaluated in the light of inclusive curricula and assessment. This must be done at course planning stage. In addition marking criteria must be explicit and robust:

> 'If the person marking is confident that the assessment mode supports and enhances the students' learning in a way that allows the student to demonstrate their understanding, then there is no requirement for complicated marking concessions which treat students differently and are difficult to standardise.' (SPACE Project, 2007)

This will resonate with many tutors who have marked deaf students' written work, especially under examination conditions. Even with a set of guidelines, it is sometimes difficult to grasp the content and the argument because of the way it has been expressed. Inclusive and innovative assessment will remove the necessity of such schemes:

> 'The inclusive approach, which does not compromise academic standards but rather improves the chances for students to fairly demonstrate their acquisition of the learning outcomes, is also congruent with the social, cultural and legislative imperatives pressing the Higher Education sector to play an active role in creating a more inclusive society.' (SPACE Project, 2007)

Conclusion

All institutions are aware of the need to provide 'reasonable adjustments' to assessments for deaf and disabled students. Issues are raised as to what constitutes a reasonable adjustment, particularly for deaf BSL users who present their own unique learning styles in that they access the curriculum via a different language to their non-deaf peer group. Reliance on written essays and end-of-course examinations disadvantages those students who struggle with English literacy, but who can, nonetheless, meet learning outcomes using different more visual modes.

Whilst 'reasonable adjustments' undoubtedly aim to 'level the playing field' for deaf students, it has been argued that many of these assessment arrangements are individual, ad hoc and have rarely been researched to evaluate efficacy and success (Waterfield and West, 2002). Moderated exam papers, extra time, language tutorials and extensions to deadlines are all necessary in the absence of more alternative assessments, but it can be argued that these adjustments are compensatory in nature, and that they single out deaf and disabled students as being 'special' or different:

> 'These compensatory arrangements, as a contingent approach, continue to bracket disabled students into a 'special' category. In this way they are both marginalised and held in a medical model of response by institutions.' (SPACE Project, 2007)

Furthermore, these arrangements still have written English as their focus, and still rely predominantly on essay writing and exam methodology. For some assignments, this will be appropriate. For others, it is likely that learning outcomes can be met in more innovative ways.

For example, deaf students could negotiate a different kind of assessment, or produce their assessment in a different format. Discussions with disability advisers, course leaders and heads of department could enable students to produce coursework and exams via BSL, replace long essay questions with shorter questions, perform signed presentations rather than written papers, undertake vivas in place of or to support exams and produce visual projects rather than written dissertations.

However, whilst alternative assessments of this type might 'minimise the impact of a disability on a student's performance' (Waterfield et al, 2006), the arrangement is still individual; the onus is still on the deaf student to negotiate change; they are still being singled out as 'different'.

According to Waterfield et al (2006) this exclusive provision can be seen:

> 'as a further facet of a broadly compensatory range of activities that should more accurately be conceptualised as only part of a changed approach to assessment.'

A more inclusive approach would be to offer a wide range of alternative assessments, which are built in for all students at course planning stage. By focusing clearly on the purpose and nature of learning outcomes and identifying the key competencies required by course and subject designers, inclusive assessments can be written into the course at the outset, to allow the whole diverse student population to clearly and fairly demonstrate their learning.

Thus, video portfolios, poster presentations, signed research projects, annotated storyboards, visual projects and live events whilst benefiting deaf students, also benefit a whole range of students without marginalising one group or making students feel that they are 'privileged or special' (SPACE Project, 2007).

Downplaying the importance of exams and essays in favour of more visual practice and portfolio work will mean that deaf students do not need as much English support work, therefore they will have more time to concentrate on the assessment task at hand. Neither will they need contingent or individualised alternative arrangements, and so compete with their peers on a far more equal basis.

Clearly this will involve a major culture shift, one which many academics are not yet ready to embrace (SPACE Project, 2007; Waterfield et al, 2006:86; Walker et al, 1996). It is recognised that change may take some time, and that each institution will have different constraints in effecting this change. Nonetheless, change is upon us. The advent of the Disability Discrimination Act 2005, which introduced the Disability Equality Duty and recent and ongoing governmental emphasis on creating an inclusive society, has meant that Higher Education Institutions now have a social, cultural and legislative responsibility to engage in inclusive teaching, learning and assessment.

Key considerations:

- It is expected that deaf students will have their support needs assessed as soon as they are offered a place on a university course; ideally, long before the course starts. In the UK, this is undertaken by members of the National Network of Assessment

Centres (NNAC). Arrangements for exams and other forms of academic assessments should be discussed alongside other support options and advice. It is necessary for Assessors to be specialists in the supporting and assessing of deaf students' support needs in order that the full range of support options, including assessment arrangements are considered.

- It should be remembered that for some students, their assessment requirements may change during the period of their study, as academic levels and the demands of the course change. Mechanisms should be in place for a review and update of assessment and support requirements.
- Each student has individual access requirements; it is not possible to be prescriptive about which method of assessment will be appropriate for all deaf students.
- Universities must employ a range of 'Language Service Professionals' (LSPs) who are trained and qualified in their relevant role (CACDP, 2005:20). How one defines this, is, of course, extremely complex. What may be deemed reasonable for one institution, may not be reasonable for another. At minimum, institutions must put into place measures to ensure the quality of language and communication support, stipulating the training and qualifications for each LSP (see CACDP, 2005:26)[27]
- Ideally, institutions should think inclusively when designing assessment instruments, so that alternatives are built in at the outset which enable disabled students to have an equivalent assessment experience (Adams and Brown, 2006:187)
- Institutions must ensure that any changes to assessment practice do not compromise academic standards nor students' 'fitness to practice' in professional programmes (SPACE Project, 2007).
- Finally, the cost of implementing inclusive assessment must be addressed. The inadequacies of the Disabled Students' Allowances are well-known throughout the sector. If true inclusive learning and assessment is to be achieved, the financial implications must be recognised by government and realistic allowances

---

[27] A Language Service Professional (LSP) is a professional whose role is exclusively to provide a language or a communication service to facilitate communication between deaf and hearing people. LSPs include: BSL/English Interpreters; Lipspeakers; Note-takers (Manual and Electronic); Speech to Text Reporters; Transcribers and Translators.
Further information about LSPs can be found on the CACDP website at
http://www.cacdp.org.uk/linkspage.asp?L1=Directory&L2=Scripts&L3=Index.asp

granted to students, or clearer guidelines as to how institutions should finance this activity.

- For further information regarding support for deaf students, see the HECFE (Consortium of Support Services for Deaf Students) website at http://www.skill.org.uk/shared/chess.asp
- DEAFLINK@JISCMAIL.AC.UK is an online forum for discussing deaf student support

Acknowledgements

I would like to thank the members of the University of Central Lancashire interpreting team for their discussions and contributions regarding the use of interpreters and translators in supporting students during assessment.

Further reading

Adams, M. & Brown S. (Eds.) 2006 *Towards inclusive learning in Higher Education: developing curricula for disabled students* London, Routledge

Barnes, L. 2005 *Assessment of deaf students: an investigation into the working practices of language tutors.* (Unpublished MA dissertation)

Barnes, L. 2006 'Formal qualifications for language tutors in Higher Education: a case for discussion' *Deafness and Education International* 8, 3, 106-124

Barnes, L. & Doe, L. 2007 'Language tutors under the microscope' in Barnes, L., Harrington, F., Williams, J. and Atherton, M. (eds.) *Deaf students in Higher Education: current research and practice* Coleford, Douglas McLean

CACDP 2005 *Guidance for awarding bodies: access to external assessment for D/deaf candidates* Durham, CACDP

Disability Rights Commission 2002 *The DDA Part 4: Examinations and assessment guide.* London, Disability Rights Commission

Doyle, C & Robson, K. 2002 *Accessible curricula: good practice for all.* Cardiff. UWIC Press.

Federation of Awarding Bodies July 2005 'Good practice guide: the application of reasonable adjustments and special consideration in vocational qualifications' http://www.awarding.org.uk Accessed 21.5.06

Harrington, F. 2001 'Deaf students and the interpreted classroom' in Harrington and Turner (eds) *Interpreting interpreting: studies and reflections on sign language interpreting.* Coleford, Douglas McLean

Maclellan, E. 2004 'How convincing is alternative assessment for use in Higher Education?' *Assessment and Evaluation in Higher Education* 29, 3: 311–321

McCarthy, D. & Hurst, A. 2001 'A briefing on assessing disabled students'. LTSN Generic Centre. Assessment Series No.8
http://www.heacademy.ac.uk/resources.asp?process=full_record§ion=generic&id=8 Accessed 09.04.06

Mole, J. & Peacock, D. 'Language issues for deaf students in Higher Education' in
Adams, M. & Brown S. (Eds.) 2006 *Towards inclusive learning in Higher Education: developing curricula for disabled students* London, Routledge
O Neill, R. 1999 'Is literacy necessary?' *Deaf Worlds* 15, 2: 2-5
Paul, P 1998a *Literacy and deafness: the development of reading, writing and literate thought.* Needham Heights, MA, Allyn and Bacon
Paul, P. 1998b 'First and second language English literacy'. *The Volta review*, 98, 2: 5-16

Sharp, K & Earle, S. 2000 'Assessment, Disability and the problem of compensation' *Assessment and Evaluation in Higher Education* 25, 2: 191-198

SPACE Project 2007
http://www.plymouth.ac.uk/pages/view.asp?page=10494 Accessed 25.2.07

The Quality Assurance Agency for Higher Education May 2000 'Code of Practice for the assurance of academic quality and standards in Higher Education'
http://www.qaa.ac.uk/academicinfrastructure/codeofpractice/section6/COP_AOS.pdf Accessed 9.4.06

The Towards Learning Creatively (TLC) Project
www.creativeassessment.org.uk Accessed: 20.2.07

Walker, L., Adams, L, Coverdale, R., McCracken, M., & Murfitt, K. November 1996 'Assessment Issues in Higher Educational settings for deaf students'
http://www.tcd.ie/disability/docs/DNA/deafassess.pdf Accessed 15.5.07

Waterfield, J. & West, B. (Eds.) 2002 SENDA *Compliance in Higher Education – An audit and guidance tool for accessible practice within the framework of teaching and learning.* University of Plymouth

Waterfield, J., West, B. & Parker, M. 'Supporting inclusive practice – developing an assessment toolkit' in Adams, M. & Brown, S. 2006 *Towards inclusive learning in Higher Education: developing curricula for disabled students* London, Routledge: 78–94

CHAPTER TEN

Integrating technology, improving access

Kevan Williams and John Hodgson

Introduction

The University of Central Lancashire (UCLan), the sixth largest in the UK with approximately 36000 students and 2500 staff located on four campuses, has a mission-led commitment to widening participation with the aim:

> 'to provide the widest possible access to those individuals who seek to benefit from its educational activities and to remove barriers to those with special needs.' (UCLan 2007)

By 2010 the University of Central Lancashire (UCLAN) aims to be one of the leading providers of eLearning programmes in the UK (UCLan 2007a). To achieve this, new and emerging technologies must be exploited and embedded as standard practice in teaching methods to enhance the learning experience. As the University eLearning portfolio continues to grow and mature, technology is becoming an integral measure of the quality of the user experience. Over the past five years WebCT has become the accepted Virtual Learning Environment at UCLAN, with approximately 20000 student users delivering over 2500 live modules.

The growth in demand for enhanced interactive learning technologies led to the submission of the University's Learning and Teaching strategy to the Higher Education Funding Council for England (HEFCE). This in turn initiated research undertaken by the University's Learning Development Unit to enable rich multimedia content to be easily integrated into the WebCT environment. Phases 1 and 2 of the Learning and Teaching Strategy outlined that:

> 'the Learning and Teaching Strategy represents an ambitious set of initiatives through which the University seeks to strengthen the good practice that currently exists both within the University and in many partner institutions. It aims to encourage greater use of less traditional methods to deliver the curriculum and a far higher profile being given to helping academic staff to improve the quality of the learning and teaching experience for students.' (UCLan 2007b)

Understanding individual approaches to learning and acknowledgment of the many different learning styles has facilitated the evolution of technology and the direction this has taken at an institutional level. This evolution has created a much more versatile, flexible and accommodating educational environment in which effective and engaging teaching and learning practice can be delivered. Technology can be applied in a wide variety of circumstances to enhance the student learning experience. This can range from basic access to online resources via a web connected PC to the implementation of a fully populated online learning environment offering access to material 24 hours a day, seven days a week. As students begin interacting with technology and engaging with online resources the demand for more effective, engaging and high quality content inevitably grows in proportion to the level of interaction.

This chapter aims to address the issues associated with the implementation of teaching and learning technologies with specific reference to the measurable benefits available to the Deaf user, and the ways in which technology has been embedded into the curriculum to offer a blended learning experience comparable to that of the traditional learner.

The development and integration of Virtual Learning Environments (VLEs) has enabled academics to create learning situations which deliver to, and exceed the expectation of the learner. Technology is not a barometer to be used as a measure of the quality of the students learning experience but should be used in a systematically integrated way to avoid the distinction between the users expectation and content that is delivered:

> 'Technology often fails to deliver results, but in the creation of e-learning environments, we are its driver. If we understand how the barriers to inclusion are being created in the profligacy of spending

> on and acceptance of poor and narrow-minded design, then we can challenge our mindsets and apply consideration to the additional needs of disabled students.' (Neumann 2002)

Embedding a live video feature into an online learning environment offers the capacity to deliver video interpretation to the user without the need for significant differences in the way the deaf learner engages with content analogous to the way other learners would interact with the content.

Adobe Acrobat Connect Professional (Connect)- what is it?

Connect is a web based communication tool which enables the combination of video, audio, software simulations, and other multimedia content to produce e-Learning and training packages that are engaging and effective, while providing useful tracking and reporting capabilities. Connect can be used to record high quality PowerPoint presentations for on-demand access and also to engage with students in a live, highly interactive online environment.

What does it do?

There are four modules in Connect, covering the following areas: Content Creation; eLearning; Web Conferencing; Seminars and Events.

Content creation

Based around Microsoft's PowerPoint software, the Connect Presenter module allows users to convert PowerPoint presentations into Flash based content, complete with voice-overs, integrated video and Flash content and the capability to add quiz and survey questions through a simple wizard-like interface. Presentations can contain notes, and are accessible for screen-readers. Users can either watch a self-contained presentation or can move back and forth via the navigation links. Presenter information, contact details and photos can be added to the presentations, as can 'talking-head' videos. A theme creator enables the user to select the style of layout, colours and logos that each presentation uses. Content that has been produced using the PowerPoint plug-in can be published to the users account on the Connect server or packaged locally for distribution on CD Rom.

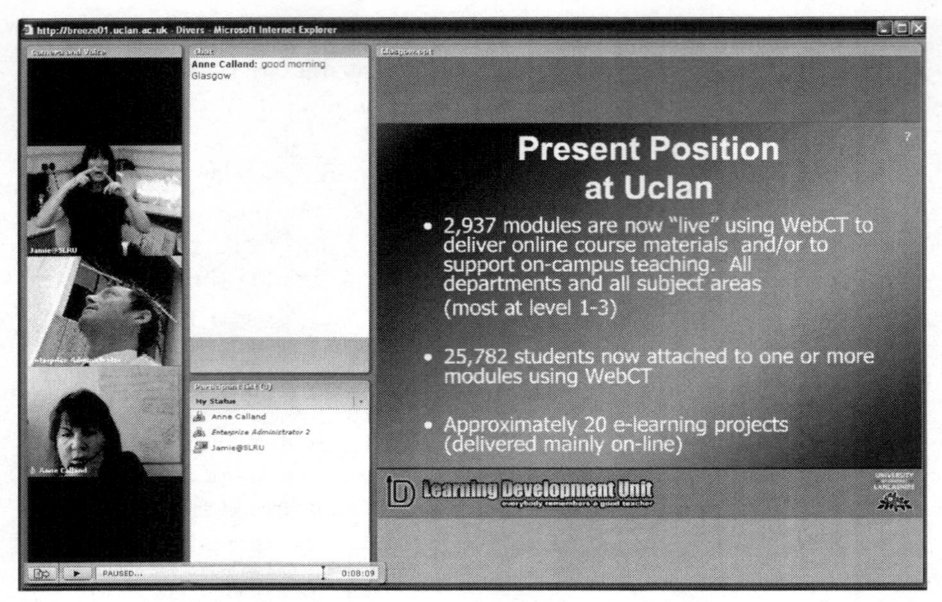

Figure 1 – Adobe Acrobat Connect Professional with interpreter top left corner

Connect content is delivered using the Flash Player technology through varying bandwidth speeds, although the preferred connection speed would be broadband 512k or above to enable the use of the complete software functionality and the quality level of the user experience.

eLearning

The Connect Training module allows you to create courses and curriculum out of the content provided through the Connect Presenter or from any Flash-based elearning Content including Macromedia Authorware generated courseware. These courses and curricula can be assigned to students and student groups, who then access the learning materials via a browser. User activity can be tracked: for example, who took in what course and when?; results of quiz and survey questions can be monitored to test understanding and progress. Each quiz can be used to guide the learner onto the next step, for example, a high pass can mean the student skips the next course section, or a failure means mandatory re-start to the whole course.

Web conferencing

Connect Meeting allows anyone with standard web cams and an internet connection to take part in real-time web conferencing. Meeting rooms can be quickly created – uploading presentations, documents, videos, and Flash content as required. All meeting participants can be take part in the video conferencing, white-boarding, polls and screen or application sharing which is a particularly useful tool for offering technical support online. A new Connect meeting room can be created spontaneously, e.g. if a student fails a course quiz, or wants to ask a question: one click and they can enter into a conference with their tutor being helped and guided through the subject. All pre-populated content remains in the meeting room e.g. notes and documents from the last meeting for approving or re-using.

The Connect Event module allows for the rapid creation, invitation and tracking of users for an online seminar, where many people can view a presentation or lecture using Connect, whether or not they are actually 'users' on Connect or not. Event facilitates the creation of customized home-pages with details of your lecture, biography and where users can register for the event. Users can also be directly invited and all users are tracked with automatic reminder emails and post-lecture emails too.

Creating and using eLearning content with Connect

Creating content is a simple process, based around the Connect Presenter plug-in to Microsoft PowerPoint. You create a PowerPoint presentation as normal (all transitions and animation effects are supported) and then select publish from the Connect menu. The menu also allows you to insert Flash files (which can contain any combination of video, animations, business functions, demonstrations and simulations) into PowerPoint – a capability much requested from PowerPoint users.

Connect Presenter allows you to easily add a voice-over to your slides, so that the presentation can run self-contained. Although PowerPoint already has this capability, Connect audio is of a higher quality and smaller file size – making the student experience that much better. There is also a friendly tool to allow you to easily edit your voice-over – removing pauses and 'ums' and 'ahhs'.

Adding a quiz or survey is a simple matter of selecting the Quiz Manager and following the wizard. There is a wide range of question types, from simple true/false to short answers to rating (likert) scales. Answers are in Sharable Content Object Reference Model (SCORM) or Aviation Industry CBT Committee (AICC) formats, allowing an LMS, or Connect itself, to track student progress. The quiz feature supports conditional branching and there is a wide array of responses you can make depending on whether the student answered correctly or not, so you retain the power to move students to different parts of the presentation, or course, or other materials to support their understanding.

The Publish button then lets you upload the content to Connect for use, or you can create the files on your PC for use on a network or CD.

Customization

Following an initial twelve month pilot project with the University's most prominent champions of eLearning, a focus group was held to determine the future viability of Connect. Academics involved in the group were quoted as saying:

> 'Connect is an important, even vital, addition to our e-learning toolbox.' (Francois Nel – Journalism Course Leader);

> 'Connect to me is an awesome product, very easy to learn and to put to use. Over the past academic year I have delivered recorded Connect presentations, conducted live group seminars and tutorials, conducted live one to one advice sessions and attended live Connect lectures. All of these have been very successful in terms of the feedback collected.' (Peter Clare – BIT Course Leader);

> 'We have been supporting online courses for three years using Web CT to deliver content and online seminars. This academic year we started using Connect, which added voice, vision from webcams, and presentation facilities. Just one semester after this experimental introduction I tried running text-only online seminars (because I did not have a webcam at the time). The student response was rapid, angry and - to me at least - almost a total shock. I had underestimated the strength of feeling that students attached to being able to see and hear their online tutors. In a matter of weeks they had come to expect this mode of interaction, to see it as a right, not a privilege, and most certainly to express a clear preference for the sort of interactivity that it allows. Of course, I raised my game to suit the new expectation, but I was left with the clear impression that the route towards greater interactivity is strictly a one-way street - there is no turning back and no standing still. The students will simply not stand for it.' (Paul Elmer - Public Relations Programme Director);

'Being able to communicate through my preferred language which is British Sign Language, I found Breeze a perfect medium as it enables a smooth online video conferencing/chat to take place. Unlike some current video conferences, where quality varies, I found Breeze more consistent with a variety of bandwidths. So this has enhanced my experience with online video conferencing and makes a big difference to my communication requirements. I use breeze for one to one sessions or one to group sessions, as well as video relay sessions - i.e. I sign to a sign language interpreter and s/he make voice calls/contacts. Other great features of Breeze for sign language users are that it has a facility to add a BSL version to a spoken presentation to enable the sign language users full access to the content, whether it be a class session or presentation by a staff member of the University.' (Clark Denmark – Lecturer British Sign Language).

Electronic notetaking software

Electronic notetakers take comprehensive notes on laptop computers and provide a legible set of notes for deaf people, who, because they are lip-reading or watching an interpreter, cannot simultaneously write notes for themselves as well (RNID 2004a). The notes are saved as text documents and passed to the student.

However, specialist software such as Stereotype or RNID SpeedText allows these notes to be transmitted simultaneously to other computers nearby either via a lead or wirelessly. Such a system can also be easily integrated into e-learning packages like Adobe Acrobat Connect and notes could be displayed during a class session.

As notetaking software is not particularly resource-hungry, neither an abundance of memory nor a fast processor are essential requirements in the computers used. For this reason low specification, inexpensive (or even second hand) laptops can be employed for the job.

Linking two notetakers laptops

Notetaking software is intended to run across two computers and for this reason it is prudent to become familiar with the variety of connection methods available. The software can utilise serial, network and wireless connections (detailed below). And whilst it is currently unavailable, future updates to the software are certain to include support for Bluetooth.

Serial cable

This is the slowest of the three connection methods, but is also the easiest to implement. A 'Null Modem' cable is used (see Figure 2) and is plugged into the Serial port on each computer (see Figure 3). The notetaking software must be configured accordingly.

Figure 2: Null modem cable

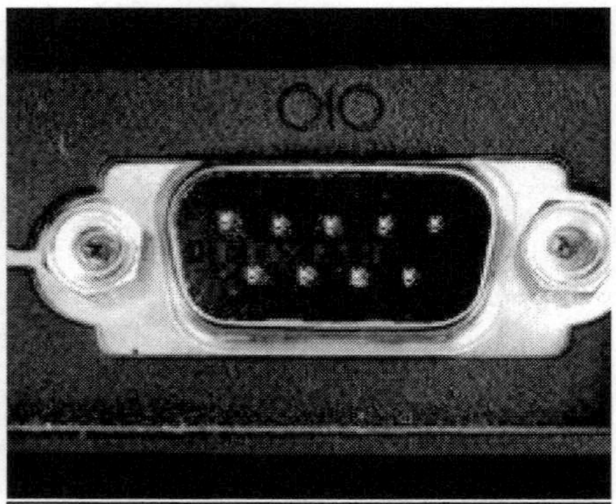

Figure 3: Serial Port

Network cable

Using a network cable will ensure the fastest possible link between laptops. The computers are connected via a Cat 5e network cable. Be sure to use a crossover cable and not a patch lead - the two cables look identical but the crossover has the 'transmit' and 'receive' connections interchanged. They can be purchased from most computer stores and are generally cheaper than null-modem cables.

To use a network cable, your laptops will need to have a network port installed (see Figure 4). If there is no network port you will need a PCMCIA network interface card. This is a credit card sized device especially designed for laptops which plugs into a slot in the side of the machine. Once inserted, the PCMCIA card protrudes from the side of the computer and should be removed prior to storage.

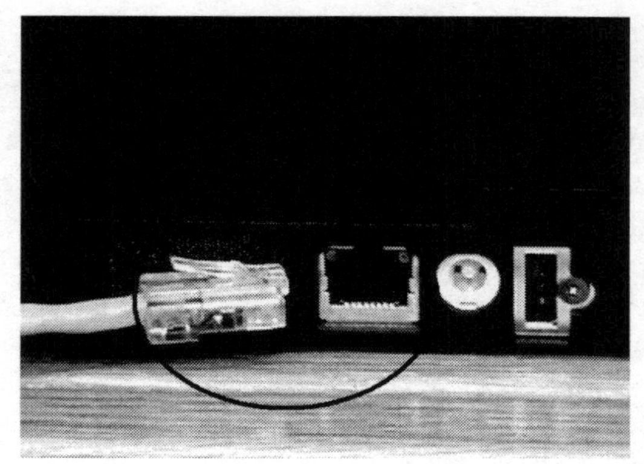

Figure 4: A Cat 5e lead and network port

Wireless

Wireless connections use low-powered radio signals to transmit data between devices. They are preferable as they offer a quick classroom setup - there are no wires to plug in and the notetaker and student do not have to be sat next to each other. A wireless connection can also facilitate multiple connections allowing the operator to simultaneously provide notes for more than one student.

You are required to setup a network between the computers in the same way that you would when using a standard network cable. However, there are additional security issues to be considered. Wireless networks can be received by anyone with a suitably enabled computer - so anyone in close proximity could potentially intercept the data. To guarantee privacy, security is built-in to wireless networks and the use of an encryption key (password) is employed on each computer. It also provides a layer of security from anyone wishing to infiltrate your mini-network. Newer laptops generally have wireless capabilities built in.

Creating a network link

Regardless of whether you wish to connect laptops together with a network cable or use a wireless connection, you are still required to setup a network between the two computers. This, however, is a once-only operation and after it has been completed, connection is quick and easy. The notetaker and student go through the setup procedure in the same way and additional students can be added at a later date.

SMIL – what is it?

The Synchronised Multimedia Integration Language (SMIL, pronounced 'smile') is a text mark-up language based on Extensible Markup Language (XML). It enables the author to precisely choreograph multimedia presentations where audio, video, text and graphics are combined in real time. These projects can easily be presented on a webpage in the same way that a simple video file might be embedded. Typical applications include real time subtitling for a video presented in sign language, subtitled video with voice-over and presentations displaying graphical information combined with video. Any combination of the above can be achieved relatively easily once the concept has been understood.

SMIL is also useful for overcoming streaming media challenges posed by the Internet's variable bandwidth. You can calculate the overall bandwidth requirements for media-integrated stream presentations, and you can adjust your SMIL files so they are targeted for one or more bandwidths, ensuring smooth playback on users' desktops (Covell 2000).

How does it work?

A typical SMIL presentation starts off by specifying the overall size (or <root-layout>) of the project.

Here is an example of how SMIL is written. This example shows a person signing, integrated into the SMIL presentation with a subtitled translation:

```
<?xml version="1.0" encoding="UTF-8"?>
<smil xmlns="http://www.w3.org/TR/REC-smil">
 <head>
  <meta content="Claire's introduction" name="title"/>
  <meta content="John Hodgson" name="author"/>
  <meta content="(c) 2006" name="copyright"/>
  <layout>
   <root-layout width="320" height="330" background-
color="black"/>
   <region top="0" width="320" height="240" left="0"
      background-color="black" id="videoregion"/>
   <region top="240" width="320" height="70" left="0"
      background-color="black" id="textregion"/>
  </layout>
 </head>
 <body>
```

```
    <par dur="0:00:37">
      <video dur="0:00:37" region="videoregion" src="claireintro.rm"/>
      <textstream dur="0:00:37" region="textregion"
src="claireintro.rt"/>
    </par>
  </body>
</smil>
```

Within the <layout> section of the SMIL file, different regions are allocated names, sizes, and locating co-ordinates. In this example, two regions have been created; "videoregion" and "textregion". This provides the structure for the project.

In the <body> section of the SMIL file, the different regions are assigned their contents via a source file. In the example, the video section refers to a Real Media video file "claireintro.rm" and the text section refers to a streaming text file "claireintro.rt". Streaming text files are also XML based and contain the content-text and information about the size, colour and font. Lines of text are assigned timed triggers allowing the author to accurately display what they want at the exact preferred time. Applications (such as Magpie®) are available to code these files quickly, but it is recommended you familiarise yourself with the format of these.

The future of SMIL

SMIL was spearheaded by Real Networks (makers of Real Player and Real Producer) and was implemented with its G2 technology. Real Networks are now working closely with Microsoft on the new version of SMIL. This new version, called SMIL Boston, will add multimedia synchronization features and functions (e.g., improved transitions between data types), and will extend the SMIL specification to enable browser-based synchronization of Web elements -such as Javascript and other dynamic HTML components (Covell 2000).

Signing avatars – what are they?

A signing avatar is the name given to a piece of three-dimensional computer animation (a virtual human) that attempts to replicate a person delivering sign language. Significant research has been conducted in this area, the most notable being those projects funded under the European Fifth Framework, part of the Information Society Technologies (IST) Program. The first of these is the ViSiCAST project (2000 – 2002) which is now complete. This included work on TESSA (Text and Sign Support Assistant) and was developed in collaboration with the Post Office.

TESSA is an interactive translation system assisting communication between a customer and a post office clerk. Speech recognition software is used to convert the clerk's words into computer text and the system suggests a list of possible phrases. The clerk chooses the appropriate phrase and TESSA, the virtual human, signs that message. The system is limited to approximately 400 possible phrases and the system cannot be used as a fully effective communication tool.

The work of ViSiCAST continued on as part of eSign, in with the aim of developing computer based signers. The system is based on databases (or 'lexicons') of signs. This means that when an individual sign has been created for one section of signing, it can be used again in other sections because as these databases of signs grow, it becomes easier and quicker to put signing onto websites (e-Sign Partners 2004; see also Zwiterslood, I. et al. 2004 for further information on e-Sign).

How is an avatar animated?

An avatar can be driven by either motion capturing or notation (synthetic signing). Motion capture utilises advanced technology such as data-gloves, positional markers and facial expression recognition systems. This equipment is expensive and is not generally available to regular computer users. The process is also labour-intensive and requires the signer to wear encumbering technical devices. However, it does offer reasonably good comprehension and has met with subjective approval from deaf users.

The second method of driving an avatar is by notation. A set of commands is used to instruct the virtual person to move their arms, hands and face in the correct way to perform a sign. The set of commands required to construct even a simple sign are complicated with estimates of two to three hours per sign. However, sign-language-editors are being developed which allow the author to draw upon previously created signs to build their sentences.

HamNoSys (Hamburg Notation System), (Hanke 2002) was developed for the purpose of driving signing avatars. Unfortunately, this is different to previously created notation systems, such as the BSL Notation system used in the Dictionary of British Sign Language/English (British Deaf Association 1992). HamNoSys has been replicated as a computer font and directly relates to a mark-up language called the Signing Gesture Markup Language (SiGML). SiGML (not to be confused with SGML, the precursor to XML) was developed by the

University of East Anglia for the eSign project and contains all the core commands required to control an avatar (see Kennaway, 2001 for more details). With this is mind, it shouldn't be too great a leap to convert more widely recognised notation systems into this format.

Feedback from these projects has been mixed. Comprehension of the signing has been described as 'adequate' and Deaf users have also complained that whilst avatars were judged to be fairly realistic, movements were still considered to be robotic. Facial expressions were also very limited (see Verlinden et al. 2001, Van der Schoot et al. 2003, Verlinden 2004a,b).

In addition to the problems mentioned, these systems would still require a programmer with well-developed sign language skills to program them. Translation of written text into both a meaningful and culturally relevant interpretation is a great deal more complex than simple transliteration of text to sign. At the time of writing no software is known to exist that can perform this function as well as a BSL/English interpreter. However, existing software can, at least, offer an English to Sign Supported English (SSE) translation.

The eSign project states that 'Virtual signing will be quicker to download than videos and does not take up lots of space on Internet servers' (e-Sign Partners, 2004). Whilst this may be the case, the recent broadband boom and availability of inexpensive hard-disk storage has meant that downloading large files from internet servers has become less of a problem and the quality of the message has come to the forefront. Modern-day computing power has also provided the regular user with wider access to video compression software.

Nevertheless, the potential for signing avatars should not be ignored. As computing power increases further and computer graphics become more advanced, their usefulness will improve greatly. The future also offers opportunities to increase translation accuracy and aesthetics through the possible integration of aspects of artificial intelligence.

The possibilities are potentially endless, although for now signing avatars remain firmly in the developmental and prototype stage.

Digital video

Video compression is the name given to the process of reducing the file size of digital video recordings. Raw digital video files are notoriously large and there are varying degrees of compression which enable the user to reduce the file size to suit the audience. For instance, if you wish to compress video for e-mail transfer, you will need to reduce the file as much as possible. However, a very high compression will also lead to greater loss of quality and the resulting video may appear grainy and sometimes jerky. It is therefore recommended that different compression ratios are experimented with to arrive at a happy medium.

Further reduction in file size can be achieved by decreasing the dimensions of the video image. Full-screen video is not essential for a message delivered in sign language and these attributes should also be adjusted to suit.

Inexpensive webcams are becoming more widely available - the quality of which is increasing due to the incorporation of CCD (charge-coupled device) rather than CMOS (complementary metal oxide semiconductor) sensors. CCD sensors allow more light into the camera increasing the image quality. It is advisable, however, that the camera should be able to record at a minimum of 640 x 480 pixels and at 30fps (frames per second). Most new webcams will come with a minimum of a USB 2.0 interface and microphone. This will allow a perfectly scalable video output suitable for many applications.

The use of video recording software (such as Real Producer) makes it easy to film using a webcam. Compression and image dimensions can be easily adjusted using functions within the application. The rate of compression is changed by making changes to the 'target audience'. The target audience is determined by the rate of bandwidth available to the end-user. This usually ranges from 56k modem up to 1Mb LAN (network download speeds) and plenty of alternatives exist in-between. Generally speaking, if you select a bandwidth setting of around 256k with an image size of about 320x240 pixels, this will offer a smooth video setup enabling sign language to be received clearly whilst ensuring the file is not overly large.

The Flash Video format (FLV) has become a widely used standard across the education industry due to the high compression rates offered without compromising on quality. The Flash Video Encoder application allows the user to effectively create FLV content from a number of uncompressed video formats and should be considered when making any decision on the most appropriate format of video for delivery over the web.

Nevertheless, a digital camcorder will offer a much better picture, vibrant colours and the ability to tackle a variety of different lighting conditions. Currently, the two main formats that exist are MiniDV (Mini Digital Video tapes are the industry standard) and MiniDVD (records straight to a DVD or CD-RW Disc).

MiniDVD video cameras have the advantage that as soon as video is recorded, the disc can be taken out and used immediately in most DVD players and computers. However, the video is compressed prior to being recorded on to disc and (at the time of writing) compression on cheaper models results in poor quality video. Also, Atkin, D. Grunin, L. (2006) tell us that optical recording media has one critical flaw in a camcorder : if any data becomes damaged, the entire disc becomes unreadable.

MiniDV camcorders record raw video directly to tape. This does have the disadvantage that the recording needs to be copied from the camcorder to a PC before you can use it. However, video is recorded at its highest quality and the resulting file is more versatile for compression into lots of different formats.

Video learning materials can be more effectively compiled by recording short conceptual clips of just a few minutes long. If the video is to be saved as part of an e-learning package, e-mail attachment or web page it is unlikely that the clips will be created in one long take. This is also the nature of filming precise information. The creation of effective electronic learning materials entails more than simply recording a lecture (and maybe providing course notes). A lecture works for the class because the students are able to interact with the lecturer. The electronic learner requires a different approach as they are learning slightly more passively. Short video clips (attached to an effective delivery medium, such as Adobe Acrobat Connect) naturally lend themselves to the creation of effective learning tools. Short clips of 'concepts' or 'objects' can be more easily integrated into teaching materials, ensuring learning becomes more interactive. Also, once the clips have been recorded, it won't necessarily require a sign-language expert to continue with the course construction.

The creation of short clips could present some continuity issues as video clips will show changes of clothes and even signer. However, it is unlikely to present too much of a problem as the real world is littered with examples of multiple signers within a website (see RNID 2004b; British Deaf Association 2006). It can also be refreshing to receive information from a number of different signers.

Remote video interpreting

Sometimes referred to as Video Relay Service (VRS) or Video Link-Up (VLU), a remote video interpreter allows a Deaf person access to an interpreter via a videophone. This means that it isn't necessary for the interpreter to be on-site. Purpose-built videophones come complete with a video screen attached and are usually used together with an ISDN phone line. More expensive video-conferencing equipment can be setup for remote video interpreting, however, a PC with a suitable webcam and high-speed broadband connection could be used as a cheap alternative. (See Figure 1)

This service can be linked up to packages such as Adobe Acrobat Connect, a lecture could be delivered with a remote interpreter in one corner of the screen. When other technologies such as electronic notetaking are linked together, then a fully accessible teaching package is created.

Conclusion

As technology develops and matures and the realisation and benefits of integration are understood, we are able to effectively engage learners in unparalleled ways. As technologists begin to understand the implications and importance of pedagogy in developments so the academic must also appreciate the capability and capacity of technology as a vehicle for effective teaching and learning.

Technology has not only allowed for the creation of pan-European cohorts of diverse students groups, effectively studying as one group online, but has also eliminated some of the barriers faced by deaf students. The integration of new communications technology in teaching practice has facilitated the availability of online sign language as a generic feature in any course development.

As the Government's Widening Participation Agenda continues to focus heavily in the Higher Education market, the common factor in all decisions making will revolve around the availability of material to a much larger community. Technology is sure to be one of the tools implemented to achieve the ambitious targets the HE sector strives to meet and this can only be a positive move for those whose potential can be realised through sustainable, transparent access to education.

The technologies outlined in this chapter can benefit the deaf learner immensely. However, true power to the learning experience will come with convergence. The future will allow for amalgamation of all these systems. Dynamic creation and integration of electronic services for deaf students is not too far in the future. They will have a huge impact on improving access not only for deaf learners but will greatly improve the access for one and all.

Key points

Electronic notetaking

The technology behind electronic notetaking allows a notetaker's work to be transmitted to computers nearby. These notes could be integrated and used as part of an e-learning package. Having notes displayed live with video, slides and interactive whiteboards would benefit all learners.

SMIL ease of use

SMIL files can be created using a simple text editor. They allow you to choreograph multimedia presentations consisting of any number of video, text or audio files and requires no video editing skills. Appendix A details how to embed a video with subtitles into a webpage.

SMIL further application

Familiarity with SMIL will enable the author to present multiple videos, text, images and sound simultaneously. For example, four people could be filmed having a conversation in British Sign Language with four separate webcams. The four pieces of video can be stitched together and displayed side-by-side as one presentation. Also, lecturer could be filmed and the interpretation filmed at a later date, these two pieces of video can be linked together providing a quick and easy accessible video. Slides for the lecture could also be added at any point.

Signing avatars

This virtual human form of providing information in sign language is still in its infancy. However, it is hoped that advances in graphics (with particular reference to the computer gaming industry) will improve quality to make this a realistic solution.

Digital video

Recent advances in digital video have arguably had the biggest technological
impact on deaf peoples lives. Video has moved from the realm of expensive professional set-ups (with video editing suites costing over £10,000 only five years ago) to a piece of software that can easily be run on a home computer.

Remote video interpretation

Interpretation can be provided remotely via specialist video conferencing systems or video phones. However, cheap systems using a PC with a high-speed broadband connection and a webcam can provide the same service.

Adobe Connect

Connect is a web-based communications technology offering the user the ability to combine Microsoft PowerPoint presentations alongside interactive animations, text chat with two-way audio and video functionality.

Virtual Learning Environment (VLE)

A VLE is a software technology that offers organisations the ability to manage large groups of students users, giving them access to online materials from any web connected PC. The majority of VLEs also allow for the integration of other technologies to create more engaging online experiences.

Integrating technology

The technologies outlined in this chapter can benefit the Deaf learner immensely. However, true power to the learning experience will come with convergence. The future will allow for amalgamation of all these systems. Dynamic creation and integration of electronic services for Deaf students is not too far in the future. They will have a huge impact on improving access not only for Deaf learners but will greatly improve the access for one and all.

Technological evolution

Moores' law (1965) states that:

> 'The complexity for minimum component costs has increased at a rate of roughly a factor of two per year ... Certainly over the short term this rate can be expected to continue, if not to increase. Over the longer term, the rate of increase is a bit more uncertain, although there is no reason to believe it will not remain nearly constant for at least ten years. That means by 1975, the number of components per integrated circuit for minimum cost will be

65,000. I believe that such a large circuit can be built on a single wafer.' (Electronics April 1965)

The primary benefit deaf learners will experience through the evolution of technology will be the capacity of the computer processor to deliver the complex requirements of new and emerging learning technologies.

Further reading

Atkin, D. Grunin, L. 2006 'Mini DVD vs MiniDV: Camcorder formats head to head'
http://www.cnet.com.au/camcorders/camcorders/0,239035915,240061716,00.htm , Date Accessed 30/4/07

Brien, D. (ed) 1992 *Dictionary of British Sign Language*. London, Faber and Faber

British Deaf Association 2006 'Sign Community'
http://www.signcommunity.org.uk/index.php , (accessed 30/4/07)

Covell, A. 2000 'Introduction to SMIL'
http://www.streamingmedia.com/article.asp?id=5598, (accessed 29/4/07)

Elsendoorn, B., Coninx, F., and Brekelmans, A., 1993 'Interactive learning technology for the deaf' (NATOASI series. Series F, *Computer and Systems Sciences*, vol. 113)

eSign Partners 2004 'e-Sign: Overview' http://www.sign-lang.uni-hamburg.de/esign/Overview.html , Date accessed 29/4/07

Hanke, T. 2002 *ViSiCAST Deliverable D5-1: Interface Definitions*. Manuscript

Kennaway, R. 2002 'Synthetic Animation of Deaf Signing Gestures'. In Wachsmuth & Sowa (eds) *Lecture Notes in Computer Science* Vol. 2298, Springer:146-157.

Murphy, D,. Walker R. and Webb, G. (eds) 2001 *Online learning & teaching with technology : case studies, experience and practice*. London, Kogan Page,

Moores, G 1965 'Cramming more components onto integrated circuits'. *Electronics* 38, 8

Neumann. Z 2002 'Visual Impairment and Technology' in L.Phipps, A. Sutherland and J.Seale (eds) *Access all areas : disability, technology and learning* (Oxford, ALT/TechDis):16-18

Parsons, M. 2003 'Howdy partner: widening participation at Newcastle University Library' *SCONUL Newsletter* Spring 2003

RNID 2004a 'Notetakers' http://www.rnid.org.uk/information_resources/communicating_better/communication_support/notetakers/ (accessed 29/4/07)

RNID 2004b 'Basic British Sign Language: Video Clips' http://www.rnid.org.uk/information_resources/communicating_better/bsl_video_clips/bsl/ (accessed 30/4/07)

Tait, J., Knight, P. (eds) (1996) *The management of independent learning* London, Kogan Page in association with the Staff and Educational Development Association,

UCLan 2007 'Widening Participation Strategy' (Section 1.1). http://www.uclan.ac.uk/other/sds/local/documents/corporate/strategies/widepartstrat.doc (accessed 29/4/07)

UCLan 2007a 'eLearning – The Revised Strategy' www.uclan.ac.uk/ldu/resources/elearnstrategy/elearning_strategy.doc (accessed 29/4/07)

UCLan 2007b 'Learning and Teaching Strategy' http://www.uclan.ac.uk/learning/introduction.htm (accessed 29/4/07)

Van der Schoot, S., Zwitserlood, I. & Verlinden, M. 2003 'User evaluation of electronic forms with signed support' in *SLN eSIGN report M6.3*, Viataal, Sint-Michielsgestel, the Netherlands.

Verlinden, M. 2004 'User evaluation of service for signed descriptions of job vacancies' in *SLN eSIGN report M6.6*, Viataal, Sint-Michielsgestel, the Netherlands.

Verlinden, M. 2004a 'User evaluation of signed information on regulations and practices' in *SLN, eSIGN report M6.7*, Viataal, Sint-Michielsgestel, the Netherlands.

Verlinden, M., Zwitserlood, I. and Frowein, H. 2005 'Multimedia with animated sign language for deaf learners' : Paper presented at the *World conference on educational multimedia, hypermedia & telecommunications*, ED-MEDIA 2005, Montréal, Canada: 4759-4764

Zwiterslood, I., Verlinden, M., Ros, J., van der Schoot, S. 2004 'Synthetic signing for the deaf: eSIGN' in *Proceedings of the conference and workshop on assistive technologies for vision and hearing impairment*, CVHI

TechDis Staff Packs
TechDis, the leading educational advisory service, working across the UK, in the fields of accessibility and inclusion has a set of useful staff packs available for download.
http://www.techdis.ac.uk

National Association of Disability Practitioners
NADP Ltd is the professional organisation for disability and support staff in further and Higher Education.
http://nadp-uk.org/

SKILL National Bureau for Students with Disabilities
The Skill Higher Education Networks are forums for sharing good practice, networking and discussing issues when working with disabled students in different regions of the country
The Information Service produces a series of booklets, which you can download free of charge
http://www.skill.org.uk/info/infosheets.asp

National Federation of Access Centres
UK-wide network of specialist services that work together to facilitate access for disabled people to education, training, employment and personal developers. *http://www.nfac.org.uk*

CHAPTER ELEVEN

Sign Language interpreting in Higher Education – a period of progress?

Sarah Obasi

Introduction

This paper is a personal reflection of changes that have taken place in educational interpreting over a twelve year period at a specific institution. The reflection was sparked by my return to interpreting at the institution after an eight year period of absence, which enabled me to see a number of the significant changes that had been made in a much more pronounced way. The paper highlights a number of important developments that have occurred in the wider interpreting field and the impact that this has had on interpreting in Higher Education. It calls for the development of a post qualifying specialism in educational interpreting and for recognition of the complexity of the role. The paper also identifies some of the changes that have occurred in relationships between the Deaf community and the interpreting profession, and concludes with a call for continued development of the profession within a more collaborative arena.

As the paper is written from a personal perspective, I would seek to make the same approach as Napier (1998), that:

> 'generalisations may be made about interpreters and deaf people which should be taken as they are intended- as generalisations.'
> (Napier 1998 :15)

1994–1996

In 1994, becoming an interpreter was something that I aspired to, but I realised that it could only be achieved after a long period of intensive study and emersion into the Deaf community. There was something about being a Sign Language Interpreter that seemed prestigious and that commanded respect, and attainment of that status was an aspiration that I shared with many of my fellow students and others around me. With the introduction of Deaf Studies as an academic subject within the institution, more deaf students were coming to study this and other courses. It was around this time that, in order to meet demand, a number of students studying BSL at the highest level available at the time (Post-Stage 2), were also offered jobs as communication support workers.[28] This meant that myself and others were 'interpreting' in classrooms within the university environment, even though we had not yet completed our own first degree.

At around the same time, the Higher Education Funding Council for England (HEFCE) were funding projects around the country looking at inclusion and access for disabled university students. Harrington (2001) was involved in one of these projects looking at educational interpreting, which revealed that many people interpreting in Higher Education at this time did so with little, if any, post secondary education qualifications. McIntire and Sanderson (1995) in their research in America also found that over thirty percent of their respondents had either no formal interpreter preparation or, preparation they had been undertaking for less than one year.

As I began working as an interpreter in lectures, I began to realise that what I had previously perceived as the prestige and respect that went with the job was in fact a fallacy. The reality of doing the job within the university soon made it clear to me that this respect and prestige was acknowledged only by those already involved in Deaf Studies and the Deaf community or those learning British Sign Language (BSL). For others present in the classroom, and for the wider university, there was at best only a passing fascination, and at worst a significant irritation at the disruption caused to their teaching or learning.

Before I started university in 1994, as with many other students, most of my BSL tuition had come from deaf people in the community. It had been taught from a culturally deaf perspective, and indeed the Deaf community was an enormous part of both my social and professional

[28] In terms of language competency, the Post Stage 2 British Sign Language course was considered at that time to lie somewhere between an intermediate and advanced level of British Sign Language (BSL).

life. An integral part of learning BSL in these settings was that it also enabled us to have an insight into the cultural life of Deaf people, an understanding of their history, and a sense of the oppression they felt as a minority community (Baker-Shenk 1993)

At this stage I think it might be useful to introduce an analogy which will run through this paper. It is one which relates the Deaf community/interpreting profession to a parent (Deaf community)/ child (interpreting profession) relationship, and the tensions that exist within the various stages of development that such a relationship must go through.

Cokely (2005) in his historical analysis of relations between the Deaf community and interpreting profession in the USA, points to this same stage in American Sign Language (ASL) learning as a period where deaf people were able to exercise a certain level of control over who did or did not act as interpreters. He also goes on to associate the move to teach ASL in academic institutions as an assault on the Deaf community's control of the teaching of their language, as many deaf people who had previously taught in the community did not possess the recognised academic credentials to teach in these more formal settings.

The analogy, identifying the parent/child relationship between the Deaf community and interpreters, is now at a point where the child is ready to progress on to school. For some parents this will be seen purely as a positive developmental step, while others will harbour anxieties about the introduction of outside influences that may conflict with the choices they have made for their child so far. In all cases, it leads to the lack of control outlined by Cokely above (2005).

Up to this point, the little training I had received around interpreting had focused on the notion of the interpreter as a machine. This approach, also known as the conduit model of interpreting (McIntyre and Sanderson 1995; Roy 2002), emphasised the notion that the interpreter should remain 'invisible', not seen to be part of the interaction (Solow 1981; McIntire and Sanderson 1995; Roy 2002). A common rationale for this was that deaf people had gone through a lifetime of being ignored in favour of the hearing person 'interpreting' for them. It was further supported by the fact that, in the past, some interpreters had exploited their position to their own advantage (Lane 1994; Ladd 2003; Cokely 2005). This approach was to have widespread implications for the interpreting arena on both sides of the Atlantic. It was incorporated into training and disseminated into practice. Solow emphasises the need for interpreters to:

> 'strive at all times to maintain a low profile, so that the attention of the participants is not focused on him or her.' (Solow 1981:5)

Another important consequence of this, and an attempt to avoid further oppression of deaf people, was the development of the notion that whatever is said to the interpreter as an individual was to be interpreted *before* being answered by the interpreter. The intention was to allow a deaf person to explain the role of the interpreter to their hearing counterpart, and identify themselves, rather than the interpreter, as the primary focus of the interaction. I would always insist on maintaining this position no matter how difficult or oppressive it felt to me as an interpreter.

These two underlying principles (of non-interference on the one hand, and communication control on the other) are just a part of the duality that was experienced by interpreters (Anderson 2002; Wadensjö 2002). Further to this, Baker-Shenk (1993) highlighted the underlying importance of reciprocal recognition of interpreter/deaf positions in her work on oppressed and oppressor people. She explored the impact these positions have on sign language interpreting, and pointed to the need for both interpreters and deaf people to consider inherent relationships between themselves and their respective positions in minority/majority group relations in order to avoid aggravation or escalation of existing issues of mistrust and conflict between the two groups.

In terms of the practicalities of interpreting in a classroom at that time, deaf students were offered the opportunity to decide where we sat as interpreters. Again the way this was articulated at the time was in terms of both 'interpreter invisibility' and of empowerment for the student, who was being given control over choice and access. Solow (1981) points out the ridiculous extremes to which interpreters would go in their attempt to remain 'invisible'. The example she provides is of an interpreter who almost passed out from an allergy, rather than interrupt a session to ask a man to stop smoking. Even the terminology used to describe interpreting had oppressive connotations, with the development of literature and training on how to 'use' interpreters appropriately. The term certainly supported the existing model, where an interpreter might be 'used' in the same way as any other type of machine.

With the benefit of hindsight, it can be seen that this approach of interpreter as machine was developed as a direct result of a move away from the previous paternalistic approaches of the interpreter as helper (See Cokely 2005 and McIntyre and Sanderson for a more detailed discussion of this development). Regardless of what were no doubt good intentions, the result of the interpreter communicating 'for' the deaf person, rather than enabling them to communicate for themselves, had often resulted in the oppression of deaf people (Scott-Gibson 1991; McIntyre and Sanderson 1995; Tate and Turner 2001; Roy 2002). As interpreting became more professionalised, and Deaf people took control of the way in which interpreters acted, the services they provided became more depersonalised, and the relationship between Deaf people and their interpreters less 'human'. What better way to do this than to behave as far as humanly possible like a machine?

In the wider university environment however, attempts to introduce best practice were just starting to filter through. Occasional (poorly attended) training sessions were held to raise awareness about how to teach deaf students, and how to work with interpreters. Teaching staff were given advice about things such as mode of delivery, pace of delivery, lighting, visual noise and the importance of providing preparation material for deaf students and interpreters. The overriding message however was still that the interpreter would not necessitate any other alteration to their teaching; that they should concentrate on the teaching and that the interpreter's job was to convey all that was said to the deaf student and vice versa.

During this period (certainly in my experience) it was extremely rare for an 'interpreter' to receive any preparation material before a session began, nor was it common practice to receive a copy of the material even during the session. We made every effort to remain 'invisible', interrupting to ask for clarification only when it was absolutely essential to the interpretation. It was normal practice to work one, two, even three-hour sessions single handed. Mostly we were given a break after one hour, but on the occasions when the lecturer was behind schedule the expectation was that we would continue working without reprieve. The research of Harrington (2000) highlights the fact that many of these issues were widespread practices across the Higher Education interpreting field nationally at the time.

Winds of change causing little disruption

In my final year at the university we studied a theoretical interpreting module which had the potential to revolutionise (or evolutionise - see Pollitt 2000) interpreting practices with its progressive approach. The module was encouraging interpreting students to, at least, recognise the existence of a number of alternative models to the machine/conduit approach that had prevailed. However this was met with resistance beyond anything other than its theoretical and ideological relevance.

McIntyre and Sanderson (1995) pointed out the significance of the impact of training on practice, stating that those who had been trained using machine/conduit interpreting would be more resistant to adapting to new approaches. Much of the existing literature influential in the training of interpreters was advocating the machine or conduit approach to interpreting (Solow 1981, Frishberg 1990, Scott-Gibson1991).

(Figure 1: McIntyre and Sanderson 1995:2)

McIntyre and Sanderson (see figure 1 above) differentiated between the models illustrated below, but the influence of this scholarship was yet to have widespread impact in the UK interpreting field.

A number of researchers (Napier 1998; Tate and Turner 2001; Roy 2002; Leneham and Napier 2003) have since written about the code of ethics and it's interpretation, and the impact that this has had on the role of the interpreter, as well as on the training of interpreters. CACDP's code of ethics, with their focus on impartiality, neutrality and the valiant endeavour not to add or omit anything from the meaning of what is said (CACDP 1996), has since been criticised for the restrictive effect it had, regardless of its well intentioned origins.

Anecdotal evidence points to the period of the late 1990s and early 2000s as a period in which many interpreters themselves recognised the conflict they faced. On the one hand they were attempting to maintain their allegiance to the code of ethics, while, on the other, they were dealing the realities of everyday practice (Tate and Turner 2001) with the result that some chose to de-register. In addition it also became clear that the dichotomous position of a reductionist approach to the process of interpretation, articulated as a simple conduit, while at the same time seeking recognition for the complexity of skills required (Roy 2002) did little to progress the campaign for professionalisation. Similarly, Dean and Pollard (2005), in their analysis of consumer provider relations, conclude that consumer expectations, based on simplistic perfunctory models of interpreting, can lead to a multitude of problems in the interpreting setting.

A more progressive approach?

In 2004 I returned to the same institution as an interpreter on a part-time freelance basis. The university I returned to was, however, very different from the one I had left eight years before. I have since noticed many positive changes.

When I left in 1996 there was only one single interpreter employed full time, directly by the institution. There is now a team of nine interpreters. In my experience, the lecturers now provide preparation material at least a week in advance. Any submission arriving later than this is accompanied by sincere apologies. A majority of lectures are now co- worked; I work regularly with other fully qualified interpreters, and have also been provided with a mentor. The minimum educational requirement for interpreting in the institution now is a graduate degree, but many of the interpreters working here also possess post graduate qualifications.

When I was leaving in 1996, talk of the establishment of a professional interpreter training course was just something that was an idea in germination. The course is now fully up and running, and is making a significant contribution to the pool of qualified interpreters throughout the UK. The percentage of deaf staff employed at the university has also increased significantly.

My reflection on my return to the institution after an extended absence, brings to mind the analogy of a relative of a small child, who they have not seen for many a year. Initial re-acquaintance evokes the response 'my how you've grown', yet for those who see the child everyday, the changes, although recognisable, are viewed in a much more incremental way, and appear much less pronounced. In discussions with other interpreters who have borne daily witness to the changes that have taken place within the institution, there is always a sense of caution on their part to counter my over optimism, as there is still so much more to be done in terms of improving the situation for deaf students, as well as raising the status of interpreting within the university.

The analogy of the growing child and absent relative is one that I think fits neatly with Higher Education interpreting, as well as the wider interpreting profession. There have been some positive developments in terms of approaches to interpreting, where now interpreters often recognise the impact they have on the dynamics of the classroom and indeed within the philosophy of the educational interpreting at this institution. Some interpreters will in fact negotiate a brief introduction at the start of the first interpreting session in order to explain the role of the interpreter as 'facilitators of teaching' (Barnes and Mowe 2005). Use of the third person on occasions that warrant it, is now at the discretion of the interpreter, as outlined by Wadensjo (1998), and these days, a comment addressed to me in the break or at the start of a session is answered without a shred of guilt on my part.

That said, this paper is written predominantly from a personal perspective. It is difficult therefore to draw any general conclusions, but I feel it is an area worthy of further study. The improvements I have seen are remarkable from my particular and unusual perspective.

1996-2004

At this stage I would like to examine some of the developments in interpreting practice and discourse which appear to have had a dramatic impact on interpreting in the wider field, as well as on interpreting in Higher Education.

Roy (2002) charts the changes in the interpreting profession, and the different metaphorical approaches used to articulate widespread understandings of the role of the sign language interpreter. She charts the progression from helper to conduit to facilitator, to bilingual, bicultural specialists to current recognition as active third party. This recognition of the active participation of the interpreting professional must also have some impact on their status. Interpreters can now feel legitimised in claiming respect as a fellow professionals in the Higher Education environment. This in turn will also have a direct influence on the whole interpreted event, as Napier concludes:

> 'the interpreter's decision making will be influenced by how he or she perceives his or her role in this discourse environment.' (Napier, 2002:286)

Napier is able to provide an insightful analysis of the position of interpreters at the time in her contention that interpreters were 'more concerned with the potential ramifications of being seen to step outside of the boundaries of their professional status' (Napier, 1998: 19). Her much cited and liberating paper on free interpretation has done much to raise awareness amongst interpreters of the potential benefit of a braver approach to interpreting in which interpreters have greater confidence in moving away from the source language to provide a culturally equivalent interpretation in the target language. Napier (1998, 2002) and Metzger (1999) refer to this distinction between free and literal translation. Free translation being 'the process by which concepts and meanings are translated from one language into another by incorporating cultural norms and values assumed knowledge about these values; and the search for linguistic and cultural equivalents' (Napier 2002:285). They make a convincing case for its wider use in our practice.
In educational interpreting too, which holds the long suffering position of the poor relation (Harrington 2005), there is now more evidence of the multitude of skills needed to carry out that task successfully (Napier 2002). There is wider recognition of the need for interpreters working in Higher Education to have completed a Higher Education qualification themselves, as well as the recognition of the complex discourse environments within which they have to function when working in the Higher Education setting, which demand particularly judicious approaches to language choice in interpreting (Harrington 2000, 2001, 2005; Napier 2002). The Higher Education environment has particular significance to interpreting that should not be lost: 'If the situational context of language interpreting is not taken into consideration in retrospective analyses, there is risk of making quite a different sense of what was said, compared to how it was originally understood, both by the primary parties and interpreter … ' (Wadensjo, 2002:355). All of this points to a need to recognise educational interpreting for its potential to develop as a post qualification specialism within the wider interpreting field. This could be done in much the same way as the growing recognition of other specialisms, including court and conference interpreting, which tend to carry much higher status (Harrington 2001).

Seal (1998) when writing about generic educational interpreting points to the way in which training is often preceded by the practice. This analysis fits well with what has happened in relation to interpreting in Higher Education. Deaf students in Higher Education are a relatively new phenomenon (Harrington 2005) so appropriate training and good practice is still emerging. Sign language interpreting has taken much of its practice from spoken language interpreting at conferences, (Pollitt 1997; Roy 2002) which, with hindsight, can now be seen as inadequate for adaptation in the interpreted classroom.

What is needed now is an opportunity to learn from the practice which has preceded. Roy (2002) in her work on the changes in the field calls for a re-examination of the theory and knowledge relating to interpreting as a profession. If the sign language interpreting profession is to develop and mature, then these significant changes will need to take place.

Conclusion

Many positive outcomes have resulted from the deconstruction of the myth of the interpreter as a neutral, invisible conduit (Metzger 1999). However developments of conduit interpreting came about partly as a result of the closeness of interpreting to the Deaf community, who themselves were advocating a move away from the benevolent but oppressive helper, and the unwarranted reflection this had on them in terms of their capability and independence (Scott-Gibson 1991 McIntyre and Sanderson 1995, Roy 2002). The conduit approach to interpreting was therefore historically a blessing in terms of the movement away from helper. In Britain, this process of development also necessitated a move away from the social work role of the Missioner interpreter. Napier (1998) points out the way in which the professionalisation of interpreting has lead some in the Deaf community to bemoan the departure of the 'fledglings'; those who had acted as interpreter (all be it via the helper mode) emanating from within the bosom of the Deaf community and had developed their sign language skills to a fluent level.

Scholarship, practice and training of interpreters have gone some way to revolutionise our work as sign language interpreters which I would purport has been beneficial to all involved. In addition, the importance of the recognition of the need for educational ability as a firm foundation to interpreter ability has also lead to the nurturing of critical thinking not only in terms of the interpreting performance, but also in terms of interpreting scholarship. Turner and Harrington (2001) and Marschark et al (2005) have suggested that scholarship around interpreting is still in its early stages of development and as such there are further developments yet to emerge that will continue to develop the field. With this I would wholeheartedly agree. My position here does however come with at least one proviso.

Continuing with the existing analogy, it could be viewed that the interpreting profession is now in its adolescent stage and has characteristically begun to put its own needs as a profession before the needs of the Deaf community, who nevertheless continue to fulfil a nurturing role. This has caused conflict between the Deaf community and the profession commonly witnessed elsewhere in parent/child relationships at this stage. Napier (1998) points out some of the actual problems caused by the difficulties, including issues of mistrust and misunderstanding, and Pollitt (2000) cautions against arrogant condemnation of deaf people who dare to express a preference for conduit, as well as against its whole scale decommissioning from our practice.

Napier (1998) also highlights the differences in perceptions and articulations between deaf and hearing people about what constitutes professional values, which she also interprets as the adopted positions of the Deaf community and interpreters. She points to the vulnerability of interpreters as a reason for resistance to the concept of free interpretation. Although it is generally easier to see the vulnerability of the younger members in a familial relationship, there are also existing and new vulnerabilities (Baker-Shenk 1983, Cokely 2005) to the Deaf community amidst all these changes.

However it is for interpreters and the interpreting profession as a whole to be mindful of the statement that 'members of the Deaf community need to acknowledge the investment that sign language interpreters make to improve their skills in order to meet the needs of their target audience' (Napier 1998 pg 22). This must also be balanced by the recognition that the Deaf community have provided much in terms of investment of time and resources to nurture individual interpreters as well as the profession as a whole. It is important that the significance of interdependence and collaboration in the relationship recognised by Pollitt (1991, 1997), Turner and Harrington (2000) Harrington (2001), Turner and Alker (2003), Napier (2006) is supported and acknowledged by all.

Where the analogy running throughout this paper must end is in the realisation that unlike the actual parental relationship which usually results in independence on maturity, no matter how established interpreting becomes as a profession, it cannot survive without the Deaf community to whom it will always need some level of attachment to their apron strings!

Further reading

Anderson, R. B. W. 2002 'Perspectives on the role of the interpreter' in Pochhacker F. and Shlesinger, M. (Eds.) *The interpreting studies reader*. London, Routledge.

Baker-Shenk, C. 1993 'Characteristics of oppressed and oppressor peoples: their effect on the interpreting context' in McIntyre, M. L. (ed.), *Interpreting- the art of cross cultural mediation* Proceedings from the Ninth National Convention of Registry of Interpreters for the Deaf. Silver Springs, RID Publications.

Barnes, L. and Mowe, K. 2005 *Facilitating teaching of deaf students*. (Unpublished Work)

CACDP 1996 Directory of Registered Interpreters. Durham, CACDP.

Cokely, D. 2005 'Shifting positionality: a critical examination of the turning point in the relationship of interpreters and the deaf community' in Marschark, M. Peterson, R. and Winston, E. (eds.), *Sign language interpreting and interpreter education - directions for research and practice*. Oxford, Oxford University Press

Dean, R. K. and Pollard, R. Q. 2005 'Consumers and service effectiveness' in Marschark, M. Peterson, R. and Winston, E. (eds.) *Interpreting work: a practice profession perspective*. Oxford, Oxford University Press.

Frishberg, N. 1990 *Interpreting: An introduction* Silver Springs, RID.

Harrington, F. J. 2001 'The rise fall and re-invention of the communicator: re-defining the roles and responsibilities in educational interpreting' in Harrington, F. J. and Turner, G. H. (eds.) *Interpreting interpreting: studies and reflections on sign language interpreting* Coleford, Douglas McLean.

Harrington, F. J. 2005 'A study of the complex nature of interpreting with deaf students in Higher Education' in Metzger, M. (ed.) *Attitudes, innuendo and regulators: challenging of interpretation*. Washington DC, Gallaudet University Press.

Harrington, F. J. 2000 'Sign language interpreters and access for deaf students to university curricula: the ideal and the reality' in Roberts, R. et al. (eds.) *The Critical Link 2: Interpreters in the community*. Philadelphia, Benjamanis Translator Library.

Ladd, P. 2003 *Understanding deaf culture: in search of Deafhood*. London, Multilingual Matters.

Lane, H. 1994 *The mask of benevolence: disabling the deaf community*. New York, Alfred Knopf.

Leneham, M. and Napier, J. 2003 'Sign language interpreters' codes of ethics: should we maintain the status quo?'. *Deaf Worlds*, 19, 2.

Marschark, M., Sapere, P., Convertino, C., and Seewagen, R. 2005 'Educational interpreter access and outcome' in Marschark, M. Peterson, R. and Winston, E. (eds.), *Sign language interpreting and interpreter education: directions for research and practice.* Oxford, Oxford University Press.

Marschark, M., Sapere, P., Convertino, C., and Seewagen, R. 2005 'Educational interpreting: access and outcomes' in Marschark, M. Peterson, R. and Winston, E. (eds.), *Sign language interpreting and interpreter education: directions for research and practice.* Oxford, Oxford University Press.

Marschark, M., Peterson, R., and Winston, E. 2005 'Preface' in Marschark, M. Peterson, R. and Winston, E. (eds.), *Sign language interpreting and interpreter education: directions for research and practice.* Oxford, Oxford University Press.

Marzocchi, C. 1998 'The case for an institution specific component in interpreting research' *The interpreters newsletter.*

McIntyre, M. L. and Sanderson, G. R. 1995 '"Who's in charge here?": perceptions of empowerment and role in the interpreting setting' *Journal of Interpretation*, 7, 1.

Metzger, M. 1999 *Sign language interpreting - deconstructing the myth of neutrality.* Washington DC, Gallaudet University Press.

Napier, J. 1998 'Free your mind, the rest will follow' *Deaf Worlds*, 14, 3.

Napier, J. 2006 '"I like it /him/her because...": An exploration of practitioner and consumer attitudes towards signed language interpreting in the community'. *Supporting Deaf People (SDP3) on-line conference*

Napier, J. 2002 'University interpreting: linguistic issues for consideration'. *Journal of Deaf Studies and Deaf Education*, 7, 4: 281-301.

Pochhacker, F. 2000 'The community interpreter's task: self-perception and provider views' in Roberts R. et al. (eds.), *The Critical Link 2: Interpreters in the community.* Philadelphia, Benjamanis Translator Library.

Pollitt, K. 1991 'Rational responses'. *Sign Post*, 4, 2 ; 24.

Pollitt, K. 1997 'The state we're in: some thoughts on professionalisation, professionalism and practice among the UK's sign language interpreters'. *Deaf Worlds*, 13, 3: 21-26.

Pollitt, K. 2000 'On babies, bathwater and approaches to interpreting'. *Deaf Worlds*, 16, 2.

Roy, C. 2002 'The problem with definitions descriptions and the role metaphors of interpreters' in Pochhacker, F. and Shlesinger, M. (eds.), *The interpreting studies reader.* London, Routledge.

Scott-Gibson, L. 1991 'Sign language interpreting: an emerging profession' in Gregory, S. and Hartley, G. M. (eds.) *Constructing deafness.* London, Pinter Publishers.

Seal, B. C. 1998 *Best practice in educational interpreting.* London, Allyn and Bacon.

Tate, G. and Turner, G. H. 2001 'The code and the culture: sign language interpreting: in search of a new breed's ethics' in Harrington, F. J. and Turner, G. H. (eds.) *Interpreting interpreting: studies and reflections on sign language interpreting.* Coleford, Douglas McLean.

Turner, G. H. 2001 'Rights and responsibilities: the relationship between deaf people and interpreters' in Harrington, F. J. and Turner, G. H. (eds.) *Interpreting interpreting: studies and reflections on sign language interpreting* Coleford, Douglas McLean.

Turner, G. H. and Harrington, F. J. 2001 'The campaign for real interpreting' in Harrington, F. J. and Turner, G. H. (eds.) *Interpreting interpreting: studies and reflections on sign language interpreting* Coleford, Douglas McLean.

Turner, G. H. and Alker, D. 2003 'Partnership in British Sign Language research and policy development' *Deaf Worlds*, 19, 2.

Turner, G. H. 2005 'Towards real interpreting' in Marschark, M. Peterson, R. and Winston, E. (eds.) *Sign language interpreting and interpreter education: directions for research and practice.* Oxford, Oxford University Press

Wadensjo, C. 1998 *Interpreting as interaction.* London, Longman.

Wadensjo, C. 2002 'The double role of a dialogue interpreter' in Pochhacker, F. and Shlesinger, M. (eds.), *The interpreting studies reader.* London, Routledge.

CHAPTER TWELVE

Hearing Education through the ears of others

Frank J Harrington

Introduction

Prior to 1997, there had not been any comprehensive investigation into the activities of interpreters working in educational settings in the United Kingdom. The UCLan project (Harrington and Turner 2000, 2001; Traynor and Harrington 2003; Harrington 2005), funded by the Higher Education Funding Council for England (HEFCE), enabled researchers to video and analyse classroom interaction for the first time, and to identify a number of different factors that had an impact on the learning of Deaf students, and other students and tutors. This chapter will draw together some of the key themes that were identified in that study and the issues that they raise for the education of Deaf children and adults (see also Winston 2004, Marschark, Peterson and Winston 2005, Seal 1997).

The videotaped data from the UCLan project also allowed the researchers to take a detailed look at how interpreters function in educational settings. Again, supported by the work of other researchers (Roy 1992, 2000, Wadensjö, 1992, 1997) the team learned much more about how interpreters function, and were able to describe the interpreting task in much more detail. Understanding what interpreters do on a daily basis (Tate and Turner 2002), and the pressures that they are put under by all aspects of the work-place (as well as the task of interpreting itself) has enabled trainers to approach the training of interpreters in different ways. In particular, trainers of interpreters, not only in the UK, but around the world, have begun to introduce much more in the way of reflective practice into their training (Turner 2005).

Having looked at the complex nature of the interpreted classroom, and the extent to which Deaf students successfully access their education, this chapter will go on to look at the changing nature of both the interpreter and interpreter training. It will look first at the origins of Interpreting in the UK, and then go on to see what might need to be developed in future, if interpreters are to attain the high level language and interpreting skills required to meet the needs of Deaf students in educational settings more fully.

Deaf students in the interpreted classroom

Activities that take place in lecture rooms and classrooms in Universities are not designed with the a-typical student in mind. They are filled with multimedia, and are used predominantly by people who are able to watch, look and listen all at the same time (Harrington 2005, Johnson 1992). The introduction of a Deaf person (and all that s/he brings) into this environment has an impact on the entire situation; the classroom dynamic, the individual learning experience of every student, and the teaching experience of the Lecturer (Harrington 2005, and see Metzger 2002). Elsewhere in this volume, a number of different types of support are explored in detail, so it is proposed here to focus on the use and activities of interpreters, rather than spend time exploring the effects of other monolingual and bilingual support services (See Turner; Barnes and Doe; McRea and Turner - this volume).

Interpreters working in Higher Education settings will find themselves in a wide variety of situations, and need to be prepared for all of these (Traynor and Harrington 2003).

To list but a few:

- A formal lecture in a lecture theatre;
- A formal lecture in a classroom;
- A seminar;
- Working with a group of students preparing for a presentation;
- Interpreting (BSL – English) for a deaf student giving a presentation;
- One-to-one tutorial with a tutor.

The dynamic and types of interaction in each of these situations is going to be very different, and will leave the interpreter constantly making decisions and choices about how to best ensure access for a Deaf student. For example, in seminars, group preparations, and sometimes in lectures, there is regular overlapping of speech, where a number of contributors may wish to comment at the same time. In this situation, the interpreter will have to decide which speaker should be interpreted, and at whose expense (Napier 2002, Harrington and Turner 2001). Any intervention on their part (e.g. to ask people to speak one at a time) will dramatically affect the group interaction and cause the spontaneity to be lost.

Another issue for consideration is that of the language of the classroom, which is itself related to the variety of topics that are taught in HE (Traynor and Harrington 2003).

To give just two or three examples:

- interpreters may find themselves interpreting in the fine arts; using a visual/gestural language to describe visual entities, some of which they may not have seen (an example of this is the description of a Thai House, as explored by Johnston 1992) and which may, therefore, look very different from the version described by an interpreter;

- They may be expected to interpret poetry, or to provide interpretations from different forms of spoken language. A particular example might be the interpretation of Shakespeare in an English class. So many layers of the source material are likely to be lost simply because the interpreter is having to work from C16th 'iambic pentameter', to modern BSL prose;

- They may be interpreting a linguistics class, with the added metalinguistic difficulty of having to talk about linguistic constructs of one language while using the differing linguistic constructs of a second language.

Three other factors that have to be taken into consideration centre around the abilities and knowledge of the interpreter themselves. Obasi (this volume) talks about the extent to which interpreter training has changed in the last decade, identifying that a much greater number of interpreters are now being educated in HE based Interpreter Education Programmes (IEPs). Although this is the case, there is no guarantee that an interpreter will have specialist, subject specific knowledge for all of the situations in which they may find themselves interpreting in HE.

To become qualified, interpreters have to attain a standard of British Sign Language (BSL) equivalent to a UK National Vocational Qualification (NVQ) at level 4. Since current BSL assessments in the UK require minimum competence to pass the qualification at the right level, it is not necessarily the case that all qualified interpreters will have high order or near native second language skills (this issue will be discussed in more detail later in this paper).

A natural part of the interpreting process is that any message has to pass through the mind of the interpreter and its meaning be understood, before it can be interpreted into the target language. As Cokely (1992) tells us, one can only interpret that which one understands, and anything that one misunderstands will be misinterpreted. A natural part of the listening process is that the mind filters what it hears in order to gain understanding, so everything that is received by a deaf student via an interpreter is, by its very nature, second hand information (Harrington and Turner 2001). While every interpreter will do their best to interpret effectively and accurately, it is widely recognised (Winston 2004, Turner 2005, Lee 2005, Harrington 2001) that educational interpreting and the access afforded Deaf students in the classroom is far from perfect.

In an ideal world, one would want to be able to put services in place that would fully meet the needs of Deaf Students. Later in this paper, suggestions will be made about the ways in which training for interpreters might change, and access for Deaf students be improved. However, to understand the need for these changes, and the impact that they might have, it is first necessary to look back at how sign language teaching and learning, and interpreter training, have developed.

Training the interpreters

Developments in Interpreter training in the UK since the early 1980's have been led by a unique set of circumstances.

In many countries, particularly in mainland Europe, interpreting emerged as a development from within the education system (Nilsson 1997). It was the Teachers of the Deaf who branched out, first into educational interpreting and then into interpreting in other settings. In the UK, almost uniquely, interpreting emerged from the welfare professions (Scott Gibson 1991, Simpson 1991) - so it was the 'community' aspects of deaf people's lives, rather than their education, which was catered for in the first instance.

In the late 1970s and early 1980s, a number of things began to happen which led directly to the identification of interpreting as a separate profession and the establishment of BSL interpreter training.

Social policy developments (in the aftermath of the establishment of the welfare state) meant that welfare services for Deaf people ,which had been the traditional domain of the church – carried out by welfare officers who were from within the Deaf community themselves, were taken over by the state (Hill 1996). New Social Work qualifications and Social Services departments were established, and the new Social Workers were removed from the direct contact they had previously had with Deaf people (Scott Gibson 1991). Deaf people became open cases to Social Services departments and, as their privacy seemed to be increasingly compromised, they began to demand a separation of the Social work and interpreter roles.

One of the main problems for the new Social workers was that they were not from within the Deaf community, and were not natural users of British Sign Language (Scott Gibson 1991). Partly in response, the Department for Health and Social Security provided funding for a three year project which had two main aims. The first was to enable interested parties (eg the new Social Workers) to learn to sign. The second was to establish a register of sign language interpreters. As a result of this project, the Council for the Advancement of Communication with Deaf People (CACDP) was formed, and BSL qualifications at three levels were established, as was the first register of interpreters (Simpson 1991).

These events also coincided with new research which was beginning to emerge into the linguistics of BSL. Mary Brennan and her colleagues began their work on the language at Moray House Institute in Scotland, later moving to the Deaf Studies Research Unit at Durham University (Brennan 1990). Work was also being carried out by Jim Kyle, Bencie Woll and others at Bristol University (Woll, Kyle and Deuchar 1981), and it was no surprise that Bristol, followed closely by Durham, went on to establish the first University based interpreter training programmes.

The recognised function of the BSL/English Interpreter is that they work simultaneously, receiving a source text and interpreting it, sentence by sentence, into the target language, or in dialogue settings where there are two interwoven source and target texts. The examination for membership of the register of interpreters was established by CACDP and, from the outset, it tested interpreting in these two forms. As the exam gave way to National Vocational Qualifications (NVQ) in the late 1990's this practice continued, and assessment for registration at present is still almost exclusively focused on these modes of interpreting (see NVQ Level 4 BSL/English Interpreting standards – CACDP 2007). It is, therefore, no surprise that most interpreter training is also designed to enhance and assess the interpreters ability to function in this way.

Second language learning

Most learners of BSL as a second language are adult learners, whose use of their first language (usually English) has been well established over many years. Literature on second language acquisition describes the learning process as one that relies heavily on what is known as 'inter-language' or 'foreigner language' (Larsen-Freeman and Long, 1991). This is a form of language which uses the grammatical features of the individual's first language to hold together lexical and other items taken from the new language that is being learned. In the case of English speakers learning BSL, they would use the grammar, sentence structure, etc of English in order to make sentences using BSL vocabulary. This is regularly seen in BSL learners who produce what is often referred to as SSE rather than grammatically correct BSL. As they continue to learn BSL and develop their understanding of the grammar and syntax of the language, their production of the language should become increasingly more BSL-like and less influenced by their knowledge of English.

When BSL classes began in the 1980's, most were being taught in Deaf clubs, and mostly (but not always) by Deaf BSL users. My own first experience of learning BSL in the mid 1980's was of being taught to sign and speak at the same time by a hearing Social Worker. Although there was an intense period of research into the linguistics of the language at that time (Brennan 1990, Kyle and Woll, 1985, etc), it is fair to say that there is still much work to be done before we have a comprehensive understanding of the workings of BSL. There are a variety of resources that can be used (the BSL Dictionary, 1991, Sutton Spence and Woll 2000) but we have to be confident that those charged with teaching the language have a comprehensive knowledge of its structures and intricacies, and the ability to convey this to their students through their teaching. This is the only way that second language learners will be able to become competent and 'near native' in their use of BSL. New initiatives are leading to a renewed interest in a corpus based study of BSL, but until these are realised, our knowledge of how BSL works will remain incomplete. (Turner 2005, Lee 2005)

The impact of second language learning on interpreting should raise a cautionary note. Neidle et al (1995) showed that where sign language is taught using the accepted rules (which may not necessarily correspond to those used by Deaf people when they sign with each other) there is no guarantee that what is produced and understood by students of the language is necessarily the same as that produced or understood by native users of the language. If this is the case, then it is possible that second language users acting as interpreters may not always convey a message using the same linguistic rules and norms as those used by native users relying on their interpretations (Lee 2005). In other words, if interpreters are not being taught BSL as it is used by the Deaf community, but rather a highbred or pigeon version of the language, they may never be able to achieve near native linguistic competence, and there is potential for misunderstanding and miscommunication to occur. Neidle et al (1995) describe just such a situation, which resulted in a Deaf person being declared bankrupt. The consequences might not be so dramatic in educational interpreting, but the potential for such miscommunication does exist.

Changing nature of the interpreting student

BSL/English interpreting is a function that many people fall into much earlier than they should, as a result of attending a BSL class, or regularly attending a Deaf Club. It is all too easy to begin facilitating communication using a simultaneous mode of 'interpreting', even though one is still learning the language, because to some extent or another, this is what's expected. As was mentioned earlier, IEPs, CACDP and other assessment bodies have traditionally supported the teaching and assessment of simultaneous interpreting as the norm, and BSL/English interpreting naturally lends itself to this mode of interpreting as there is no perceived overlapping of speech during the process. (CACDP 2007)

To an extent this was not deemed problematic in the past, since many students coming through the newer IEPs had already held advanced level BSL certificates (CACDP Stage III) for some years, and had also been working as interpreters before enrolling on the programmes. The fact that they seemed to be able to carry out the simultaneous role fairly well disguised the fact that simultaneous interpreting might not always be the best mode of interpreting to use (Seleskovitch 1998).

As time has gone on, and these interpreters have passed through the training system onto the Register of Interpreters, they are being replaced by a new type of student. It is now much more common for students to come forward having only just completed their advanced BSL certificates (NVQ level 3), and with little or no experience of working as interpreters. Since there have been no significant changes to the assessment of interpreters or the content of IEPs, they are being taught and assessed as near native BSL users working in a simultaneous/dialogue mode of interpreting when they may not be highly skilled either in their language usage or their interpreting ability. With this in mind, perhaps the time is right to review the way in which interpreter training in the UK is designed and delivered, and also the way in which students wishing to become interpreters are recruited into IEPs

Meeting the training needs of interpreters in the 21st century

As we have seen above, in terms of educating interpreters, there are issues relating to language learning, to the experience that current students bring with them to their IEP, and to the skills being taught and encouraged both by their trainers and assessors. This paper will now explore some of the potential responses by trainers and assessors to the issues raised.

It is increasingly the case that IEPs are being based in Higher Education Institutions. Obasi discusses the difficulties that have been faced in the past by the Deaf community and those learning BSL in relation to ownership and teaching of the language.[29] However, if IEPs are to deliver interpreters with the quality of skills required to undertake the role appropriately, then the HE BSL curriculum needs to be robust in both its content and delivery, and of a comparable level with other modern foreign languages taught in such institutions. (Turner 2005, Lee 2005). Recent collaborative projects such as Sign On, Sign Online and BSL:QED (Quality Embedding of the Discipline), have come a long way in delivering the type of resources required in HE, and any future corpus-based study of the language can only further enhance this. [30] The task now is for IEPs to take these developments to heart and review the ways in which they teach BSL as a second language to interpreting and other students. In terms of interpreting processes, Hatim and Mason (1997) Hatim (2001) and Mason (1999) discuss the differences that exist between different modes of translation, consecutive interpreting, simultaneous interpreting and dialogue interpreting.

Translation is a process whereby the individual undertaking the work is in possession of the complete text to be translated before they begin the work of translating that text. Although there may ultimately be a limit in terms of the time available for the translation to be undertaken, the process is one that can be done with care and revision up until the final translation is delivered (Hatim 2001).

In consecutive interpreting, as with translation, the text is received in full in the source language (SL) prior to the interpretation being delivered in the target language (TL). The difference is that the interpretation is

---

[29] See Chapter Eleven of this publication

[30] These projects have all resulted in web based resources being developed for the teaching and learning of BSL. For further information see the website details in the references section at the end of this chapter

expected to be delivered immediately following the reception of the SL text. The interpreting process, as a result, will be more complex, as the interpreter will have to analyse quickly the content of the message, use some form of notation of keywords and concepts, and have an overall awareness of the structure of the piece in order to recall detail when giving their interpretation in the TL (Hatim and Mason 1997).

Simultaneous interpreting requires the interpreter to partially receive a SL text, understand it, reconstruct it, and deliver it in the TL whilst receiving the next part of the text. It is immediately clear that this process is far more complex and quite different from that described above either for translation or consecutive interpreting. The interpreter cannot focus on the structure of the text as a whole, and has to rely much more on its texture - the way sentences are structured and woven together to give meaning (Ibid).

Finally in dialogue interpreting (the task most often undertaken by the BSL/English interpreter), the complexity is increased by two factors. Firstly the speech is live and interactive, moving in two directions. Secondly, it is unstructured, as each utterance is dictated by the previous utterance. There is no overall pre-designed structure to the discourse (Mason 1999).

Writing about the training of spoken language interpreters, Danica Seleskovitch (1991, 1998) suggests that interpreting students should begin by learning the art of translation. They should practice this art for a significant period of time until they are proficient at it. Only then should they move on to consecutive interpreting, which again they should practice for a significant period of time until they have honed their skills. She goes on to suggest that, for competent students and interpreters ..."simultaneous interpretation can be learned quite rapidly, assuming one has already learned the art of analysis in consecutive interpretation". (Seleskovitch, 1998, 30).

This notion, that Simultaneous interpreting is only possible after the other forms of Translation and Consecutive interpreting have been mastered, is a far cry from the current norms for training sign language interpreters. It is certainly the case that the re-design of IEPs around the country to place much more emphasis on these different modes of translation and interpreting is certainly not imminent. However, if we are to see the improvement we want to see in the language and interpreting skills of the modern interpreting student, perhaps a three or four step approach to their training might be appropriate.

- Step one would ensure that they are secure in their use of both English and BSL;
- Step two would hone their translation skills;
- Step three would move them into interpreting by first enhancing their consecutive interpreting skills;
- Finally strep four would move them into the more complex art of Simultaneous and Dialogue interpreting.

In many settings, including education, trained and qualified interpreters might then be required to undertake specialised, setting-specific training, to properly equip them for work in these areas. For too long interpreting has been seen as an easy task, and something that every sign language student has the right to attempt. In reality it is a highly specialised and difficult task, not always successfully executed by students of the existing training and assessment systems.

Finally, and crucially, if changes are to be made to the ways in which interpreters are trained, and which will no doubt overflow into the workplace, then Deaf and other consumers of interpreting services need to be given the opportunity to understand and experience those changes too. It might be, for example, that a particular lesson or assignment would be best handled using a simultaneous mode of interpreting. If this were the case then the principal participants in the interpreted interaction would need to understand that process and be comfortable with it. This will not happen if the expected norm continues to be that Simultaneous or Dialogue modes of interpreting be used.

Key points

- BSL curriculum needs to be designed to meet the needs of second language learners in HE;
- Greater emphasis needs to be placed on translation and consecutive interpreting theory and practice in interpreter training;
- There needs to be a move away from simultaneous/dialogue interpreting as the norm both in training and assessment, end within the field;
- Post qualification training will be essential – There should be highly qualified specialists working in education, and a variety of other settings;

- In terms of assessment of student interpreters, we need to see a move away from the traditional standpoint of looking for minimum competence;
- Educational Interpreting should be seen as a specialism, not as a practice ground for trainee Interpreters.

Further reading

Brennan, M. 1992 'The visual world of British Sign Language: An introduction' in Brien, D. (ed): *Dictionary of British Sign Language/English*. London : Faber and Faber

Brennan, M. 1990 *Word formation in British Sign Language*. Stockholm : University of Stockholm

Brien, D. (ed) 1992 *Dictionary of British Sign Language/English*. London : Faber and Faber

CACDP 2007
http://www.cacdp.org.uk/Qual_Training/Scripts/assessments.html

Cokely, D. R. 1992 *Interpretation: A sociolinguistic model*. (Linstok Press Dissertation Series) Silver Spring, MD : Linstok Press.

Harrington, F. J. and Turner, G. H. 2001 *Interpreting interpreting: studies and reflections on sign language interpreting* Coleford : Douglas McLean

Harrington, F. J. 2005 'A study of the complex nature of interpreting with deaf students in higher education' in Metzger, M. and Fleetwood, E (eds) *Attitudes, innuendo, and regulators : Challenges of interpretation*. (Studies in Interpretation Series 2) Washington, DC : Gallaudet University Press

Harrington, F. J. 2001 'Sign language interpreters and access for deaf students to university curricula: the ideal and the reality' in Roberts, R et al (eds): *The Critical Link 2: interpreters in the community*. Philadelphia: Benjamins

Hatim, B. and Mason, I. 1997 *The translator as communicator*. Longman: London

Hatim, B. 2001 *Teaching and researching translation*. Longman: London

Hill, M. 1996 *Social policy: a comparative analysis*. Prentice Hall: Hemel Hempstead

Johnson, K. 1992 'Miscommunication in interpreted classroom communication' in Cokely, D. R. (ed): *Sign language interpreters and interpreting*. (SLS Monographs) Silver Spring, MD : Linstok Press

Kyle, J. and Woll, B. 1985. *Sign language. The study of deaf people and their language.* Cambridge, New York : Cambridge University Press

Larsen-Freeman, D. and Long, M 1991 *An introduction to second language acquisition research.* London, Longman

Lee, R. G. 2005 'From theory to practice: making the interpreting process come alive in the classroom' in Roy, Cynthia B. (ed): *Advances in teaching sign language interpreters.* (Interpreter Education Series) Washington, DC: Gallaudet University Press

Lee, R. G. 2005 'The research gap: getting linguistic information into the right hands - implications for deaf education and interpreting' in Marschark, M., Peterson, R. and Winston, E. A. (eds): *Sign language interpreting and interpreter education : directions for research and practice.* Oxford: Oxford University Press

Marschark, M., Peterson, R. and Winston, E. A. (eds) 2005 *Sign language interpreting and interpreter education : directions for research and practice.* Oxford: Oxford University Press

Mason, I. (ed) 1999 *The Translator*: special issue on Dialogue Interpreting Volume 5: Number 2

Metzger, M. 2002 *Sign language interpreting: deconstructing the myth of neutrality.* Gallaudet University Press: Washington DC

Napier, J. 2005 'Linguistic features and strategies of interpreting: from research to education to practice' in Marschark, M., Peterson, R. and Winston, E. (eds) *Sign language interpreting and interpreter education : directions for research and practice.* Oxford: Oxford Univ. Press

Napier, J. 2002 *Sign language interpreting: linguistic coping strategies.* Coleford: Douglas McLean

Nilsson, A. 1997 *Forskning om teckenspråkstolkning - en översikt.* TÖI Rapport nr 6. Tolk- och Översättarinstitutet. Stockholm : Stockholms Universitet

Pöchhacker, F. and Shlesinger, M. (eds) 2002. *The interpreting studies reader.* London: Routeledge

Roy, C. B. (ed) 2006 *New approaches to interpreter education.* (Interpreter Education Series: 3) Washington, DC: Gallaudet Univ. Press

Roy, C. B. 1992 'A sociolinguistic analysis of the interpreter's role in simultaneous talk in a face-to-face interpreted dialogue' *Sign Language Studies* 21: 74: 21-61

Roy, C.B. (ed) 2000 *Innovative practices for teaching sign language interpreters.* Gallaudet University Press: Washington DC

Roy, C.B. (ed) 2005 *Advances in teaching sign language interpreters.* Gallaudet University Press: Washington DC

Scott-Gibson, L. 1991 'Sign language interpreting: an emerging profession' in Gregory, S. & Hartley, G.(eds.) *Constructing deafness.* Pinter Publishers (in association with the Open University): Milton Keynes

Seal, B. 1997 *Best practices in educational interpreting*, Allyn and Bacon: Boston

Seleskovitch, D. 1991 'Fundamentals of the interpretive theory of translation' in *Expanding Horizons.* Proceedings of the 12th National RID Convention 1991, RID Press

Seleskovitch, D. 1998. *Interpreting for international conferences*, (3rd revised edition), Pen and Booth, Washington DC.

Shepard-Kegl, J., Neidle, C. and Kegl, J. 1995 'Legal ramifications of and incorrect analysis of tense in ASL' *Journal of Interpretation* 7: 1

Simpson, T.S. 1991 A stimulus to learning, a measure of ability, in Gregory, S. & Hartley, G.(eds.) *Constructing deafness.* Pinter Publishers (in association with the Open University): Milton Keynes

Sutton Spence, R. and Woll, B. 2000 *The linguistics of British Sign Language: an introduction.* Cambridge: Cambridge University Press

Tate, G. and Turner, G. H. 2002 'The code and the culture: Sign language interpreting': in search of the new breed's ethics' in Pöchhacker, F. and Shlesinger, M. (eds): *The interpreting studies reader.* London : Routledge

Traynor, N. and Harrington, F. J. 2003 'BSL/English interpreting in higher education: is access to the university curriculum a reality for deaf students?' in: Gallaway, C. and Young, A. M. (eds): *Deafness and education in the UK : Research perspectives.* London : Whurr Publishers Ltd.

Turner, G. H. 2005 'Toward real interpreting' in: Marschark, M., Peterson, R. and Winston, E. A. (eds), *Sign language interpreting and interpreter education : directions for research and practice.* Oxford: Oxford University Press

Turner, G.H. and Harrington, F.J. 2000 'Power and method in interpreting research' in Olohan, M. (ed) *Intercultural faultlines*. Manchester: St Jerome Publishing,

Venuti, L. (ed) 2000 *The translation studies reader*. London: Routeledge

Wadensjö, C. 1992 *Interpreting as interaction: on dialogue interpreting in immigration hearings and medical encounters*. Linköping: University of Linköping.

Wadensjö, C. 1998 *Interpreting as interaction*. London & New York: Longman.

Winston, E. (ed) 2004 *Educational interpreting : how it can succeed*. Washington, DC : Gallaudet University Press

Woll, B., Kyle, J. and Deuchar, M. (eds) 1981 *Perspectives on British Sign Language and deafness*. London: Croom Helm

Web Based BSL resources

http://www.signonline.org.uk/

http://escalate.ac.uk/2752

Section Three:
Deaf students in post-graduate study

CHAPTER THIRTEEN

A bridge too far? The issues for deaf students in research education

Val Farrar

Starting out

To begin doctoral study is to set out on an expedition to the pinnacle of educational achievement. About 12,000 graduates embarked on the PhD route in the UK in 2005. Those who select candidates for a postgraduate research degree have high expectations of the people they choose. There is likely to be a tacit assumption that graduates who have travelled to this point have acquired the skills, knowledge and tenacity to succeed at the highest level. They will be expected to be, or to become, wholly independent travellers. If they are deaf candidates, then previous educational experience will have fitted them for the journey. It may be supposed that they will have in place the learning management strategies, including support, which will enable them to complete the journey.

During 2003 to 2005, a project based at Newcastle University and funded by HECFE (the Higher Education Funding Council for England) set out to improve postgraduate research provision for deaf and disabled students across the sector.[31] The team began by trying to discover if there were particular barriers to research education - whether research posed different issues from undergraduate study. We talked with 31 deaf and disabled postgraduate research students and asked them to tell their stories in questionnaires, interviews and case histories. Their experiences informed the design and content of staff development and student resources which we hope give voice to their concerns.
This chapter will:

---

[31] Premia (Postgraduate research – making it accessible).

- look at the extent of deaf people's participation in research education;
- identify some of the issues they face in research environments;
- explore ways in which institutions, and external agencies, might tackle some of the barriers deaf research students have encountered.

How many deaf research students are there?

From 2002 the numbers of deaf students entering Higher Education as undergraduates steadily increased. That increase was in line with the growth of the whole cohort. When we analyse the figures starting a research degree programme, there has been only a modest increase. But at a time when there was a slight reduction in the numbers of hearing graduates starting on research degrees (15,395 in 2003/4 to 14,875 in 2004/5), the numbers of deaf researchers grew (from 40 to 50).

Table 1

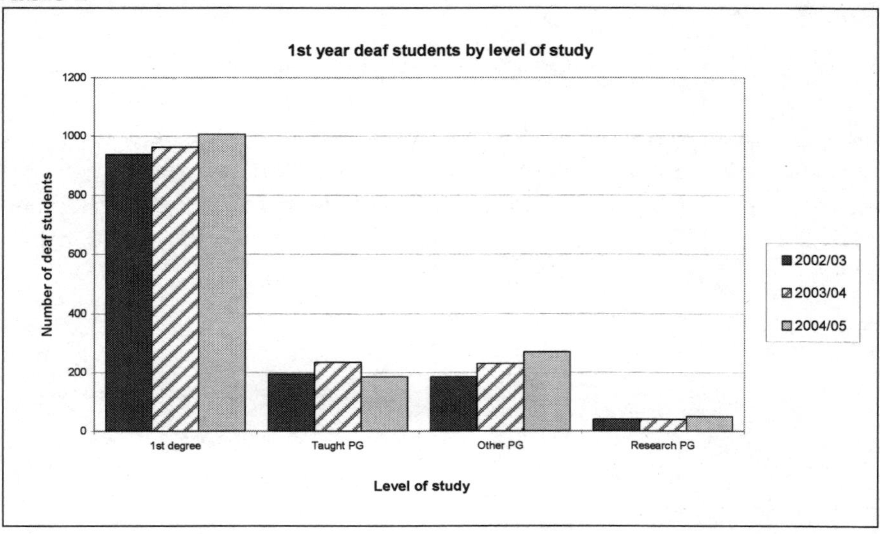

Source: HESA(Higher Education Statistics Agency) Student records 2002/3, 2003/4, 2004/5

Table 2

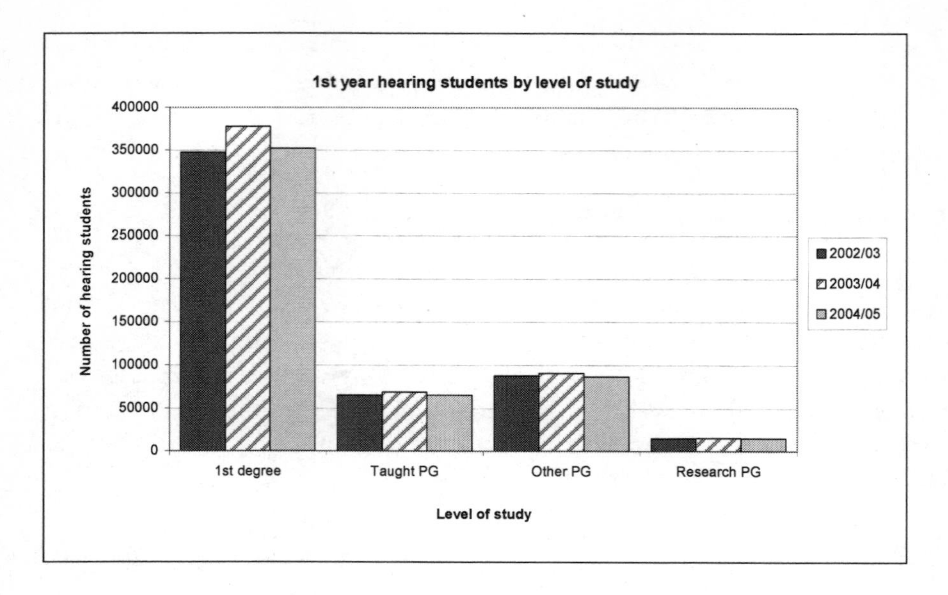

Source: HESA student records 2002/03, 20003/04, 2004/05

There is a more significant trend when we look at the percentage of deaf graduates who remain in Higher Education after graduation both as their main activity and combined with work. Just over 25% of deaf graduates opted for continuing study – a very similar pattern to other graduates.

Table 3

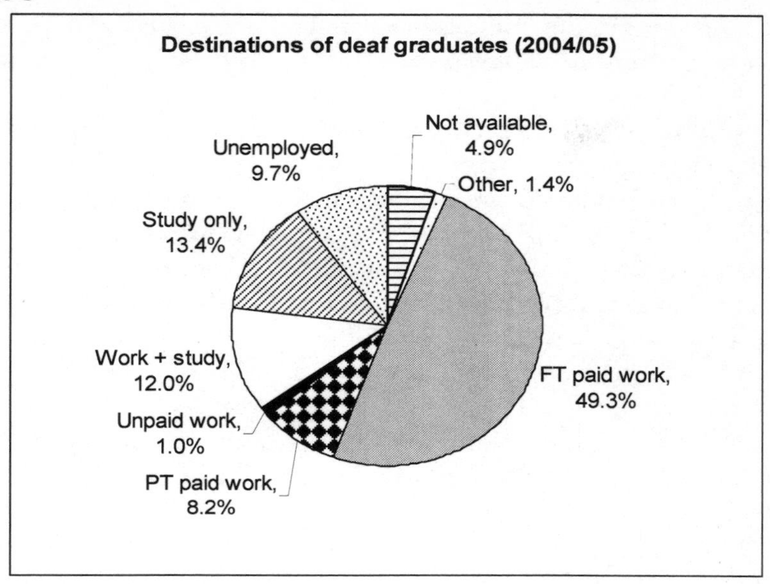

Source: What happens next? A report on the destinations of 2004 graduates with disabilities (AGCAS)

The year on year increase in the numbers of deaf students starting out in Higher Education suggests that, in the absence of significant barriers, there will be a similar increase in the numbers of deaf researchers. But that makes it all the more urgent to identify the potential hurdles and work towards a research community which understands and engages with deaf issues.

The nature of research

All those who took part in the research phase of the Premia project confirmed that their experiences as undergraduates were distinctly different from their lives as research students. The application process, the activities of research, the personnel who are crucial to their success, the nature of relationships with staff and the expectations of others defined those differences. For example, an application for a research degree often demands a complex written proposal which shows foreknowledge of the research process as well as its subject matter. A research supervisor monitors progress and interacts with a student very differently from a tutor marking and feeding back on an undergraduate essay. The planning and time management required to complete a PhD are far more complex than those needed in a first degree.

Taylor and Beasley (2005) state:

> 'Historically ...doctoral supervision has been based upon the assumption that, by virtue of having made it on to a doctoral programme, candidates would necessarily have the confidence to cope with its academic and social demands. This assumption was arguably always dubious, as demonstrated by high non-completion rates and long completion times two decades ago when the candidate population was highly elitist. But it is even more so in the context of a diverse population ... '.

The students who spoke about their experiences were studying at a range of UK universities, both traditional, research-intensive institutions and newer Higher Education Institutions where there were far fewer PhD candidates. They also represented a wide range of academic disciplines. What became clearer in the later stage of the project, particularly in the dissemination of the findings, was that the research community has been less exposed to disability and deaf awareness. It may not be a prominent concern where funding, status and academic recognition are likely to be priorities.

Deaf research students in subjects where there may have previously been very few deaf researchers may find themselves outside their usual zone and distant from a Deaf community within the institution. They may well be pioneers. But that role can be time-consuming and divert energies away from the concentrated, highly focussed sphere of the research project. The emphasis should rather be placed on the need for structural change in an academic environment where tradition has firmly helped to shape the structure.

The nature of barriers

Pre-entry

> 'A research PhD appeared to be based on few or no lectures, which makes it ideal for me as most of my work would be independent and any discussions one to one. It is group discussion or lecture rooms that create problems for me.'
> (A deaf PhD student)

When undergraduates are making decisions about life after graduation and the option of research study, each one needs to have clear, unambiguous information about: what it involves; where to go for advice and guidance; whether they have the skills and motivation to undertake research; how they apply and what will be expected of them. A deaf student needs additional information about the funding of support, the openness of the research community to deaf applicants, and whether research will present different issues from undergraduate study. They may also wish to seek advice about putting together a research proposal which will be a statement not just of their subject but also of their ability to express complex ideas fluently and effectively. All that information will ideally be placed within mainstream research education web pages and prospectuses.

Induction

> 'When I arrived at university, there was a series of introductory lectures and other lectures intended for research students. I skipped all of them except for the first one. The main reason was that any support I wanted (which would have been an audio typist) would have been a nightmare to get.' (A deaf PhD student)

The first few weeks of a research degree programme should enable the new student to acclimatise to the new and very different learning environment. It is when they discover what they can expect and what is expected of them. They will learn where to locate the central services like the library and IT support; the nature of the supervisory relationship; how to plan their research; the important milestones and the shape of research degrees. Additionally they meet their peers and have the opportunity to create informal support networks.

The funding of support for deaf and disabled postgraduate students in the UK does not mirror the process for undergraduates. There may be a time lag between being accepted on to a programme, being assessed for support requirements and then receiving funding. Institutions need to make interim arrangements to ensure that all students are able to participate fully in an introduction to research. Research can be an isolating experience. It is vital that students do not become more isolated because support is missing at this crucial early stage.

The language of research

> ' … people who are high up in academia do [….] use long words where I would use short ones. When they are doing this all the time in every sentence, it can take me ages to realise what they are saying because I am not used to these words being used. I found the theory rather difficult to take in at the start of my PhD and most of my colleagues tend to use very technical terms which are difficult to understand without knowing all the related theory. This was rather a vicious circle.'
> (A deaf PhD student)

The currency of the research community is the language it uses to exchange, explore and debate ideas. Ownership of that language is one of the keys to the academic kingdom. It gives status, validity and membership. It may be assumed by the community that the language of research will be acquired through discourse and reading. It will be absorbed incidentally by listening to academic staff and peers. The importance of this process should not be underestimated. Mastery is essential as Grix (2001) advises research students:

> 'If you command the basic vocabulary of generic research, you are far more likely to choose the correct theories, concepts or methods to use in your work. By grasping the core tools used in research, much of the mystery that can surround it begins to disappear.';

> '[...] knowledge of the 'nuts and bolts' that make (scholarship) up can go a long way to ensuring that the tools of research are used properly. If you have the right tools and you know how to employ them, the research process becomes a great deal easier and *quicker*.'

For deaf students the use of complex terminology can be a real barrier to understanding and to clear, unambiguous communication between tutor and learner; it can inhibit the development of a professional partnership between research supervisors and students and even the progress of the research project. Students, interpreters and communication support workers need to know the word but also to have a clear understanding of its meaning. Only then can it be spoken, interpreted, comprehended, absorbed and internalised.

Paul Haan, a BSL/English interpreter, wrote about this issue for the Premia resources:

> '[...] the supervisor and tutor need to bring the intended (denotative/connotative) meaning to the surface making it more accessible to the Deaf ...student. A good tutor will provide examples and analogies to unpack meaning (situate the example in real life). This goes a long way to supporting the interpreter and student and enhancing the learning experience. Once a concept or term is understood usually a Deaf student creates their own sign that can be used. This encapsulates the essence of the meaning and if embraced by the Deaf Community can become part of the BSL lexicon.'

While there are now comprehensive signed subject glossaries in existence to which students can be directed,[32] there remains a need for research supervisors and research skills developers to acknowledge and work with this potential barrier. It is a hurdle that may be presented at the outset in the selection interview and that can reappear right through to the viva. If subject terminology is not accessible, then the student can be stopped at the threshold. From the doorway, the research community can appear to be a very exclusive society.

Intensive reading

Anyone beginning supervision with a doctoral student will probably expect a level of reading corresponding to the highest level of study. It will be assumed that here is someone who can construct meaning from what they read; infer unstated meanings; assimilate learning; extrapolate arguments; draw conclusions; and relate the authors' ideas to their own hypotheses. The supervisor may also assume that students can do all this instinctively and efficiently.

Many research students will be used to skim reading, extracting key information and retaining it for use at a later date. They may be able to assess the relevance of the literature by rapidly scanning an index or the abstract of an academic paper. But the sheer volume of the reading required for a research degree – and the breadth and depth of that reading - may have an impact on deaf students. Supervisors may anticipate that deaf people arriving at doctoral study are functioning at a

[32] http://artsigns.ac.uk/, http://www.sciencesigns.ac.uk/default.asp and http://www.engineeringsigns.ac.uk/home_glossary.asp (Accessed July 2006)

relatively advanced level. However, reading may remain a difficult and time-consuming task for some deaf students.

One research student described a book list they given by a supervisor as taller than them and very daunting. But research supervisors and language support workers can demystify this formidable task by helping the student to prioritise their reading; by identifying key texts which really are essential reading; by assisting the student to devise reading plans which are realistic and achievable - and regularly reviewing the schedule with the student; by locating journal articles and signposting a student to them; by confirming with students in supervision meetings that they are interpreting the meaning of the literature effectively. None of these interventions need undermine the student's autonomy or academic standards. They simply create parity.

Writing the thesis

There is a huge step to be taken when students commit their ideas to paper. Every academic writer knows something of the uncertainty: fears about how the work will be received; indecision about phraseology; doubts about conveying adequately in words what has been reflected on for months or years; apprehension about the ability to do justice to the subject matter.

We can perhaps add to that list a fear of criticism. How much more are those uncertainties increased if there are difficulties with sentence structure, spelling and confident use of an academic style?:

> 'The issues are […] having confidence in my English skills. Are they up to academic level? Has my poor school education affected me in later life, especially grammar? If I do not meet academic levels, will this be related to being Deaf or that I simply do not meet the required standards?'
> (A deaf PhD student)

A deaf doctoral candidate who was about to enter the writing up phase of their PhD said:

> 'Not surprisingly my written English and grammar are poor. … I felt it took me longer to write my first year literature review report than it did take my hearing peers and I had to rely on my partner to make grammar corrections. I have concerns that my thesis may take longer than usual.'

A research environment, whatever the discipline, is a world where language is the only accepted means for the communication and dissemination of ideas. Whatever additional gifts and insights a student may bring, language is the medium they must use to demonstrate those gifts and insights. So how can research and support staff assist deaf students with written language difficulties to communicate through their thesis the findings of their research? How too can deaf researchers make sure that they efficiently manage the production of their theses?

Supervisors need to encourage students to start writing from the outset of their research. Supervision meetings can be used to plan out a writing schedule with agreed targets for the next meeting. This emphasis on writing things down means that students can build up their confidence gradually. The students learn in stages about writing style and the construction of a complex written argument. They also acquire the discipline of writing which will serve them well when they come to the 'writing up' phase. Supervisors can also encourage the production of chapters from year one which removes the time pressures that can affect the quality of the writing.

Early intervention by language or learning support tutors and/or disability advisers can result in the funding of proof-reading from the beginning, freeing supervisors to give feedback on the quality of the structure and content. It also enables the supervisor to concentrate on the positive features of the work, while at the same time giving constructive feedback on areas for development. It means that potential difficulties which could have an impact on successful completion are identified and addressed promptly.

Academic networking

Informal and formal networking is the life-blood of academia. Advice given to students in handbooks and the literature is to establish their own informal networks while participating in formal ones like professional associations and conferences. Such networking can counteract isolation, stimulate and motivate by placing individual research in a wider context. It can create opportunities for attending conferences and giving papers and develop skills which will enhance employability.

Effective networking demands strong written and spoken communication. It also needs the student to be confident and assertive, ready to maximise opportunities for the exchange of knowledge and ideas. Above all, it requires recognition by the student that they have something of worth to contribute.

No-one feels entirely comfortable meeting strangers for the first time. But there are strategies for enabling deaf students to develop networks. Supervisors can let students know about email professional lists; introduce students directly to people in their own networks; help to set up meetings with individuals and, with the student's permission, prepare the contact for the meeting – explaining, for example, that the student will come with an interpreter or lip-speaker and how to manage communication. Supervisors can prepare the student for a seminar at which they are expected to contribute; encourage the student to participate in research and generic skills development programmes in-house or regionally in the UK through the UK GRAD programme.[33] These strategies will help the student to create informal networks in and outside the institution. In turn these networks can help keep problems in perspective and counteract personal and intellectual isolation.

Access to informal learning

> 'With my PhD everyone goes for a coffee break twice a day. It's a big room. We call it the conference room and it has rows of chairs that face each other. People just sit on these. The couple of people opposite me – I can hear them. But as all the teams tend to sit together in big groups, I am just lost so I don't bother going for coffee. They probably think I am a bit anti-social.'
> (A deaf PhD student)

In research, perhaps more than in any other level of study in Higher Education, informal and incidental learning opportunities abound. Learning from peers in social and work-based settings, networking within the institution and across interdisciplinary academic teams all contribute to a vibrant learning community.

The exchange of ideas, methods and knowledge can take place in shared offices or laboratories and in everyday social settings. If those places and opportunities are inaccessible, then the whole research experience is narrower and is defined by its boundaries.

It is important that, when support requirements are assessed, access to the whole research environment is considered. For example, can the student be enabled to communicate with other members of a research team in informal settings as well as more formal team meetings? Are shared offices arranged to make communication possible? Are all members of the team aware of how to communicate effectively? Is

[33] UK GRAD Programme can be found at www.grad.ac.uk (Accessed June 2006)

equipment in place to maximise communication? Are there other forums, like email lists, for research students to exchange ideas and discuss their research?

Managing the viva

> 'The last viva I had was with [an examiner from another European country]. I chatted to them off and on about my project throughout the year and I never understood a word they said. I was terrified about the viva but I got through it. There was a moderator, my supervisor and this person [. . .] Every time I couldn't understand them, I would just say so and they would repeat it. Occasionally my supervisor would chip in and repeat what they said. This person also had a habit of starting the question, carrying on and talking about their opinion on something and then just looking at me questioningly. I had real trouble understanding the question.
>
> [. . .] If I can get through that, I can get through anything.'
> (A deaf PhD student)

> 'You need a fluent signer to be the examiner.'
> (A deaf PhD student)

The final hurdle for all students in the UK who are examined by thesis is the viva voce. This is the oral defence by a candidate of their thesis, where the candidate faces examiners, at least one of whom is external to the institution. For some deaf doctoral students this form of examination will present additional challenges and anxieties – challenges that hearing candidates do not face. One of them may be the examiners' unease with communication methods outside their experience. Another may be a university's discomfort about making adjustments to a process which has been honed by tradition and institutional practice.

The viva assesses a student's ability to place their research in the broader context, identify its contribution to knowledge, show detailed knowledge of the thesis and prove that it is the student's own work. During the viva examiners expect the candidate to defend their methodology and findings of the thesis, as well to be aware of their limitations. If it is to be an opportunity for the candidate to demonstrate all those facets, not only the student but also the examiners and interpreters need to be well-prepared and confident in the process.

For example, the key adjustment for a BSL user is the use of an interpreter within the viva. However, that adjustment will only work if all the participants in the viva are confident with and in the interpretation process. The interpreter(s) needs to know the content and context of the viva and subject terminology if the communication is to be effective. The examiners and chair need to know how to work with the interpreter. The student needs to be confident that the interpreter has sufficiently high level signing skills to be able to function in this academic context and that the examiners know how to manage communication.

Examiners will have to be prepared to work with two interpreters, who will change over during the course of the viva, or agree breaks. Each interpreter will need to know the subject terminology; examiners will have to be ready to explain and unpack the meaning of their words during the viva.

It is vital that planning for the viva is a collaboration involving all the interested parties – student, main supervisor, interpreter, disability/deaf students' adviser, administrator, the chair of the panel, external examiner. While one co-ordinator manages the planning, all need to be informed and confident in the arrangements.

Funding

Many of the adjustments suggested throughout this chapter will carry with them financial cost. The use of interpreters, communication support workers and language support tutors need significant funding. The current funding available to deaf postgraduate students in the UK who are **not** in receipt of a bursary from a research council is capped at a level much lower than the undergraduate DSA (Disabled Students' Allowances). Only a small proportion of postgraduate research students are supported by the Research Councils and are entitled to DSA at a similar level to the local authorities' undergraduate DSA.

This anomaly may be the main barrier to deaf graduates' participation in research. Structural, environmental and attitudinal changes are all achievable. The research culture is increasingly diverse and there are external pressures to encourage diversity. However local authority funding to meet the support requirements of deaf researchers is inadequate. Without a shift in policy it is difficult to envisage a major growth in the numbers of deaf researchers.

Conclusion

> 'Although I am more than capable at the academic and teaching part, I do need support, and if that isn't in place, I am not efficient or capable. I am, indeed, disabled! There is a very tacit but very real pressure never to admit this and to stay strong, to put on a mask and pretend that all is well. It is a big issue for me and one that I negotiate on a daily basis.'
> (A hearing PhD student)

This student is not deaf, but they draw attention to the very competitive nature of a research career, the emphasis on independence and self-direction. There can be a tension between the need for autonomy which is inherent in research study and the requirement for support. There are growing numbers of deaf and disabled researchers who are setting precedents and demonstrating the immense value of diversity to the research community. Inclusion means that the best intellectual talent is available to academic institutions.

Summary

- The challenges to all students presented by research education are different from undergraduate or taught postgraduate courses;
- The nature of research activities demands self-direction and the research community values autonomy. But deaf research students have requirements for support to enable them to become independent learners;
- Institutions need to be aware of the responsibility to support deaf researchers;
- Research supervisors are key figures in the research students' experience. They may need support through staff development in supervising deaf researchers;
- Current DSA funding of postgraduate research students available through local authorities may fall short in meeting the requirements of deaf research students;
- The whole research environment includes informal learning places, national and international conferences, skills development programmes and academic networks. Access to research needs to encompass these other places;
- The research community can be enriched and enlivened by the diversity of its members.

Further reading

Christie, F., Leacy, A. and Tunnah, E. 2006 *What happens next? A report on the destinations of 2004 graduates with disabilities.* AGCAS.

Grix, J. 2001 *Demystifying postgraduate research.* Birmingham, Birmingham University Press

Haan, P. June 2006 *Premia Resource Base.* Accessed at:http://www.premia.ac.uk.

HESA (Higher Education Statistics Agency Ltd) June 2006 'Student records 2002/3. 2003/4, 2004/05' Accessed at www.hesa.ac.uk

McAlpine, L. & Norton, J. 2006 'Reframing our approach to doctoral programs: an integrative framework for action and research' *Higher Education Research and Development* 25, 1: 3-17

Pearson, M. & Kayrooz, C. 2004 'Enabling critical reflection on research supervisory practice' *International Journal for Academic Development* 9, 1: 99-116

Phillips, E. and Pugh, D. 2005 *How to get a PhD.* 4th edition Buckingham, Open University Press.

Premia Resource Base – resources for research and support staff and for deaf and disabled research students. http://www.premia.ac.uk

Rugg, G. and Petre, M. 2004 *The unwritten rules of PhD research* London, Palgrave.

Taylor, S. & Beasley, N. 2005 *A handbook for doctoral supervisors.* London, Routledge.

CHAPTER FOURTEEN

The loneliness of the long-distance post-graduate research student

Dr Steve Emery

Is it worth it … really?

The following chapter is an account of my experiences as a post-graduate student at the University of Central Lancashire (UCLan), where I undertook a doctoral thesis on *Citizenship and the Deaf Community*. I began this just after the 2002 football World Cup had finished, and the thesis was completed just as the 2006 World Cup drew to a close. I make this point for, as the title suggests, this has been a long and lonely journey, not to mention an arduous one. I have often asked myself, 'Iis it worth it … really?'. My life has been centred on my thesis during these four years, but there were lots of dramatic news and life events. During this period I've moved from Wexford to Preston to Manchester to Edinburgh; and other personal events have happened, some exciting, others stressful.

In spite of all the ups and downs, I have continued to work on my doctoral thesis. I had many means to keep me going. There is one, in particular, that I had not realized was also a way to keep the PhD student (or PhD Candidate as they often say) ticking over. It is Butterworth (1998) who advises, in *I did a PhD and did NOT go mad*: 'if all else fails, eat chocolate'.

The secret is out!! Butterworth continues:

> 'There is no problem known to science that cannot be cured by the liberal application of chocolate. Leading doctors have testified

> to its mystical curative powers -- it is known to contain all sorts of wholesome, bracing chemicals that get straight to the happiness centres of your brain and get them working at full pitch, scattering love and joy and contentment all through your cortex.' (Butterworth 1998)

It didn't quite work that way, but you get my point? I ate chocolate, lots of it (it was certainly more than a 'liberal' amount) and people were saying to me recently: 'crickey, you've put on weight'. And I did, it's true. I thank my friends though for buying me lots of chocolate presents, to keep me going.

At this point I have to pause for thought, because I haven't yet sat the viva as I write this article (although I have submitted and the examination is soon to come).[34] In the context of 'going mad', however, effects on my mental health have been apparent, so while concepts such as 'madness' and 'crazy' are meant in jest, there are potentially real effects. This statement is not meant to alarm the reader, since everyone will be affected differently to the pressures of undertaking a PhD, but this reminds the post-graduate student to be aware and take care.

Reading up on information about doing a PhD seems designed to put one off from doing it. The work I read on the subject of undertaking a doctorate thesis tends to reflect on the potential problems and pitfalls that can arise. This is an example, written by Howard (2004):

> 'Perhaps the very first question you should be asking is if you really should do a PhD. It's hard work, expensive if you don't get funding, will eat several years of your life and probably drive you half crazy in the process.'

Hmmm, encouraging! At a website that I visited in June 2006 (43things.com) 352 people listed that they wanted to 'finish my PhD' (which had increased to 438 by November 2006). Looking at the site, one man has his face covering his hands stating 'I did it', which seems to be a symbol of what the post-graduate student is letting themselves in for.

With all those health hazard warnings it is a wonder so many people take on the task. I therefore hope that this chapter will give an insight into some of the issues that the post-graduate student may be faced with.

---

[34] Editor's note: Steve Emery was awarded his PhD in 2007 soon after completing this chapter

At the same time I will reflect on a personal process and journey that as unique to me, which is to suggest that each student will have their own way of getting through theirs.

Forever running – battling at citizenship while working in research

Throughout this chapter I will interrupt the narrative with examples (indicated as 'narrative-interruptions') of the ways in which Deaf communities are engaged in struggles for citizenship rights. This seems appropriate, as the focus of my PhD is on citizenship and I was also, sometimes directly, involved in these struggles. Their relevance within this chapter may not always be apparent in a personal account of undertaking a PhD, but they are important to me in a significant sense. These kinds of issues and events provided a 'distraction' to me all the while I was undertaking post-graduate studies. They represent a stark reminder of the reality of Deaf lives; the practical ways in which the quest for citizenship is expressed.

The first 'narrative-interruption' concerns the story of UCLan students who, in late 2002, leafleted the university management demanding that more sign language interpreters be employed by the university. This action caught the attention of the local media and a full page article highlighted the issue. There was a photograph published of Deaf students caught jumping in celebration of this success. The management of UCLan agreed to some of the most important demands and the Deaf Students' Society forged stronger links with the National Union of Students. The action highlights that citizenship is not something confined to a narrow focus on elections or organized demonstrations that have the agreement of authorities – it can arise spontaneously, and take on forms that protestors define, including direct action. In my research on citizenship I was therefore constantly reminded of the need to think of citizenship in the context of power relations in society. My PhD research was therefore informed by such actions, and not only on a reading of the literature or empirical research.

So … on becoming a PhD student/candidate

How did I get started on doing a PhD? This is a question I am commonly asked, and so it seems a good opportunity to cover this here. A studentship on *Citizenship and Deafness* was advertised in the *Guardian* newspaper and the Deaf-UK e-group network, and I decided to apply. It was funded for three years – the grant advertised was nearly £8,000 per annum but it was tax free and there was exemption from having to pay national insurance – plus the grant would cover all tuition fee costs. I didn't live the 'life of riley' so felt confident I could cope with a low annual income. These costs do not include funding for interpreters and access – I will return to this later – but a fund of £1,500 was provided to pay for books and other important expenses, such as travel costs while undertaking fieldwork.

I had applied for an MPhil/PhD, so I enrolled as an MPhil student and eventually transferred to a PhD; it was always my aim to have a crack at a PhD but at the time I was open-minded about whether I would apply for a transfer. My aim was to go three years (or more) trying for a PhD, but I was unsure if I could really go all the way. A lot would depend on whether an original piece of work could be produced.

Applying for a studentship is not the only route to getting into PhD research – if you have a strong desire to research something that is close to your heart, you can write up a proposal and send it to a university where you would like to do the research (or be supervised). Different universities have different criteria – for example, when I was thinking of applying for a PhD at the end of the 1990s, Bristol University required potential students to write a 3,000 word essay proposal. If the university accept the proposal and you have a supervisor willing to see you through it, then it would be a question of getting funding – either from the university you apply to, a body willing and able to provide the funds, or more likely from your own pocket. My funding was provided by UCLan. Research studentships are advertised fairly regularly, although they tend to be related to psychological or medical research in the case of deafness, or are narrowed down to a specific area – in my case citizenship and deafness. I therefore consider myself extremely fortunate in this respect, in that citizenship is, to me, a politically related concept, and that is an area I enjoy exploring.

I was also fortunate to have a group of supervisors who were flexible enough to allow me to pursue the topic within frameworks and methods that I wanted to use. They were eager to see me follow an independent line of work and they would supervise and advise me all the way. Luckily, too, they have been there from the very beginning, and remain there...to...the...bitter...end (signed with stiff hands, or with clenched teeth if you are hearing) as I strive to finish it.

Having fun

It was, of course, also possible to have fun, and the post-graduate student should seek out opportunities to take time out from their post-graduate studies. I got onto the 'Preston Vicar's' Quiz team, and headed for the competition at Manchester Deaf Club with Deaf students from other universities. For those who don't know, the sign for Preston is the same as 'vicar' because of the existence of numerous practices for religious worship in the city. And so it was that we dressed in black shirts and folded white paper round our necks in true 'dog collar' fashion. I didn't top our group for knowledge, that accolade was held by a first year undergraduate student. There seemed some expectations of me as a PhD student – but in fact everyone else knew just as much as I did regarding answers to the questions. Our supporters, who came in numbers and proudly displayed the Preston banner, were ordered to stand behind us after (false of course) accusations of feeding us answers! The rowdiness was a joy to behold; total chaos, marvellous! We won our heat (to great acclaim) but didn't receive as many points as the other two groups that won, so didn't make the final, but a good time was had by all nevertheless.

Narrative-interruption: the recognition of British Sign Language (BSL) – a great advance towards equal citizenship rights … or was it?

British Sign Language was acknowledged to be a language by the UK government just five months (18 March 2003) after I had began my PhD, but my celebrations were on hold, and I know several others were also not celebrating. Not only was it uncertain that the recognition statement released by the government would lead to long term change, but the bombing of Baghdad began the following day. How could I celebrate the achievement of recognition (which had been the result of demonstrations and campaigns) knowing that a far more devastating event was occurring in another part of the world? Myself and others took part in the demonstrations against the US/UK intervention in Iraq. As two million people took part in the London march on 15 February 2003 (one of a number of simultaneous protests around the world), myself and three friends were present at the largest demonstration ever seen in Glasgow, where Tony Blair was addressing a Scottish Labour Party conference. At other times I also took part in several further demonstrations against the Iraq war.

In July 2003 I was a steward on the large march held in London to celebrate BSL recognition … but the main positive memories of celebration were those held on the anniversary of the government statement announcement. On the first anniversary of the statement, an evening of celebration was held, and Deaf people from the north-west gathered in a pub in Preston. We watched Sky television broadcast a special programme to commemorate the event. In 2005, a one-day BDA conference was held, again in Preston; the following year an evening of signed poetry and drama was put on by UCLan. Although disappointed that the recognition was weak and coincided with a horrific war, these events are nevertheless an inspiration and reminder that taking action (and being an active citizen) does sometimes lead to government action.

Without effective supervision … forget it

I cannot stress enough how vital supervision is to the whole process of doing a PhD. It is vital to make sure your supervisor is going to be there, from the birth of the thesis to its 'death'. Of course, it may well happen that something will change that means you will have to discontinue seeing your appointed supervisor – so then make sure you have the means to continue with other supervisors thereafter. If this can't be done, forget about doing a PhD. Look elsewhere. Move on. Forget you ever thought about it. Look for another job. Try to improve your existing job. Go see the world. Or do something else, anything, because supervision really is that important. Don't take my word for it – ask others.

Supervisors – Deaf issues, hearing issues

As I write this, there are very few Deaf people in the UK who hold a PhD; the numbers of hearing people who have a PhD in a Deaf-related field are far larger. I did ask one of the few Deaf academics if it was possible to offer me supervisory support, but a heavy work commitments meant it was could not be guaranteed. I was, however, encouraged when the academic reassured me that I would make progress. This encouragement was given on the basis of reading a presentation I had given and was an important boost to my confidence. I was still fortunate to have a team of three supervisors, one of whom has a vast experience of academic work in the field of Deaf Studies, another with experience of research and supervising other PhD students, and a third who obtained his PhD on citizenship (and has also written books and articles on the subject). At different stages throughout the life of my PhD, all three had varying degrees of input. Towards the end, when the key supervisor left to work at a different university (but who continued to offer supervision support), another person was asked to be part of the supervisory team. All in all, therefore, this worked very well. My leading supervisor was fluent in BSL, and while the others weren't, they were experienced in their area of expertise and that was just as important as to whether or not they could use sign language.

So what was supervision like … really?

The importance of supervision cannot be expressed enough in words. I'm working alone, so supervision is virtually the only measure I have of knowing that I'm on the right track. Supervision sessions could be nerve-wracking experiences. Often my expectations of meetings varied – i.e. at the beginning of the research I expected detailed questioning of the subject and prepared on this basis, but the meetings were mainly to ensure I was clear in myself what I was doing. Questions were focussed on issues such as: what I would read, what I would look for, how I would go about fieldwork research, and what timetable I would use, and so on. During the early period it was a case of being organised, having a timetable, for example, and to consider other duties I could be involved with (such as lecturing, assisting with setting up workshops, attending conferences, giving papers, going to research lectures).

During the literature review stage (that is to say the first six to twelve months) I would read and write down ideas, search for articles and literature on citizenship, soon this moved on to submitting written work, and towards the end I was given detailed critiques of my written work. However well I felt I had prepared for academic criticism, it sometimes felt very hard to take. I learnt that a vital part of doing a PhD was to be open to listening and responding to criticism. One of the most surprising experiences was consistently being asked to take greater care with how I used language. It was pointed out to me that the PhD was weakened if the language was not 'tight' (i.e. academic) because this would leave the thesis open to sharper criticism.

Narrative-interruption: Citizenship – life or death and the right to remain in the UK

Two Deaf young people and their families were threatened with deportation in the summer of 2004 and a campaign was started on their behalf by activists in Manchester, where the two were staying. They and their families were threatened with violence if they returned to their homeland. Lively meetings were held to organise support for the two young Deaf people. People would converge on the court when their case was heard. Petitioning was organised and took place in Manchester on some Saturdays; I was involved in some of these actions, and drew on my experience of petitioning over similar issues in the 1980s. The general consensus in the UK does seem to be non-supportive of asylum seekers if the tabloid press are to be believed; but in my experience, there is also a large number of people who are prepared to be supportive and sign their signature onto a petition. This particular case no doubt benefited from the support of the campaign team and those involved with it; eventually the campaign was successful and the two young people were allowed to stay in the UK.

Access issues

Obviously as a post-graduate student there are several key meetings and events I would need to attend for which a sign language interpreter is necessary – supervision meetings, courses, conferences or seminars, and so on. I may also have required a notetaker on some occasions. There are Disabled Student's Allowances (DSA) available for post-graduate students which is roughly one-third of that of an undergraduate entitlement. I have come across several D/deaf people who have simply been unable to continue their post-graduate studies because this funding is insufficient for their access needs. UCLan recognised my need for more funding after I drew up a projection of my annual support needs and associated costs and they kindly agreed to top up the funds to the same level as the undergraduate entitlement. To my shock, I was then informed that if UCLan matched DSA monies those administering DSA funds would withdraw their allocation! Talk about pulling the rug from under your feet – that's supposed to make people laugh, but it wasn't funny.

UCLan management, however, to their credit, eventually agreed to provide sufficient funding to ensure all access costs were paid – particularly sign language interpreting costs. The total they agreed to provide was the same as the annual undergraduate DSA entitlement.[35] I do know of one other university which has agreed to fund, in full, a Deaf post-graduate student's access allowance. Whether any more than the minimum legitimate DSA funding is obtained will, therefore, depend on the individual university agreeing to meet *all* access costs; i.e. they can't simply top up on what DSA the post-graduate student receives. Legislation could increase DSA funding or the university could become legally-bound to pay for all access needs, but as of 2007 there seems little likelihood of that happening.

---

[35] Details of the amounts available through DSA are given at the end of this chapter

Implications of taking on the research … issues of empowerment

The methods that I used to undertake my research on citizenship do, arguably, demonstrate a commitment to the community I am a member of. The framework is empowering research, and I use a critical discourse analysis perspective; these are tools created and established by mainstream academia but which have rarely been used within research in Deaf communities. The way in which I have approached the research and carried it out do, I suggest, demonstrate some involvement of the community in the research. I have given an interpretation of the findings, so it remains to be seen how the research is received, as due to following empowering methods I am still in the process of feeding back to those who were interviewed for the research.

It feels to me that I will 'live or die' by what I have produced in my doctoral thesis. I will only know that, however, if I involve and report to the community with whom I am engaged in research. The community, surely, has some right to know what is being made of the information that has been collated in their name.

Issues related to the research process

I am continuously asking myself: is the research I'm doing 'worthwhile'; does it meet PhD criteria?; could I be doing it differently?; and all kinds of similar questions. That is when it can be a lonely process, for ultimately only I am able to answer these questions. I have never understood or overcome the question of whether all angles of my argument have been covered; but ultimately, there always seemed to be more I could be doing. Eventually something struck me: what I was doing must be akin to writing a book. This was a very strange feeling to have had. I had always wanted to write a publication for it is a lifelong ambition but although I made several attempts to start doing so in the past, these were works intended to be fiction … and they never materialised. Eighteen months into the PhD I realise I'm writing a book, right now! That is because the thesis I am writing has to be of 80,000 words (since it is within the sphere of social science), a book-length in itself. When attempting works of fiction I prepared myself for writing by reading several 'how to write …' books and I seemed to be going through processes that I had read about within these works. The feeling of loneliness is the obvious one, but there are also times when, for example, I just cannot think of anything to write, and spend hours staring at a blank sheet of paper, or scribbling notes that lead no-where. At other times I would be unable to feel I could stop, working well into the night (during one crazy period I went three full nights without any sleep – definitely not recommended!) If I was writing and I had a strong hunch urging me to carry on, but then stopped, I would find it very hard to get back into what I had started to write – and so I continued.

Being a research student and beyond – issues of power

I have already mentioned the issue of responsibility to Deaf communities; how important is it to be conscious of the role as a (Deaf) researcher working on research in the Deaf community? Certainly I feel that as a student undertaking qualitative research this is particularly vital, and may even be so if I was carrying out quantitative research too. The researcher (who on completion of a PhD will then be categorised as an 'expert' on the topic), carries out research and if a doctorate or MPhil is awarded, he or she becomes a recognised 'authority' on their subject. This is the case whether the researcher wants such a label or not. With the title of 'Dr', society looks at the person as being somehow different from others; they will hold that bit more power. In this case the research has involved and included members of a minority community, many of whom are known and will continue to be known by me. I stress this because it is something that I was always conscious of, and therefore that duality of purpose I wrote of earlier meant two things – firstly, the attainment of a PhD in the UK is a recognised individual achievement; but that secondly, it matters also to a community who (as my research indicates!) continue to feel second class citizens. It is of course possible to state: this is what I have done, it is my work, and I have worked hard to achieve it. There is also the possibility that such work simply would not have been possible without:

- work that has been done previously on the subject by others;
- the input of those who agreed to take part in the research

In that sense the researcher, arguably, has a responsibility to share such work and not take it upon him or herself to present an 'it's-mine-all-mine' in the name of the community in question.

A good example of how it is easy to slide into such a state came when I recently presented at a conference on the minority linguistic status of the Deaf community. The audience was entirely hearing (save for one other Deaf person), many of whom had possibly not come across the concept of sign language as a language previously. It struck me just how fortunate I was in being able to present this subject: I was coming from a basis that has already begun to gain influence thanks to the work that others have carried out in the previous 30 or so years. Often they were in a far more isolating situation and were having to argue their case in the face of robust opposition. It is also very easy, in these circumstances, to come across as the sole and prevailing 'expert' on Deaf issues. I am the only deaf person there, with no-one to contradict anything I claim as the truth and so I can (supposedly) sign what I like. As is so commonly my experience, just being there and signing (never mind what the content of the presentation is), is a powerful message all by itself; but it is equally important to feed back or stay tuned in with the community, to ensure dialogue remains.

These issues relate to questions of power – what becomes acknowledged epistemology within the field of Deaf Studies, who is seen as representatives of this knowledge, and how do they become to hold this position. In other words, it goes beyond an issue of research methodology and power, and into the boundaries of politics.

This is partly why I used a Critical Discourse Analysis (CDA) approach (van Dijk 1993); there are a number of different approaches to CDA, but the one I adopted was that which made explicit the power relationships that formed the background to the study. CDA has itself come in for sharp criticisms from academics; unfortunately space limits me from exploring this topic in depth here, but see Toolan (1997) for an example. My intention in using CDA was to carry out rigorous research but at the same time not to leave issues of power and method untouched. It was hard to believe research could be entirely neutral when one reads Lane's (1999) outline of psychological research that has typically been carried out *on* Deaf people and supposed to be quantitative (and therefore scientific, empirical, factual and impartial).

A doctoral thesis is an apprenticeship to becoming a trained researcher. I was using a qualitative research approach, which entails seeking to ensure the methods I use are rigorously applied, so as to become robust and valid within the research community. That is why the mix of empowering research methods also appealed – and it then remained for me to use and work with these in the real world of the Deaf community.

Narrative-interruption: Appealing to the trade union movement – citizenship within social movements

A motion went before a large union conference in the summer of 2004 and this was of particular interest to me personally because I had been involved with trade unions prior to becoming a research student. The motion was to propose more research be undertaken on cochlear implants, particularly in light of the fact that their fitting had been responsible for the death of several children (who had contacted meningitis on being fitted with an implant). Only one Deaf person would be at the entire conference of 3,000 elected delegates, so I decided to go along and report on this as a representative of the Federation of Deaf People (FDP). The entire conference was accessible via the provision of sign language interpreters for all sessions; and all screens showed subtitles too. The person proposing the motion was supported by the disabled section of the trade union, as he had been delegated to attend from the disabled members' conference. He signed at the conference, and the motion was opposed by some delegates, but won an overwhelming majority of the conference. I wrote a report for the Voice magazine on this occasion and was proud to be there where history was in the making, as nothing like this had ever been attempted before. I do recognise that the Deaf delegate had support from the disabled members group (as well as other Deaf people within the Deaf community), but he was just one Deaf person, and look what he had achieved, as the only Deaf delegate there!

In conclusion

In this article I hope to have shown, in perhaps a small way, the experiences of being a Deaf post-graduate student. I have charted my process of accepting the research studentship, the importance of supervision, and some of the issues I deem to be important in the process. In between giving these outlines, I have also told some stories, where I have witnessed a variety of political events, as well as having taken part in some of these. It is perhaps ironic that the title of my thesis is on citizenship – and here I have demonstrated how I am as a Deaf citizen in the UK of the twentieth-first century. There is much more research to be undertaken, to collect and collate material, to build up a 'Deaf epistemology', and I hope the account of my experiences in this chapter will have added to this growing body of knowledge.

Summary – ten key issues to consider

1. Ensure the topic you choose to research is something that you are enthusiastic about – enough to spend at least three years full time or six years part time studying.

2. It is extremely vital to find a supervisor you respect and can work with over the course of the doctorate – consider having a 'back-up' in place in case your agreed supervisor has to stop for some reason.

3. Do give thought to issues of access to your research findings – how will the Deaf community learn about your research?
4. Have a network of friends/family to support you for the duration of the study; people who you trust and can turn to in times of crisis.

5. Make a plan of action or draw up a timetable for the research – and discipline yourself to follow this as strictly as possible; even if you know this won't be strictly followed, you can always re-write it.

6. Take up offers to present your research, particularly to other research students – this will enable you to receive feedback and give you a good idea of how your research is progressing.

7. Agree to teach when possible, as this will encourage you to keep abreast of the broader issues relevant to your research – but do try to avoid doing too much (be assertive and say 'no' if necessary!).

8. Ensure you have healthy distractions, such as a hobby, for example.

9. If it seems that the study is getting on top of you do not hesitate to take time out – you should ensure you take regular breaks.

10. Treat yourself regularly, especially when achieving goals or obtaining results.

And if all that fails … eat chocolate.

Note
There is one single maximum allowance for post-graduate students to cover all access costs available and totals £5,780 for the 2006-2007 academic year and increases to £5,915 for the 2007-2008 academic year. This should be contrasted with a maximum £18,965 that a full-time undergraduate can claim during the 2007-2008 academic year (which includes specialist equipment, non-medical help – which would cover sign language interpreting and is £12, 420 of the total cost – and general disabled students' allowances). Source: http://www.direct.gov.uk (widest

range of government information and services online) © Crown Copyright.

Further reading

43things.com 2005 'Finish my PhD'. [online] http://www.43things.com/things/view/14 [cited 25 November 2006]

Bell, J. 2005 *Doing your research project: a guide for first-time researchers in education, health and social science.* (4th ed). Maidenhead, Open University Press

Butterworth, R. 1998 'I did a PhD and did NOT go mad'. [online]. Middlesex University, London. http://www.cs.mdx.ac.uk/staffpages/richardb/PhDtalk.html [cited 25 November 2006]

Cameron, D., Frazer, E., Harvey, P., Rampton, M. B. H., & Richardson, K. (Eds.) 1992 *Researching language: issues of power and method.* London, Routledge

Eisenberg, S. 2006 'Chocoholics unite!' *This green life.* National Resources Defense Council Newsletter. [internet]. February http://www.nrdc.org/thisgreenlife/0602.asp [cited 25 November 2006].

Howard, S. 2004 'Planning to do a PhD in History?' [online]. Posted on 28 September 2004, 11.18pm http://www.earlymodernweb.org.uk/emn/index.php/archives/2004/09/planning-to-do-a-phd-in-history/ [cited 25 November 2006]

Ladd, P. 2003 *Understanding deaf culture: in search of Deafhood.* Clevedon, Multilingual Matters

Lane, H. 1999 *The mask of benevolence: disabling the deaf community.* San Diego CA, DawnSignPress

Phillips, E., & Pugh, D. S. 2001 *How to get a PhD: A handbook for supervisors and their students.* (3rd ed) Buckingham, Open University Press

Sillitoe, A., 1959 *The loneliness of the long-distance runner.* London, Pan Books

Toolan, M., 1997. 'What is critical discourse analysis and why are people saying such terrible things about it?' *Language and literature.* 6, 2: 83-103.

van Dijk, T. A., 1993. 'Principles of critical discourse analysis' *Discourse and Society* 4, 2: 249-283.

Conclusion: Where to next?

CHAPTER FIFTEEN

Developing services and inclusive practices for deaf students

Jannine Williams and Hayley Quinn

Introduction

Within this chapter we will first consider the key drivers in the development of services for deaf students, review the development of disability studies and the social model of disability before considering what a narrative approach to researching deaf students' experiences in Higher Education can offer. Being both Disability Advisers and deaf students ourselves we have supported the development of, and participated in, many student feedback and survey exercises which were generally based upon the social model of disability, emphasising the environmental and social barriers faced by deaf students. However, we felt such approaches did not seem to capture the richness of our experiences as students or the complexity of the observations we had made in our working roles. This interest has drawn us to explore alternative ways of researching deaf student experiences to inform our professional practices and other student involvement activities, and thus we were drawn to the literature on disability studies and narrative inquiry.

In doing so, we hope to suggest an approach to future research into the needs of deaf students and the services provided to meet these needs. We do not offer a 'model methodology' but we feel that the field of support for deaf students in Higher Education has much to gain from rooting itself in a Disability Studies and narrative framework. By doing so, it is hoped that future provision might more closely consider the views, opinions and experiences of deaf students.

Key drivers for service developments

It is important to acknowledge the journey that support services for deaf and disabled students has undertaken during the past fifteen years and understand the key milestones and policy drivers that have progressed access to Higher Education for deaf and disabled students. Students attending universities prior to 1993 received ad-hoc support services and relied heavily on individual goodwill rather than on institutional policies and practices. Barnes (1991 in Tinklin et al, 2004) found that:

> 'the majority of British colleges and universities were inaccessible and many were unwilling or unable to provide the necessary support services to make them accessible.' (1991: 638)

In 1993, the Higher Education Funding Council for England (HEFCE) embarked on a programme of investment with the implementation of the widening participation agenda. This was a direct attempt to shift the focus from marginalised groups identified by social class and/or disadvantage to directly address the needs of disabled students. In Scotland the Further and Higher Education (Scotland) Act 1992 required further and Higher Education institutions to `have regard to the needs of disabled students'.

The introduction of the Disability Discrimination Act (DDA) in 1995 made it unlawful for employers and providers of services to discriminate against disabled people without placing legislative duties on educational establishments and institutions. Part 4 of the Act only required the publication of disability statements setting out an institution's policies and practices detailing current and future activity and policy development in relation to access for disabled students. At the time this was viewed as a positive move and a useful tool to raise the profile of disabled students accessing Higher Education. The first of these statements was produced early in 1997 in Scotland, where they were seen as having had a positive impact on raising awareness of disability issues among senior management in Higher Education (Tinklin and Hall 1999).

The amendment to Part 4 of the Act (Special Educational Needs Disability Bill, 2001) brought education into the heart of disability legislation and mirrored the focus placed on employment and service providers in 1995. This meant that it became unlawful to discriminate against an individual on the grounds of their disability and the additional responsibility to make anticipatory adjustments. Thus institutions are now expected to give attention to service planning and provision, which may be required by future disabled students or applicants and make these adjustments in advance. The major part of the Act was implemented in 2002; adjustments requiring the provision of 'auxiliary aids and services' (such as interpreters, lip speakers, notetakers, etc) have been required since September 2003 and the physical access to buildings duties came into force in October 2005.

In the context of supporting deaf students, we are aware that there are communities of deaf students at some UK institutions who benefit from highly evolved support services. It should not be surprising that deaf students may gravitate to these providers' not only to benefit from these services, but also from access to a community of students with similar experiences and backgrounds. This does pose a challenge for those institutions with lower numbers of deaf students when attempting to develop their provision and is a dilemma we were aware of during our experiences as Disability Advisers; 'Which comes first: the student or the service?' Within the new legislative framework, Higher Education Institutions (HEIs) must anticipate the access requirements of disabled students; how HEIs respond to this new responsibility is yet to be seen. However we may anticipate there will be a wide variation in approaches.

A study conducted by Nottingham Trent University (1996-1999) identified three main models of support for deaf students within the UK Higher Education sector:

- a university-based support service (in house);
- a service based on collaboration with further education (partnership);
- a city-wide service. (external).

The report suggests these models focus upon how services are commissioned, as the service available is likely to fit the requirements of the individual HEI, the deaf student profile, and the extent to which the disability or student service offices are well established and resourced. Within these three broad models we can identify a range of services for deaf students which may be included in any of the models.

Note-taking is probably the main type of access support provided across Higher Education Is, although Brennan et al (2005) suggest that by no means all of the notetakers currently used in Higher Education are qualified to the Council for the Advancement of Communication with Deaf People (CACDP) standards. Other direct forms of support for deaf students include electronic note-taking, BSL/English Interpreter, Communication Support Workers and lipspeaking. More indirect forms of support for deaf students identified by the Nottingham Trent study include language tutorials, video transcriptions, arrangements for the provision of technical equipment, assistance with claiming Disabled Students Allowance, examination/assessment support and study skills.

There is a range of existing quality assurance mechanisms used to identify the tools institutions use to 'measure' the student experience. The Quality Assurance Agency's (QAA) 'Code of practice for the assurance of academic quality and standards in Higher Education' (generally known as 'The code') provides a comprehensive framework against which HEIs can assess their internal mechanisms for quality assuring disabled students' learning experience. The recently introduced 'National Student Survey' enables students to give feedback on the quality of their academic courses from a service-user's perspective. Higher Education Institutions may also choose to survey their whole student body to elicit feedback on the student experience in more detail.

The contributors and participants in the Nottingham Trent study measured the quality assurance of the student experience through questionnaires, satisfaction surveys, and similar participation opportunities for students to give feedback. These are common approaches in Higher Education to seeking student feedback at an institutional or at service/operational level, and recognize the importance of student views:

> 'The experiences and perspectives of deaf students and ex-students should play a key role in developing policy and practice in providing access to Higher Education for deaf students.' Brennan et al (2005:23)

However, the extent to which such approaches effectively capture the experiences of deaf students depends upon a number of factors, including student participation rates; whether the HEI is able to cross-tabulate the results to assess differences between disabled and non-disabled students; and whether they then disaggregate the results into impairment categories, in order to assess the different experiences of deaf, blind or dyslexic students for example. It is at this point that the low numbers of deaf students in Higher Education may prevent any differences in experience from informing effective change, especially where HEIs rely upon the statistical significance of results.

Changes to the legislative framework noted above, the shift to student fees and a subsequent desire to improve the student experience may have a strong influence on the development of future provision. The emphasis on quality will need to reflect the wider student experience, including experiences which are not tied to the immediate learning environment and, we will argue below, are not limited to the concept of 'barriers' as emphasized in the disability studies literature.

Disability Studies

Following the development of disabled people's activism, and the publication of 'Fundamental Principles of Disability' by the Union of the Physically Impaired Against Segregation (UPIAS) in 1975, the UK Disability Studies field grew to be the academic arm of the disabled people's movement (Barnes, 2003). UPIAS called for the separation of the effects of impairment upon an individual from disability, citing disability as:

> 'the disadvantage or restriction of activity caused by a contemporary social organization which takes no or little account of people who have […] impairments and thus excludes them from participation in the mainstream of social activities […] disability is therefore a particular form of social oppression' (UPIAS, 1975:14).

This redefinition of disability was theorised by Mike Oliver in 1983, leading to the development of the social model of disability. This has become the dominant approach to researching disabled people's experiences in the UK within the disability studies field (Thomas, 2004: 581). What distinguishes disability studies from other approaches to researching disability is 'an explicit commitment to assist disabled people in their fight for full equality and social inclusion', self determination, and a call for an emancipatory strategy to achieve this (Thomas, 1999:571).

Barnes (2003:5), when reviewing approaches to researching disability, restates the social model as:

> ' "nothing more or less fundamental" than a shift away from an emphasis upon individual impairments towards the way in which physical, cultural and social environments exclude or disadvantage people labelled disabled.'

Historical and materialist theories are most common in early disability studies research, focusing primarily upon the structural and material barriers that restrict disabled people's participation in all aspects of society (Gabel and Peters, 2004). However, the 1990's saw a number of additional approaches emerging, for example feminist and postmodernist, which Gabel and Peters (2004: 586) suggest 'heralds the beginning of a paradigm shift … that welcomes diverse paradigmatic representations'. Shakespeare (2006), in outlining a critical realist approach to disability, suggests there have in fact always been a number of 'social models', rather than the single predominant, or 'hard' social model. In reviewing the paradigmatic and theoretical basis of the social model Gabel and Peters (2004) argue the literature:

> 'does not inhere within one paradigm and, in fact, can be found moving fluidly between and among paradigms.' (2004:587).

Whilst it is not within the scope of this chapter to fully outline the competing approaches to disability, we would like to highlight the work of two particular authors, whose critiques have informed our views.

Thomas (2004) suggests that whilst the social model definition has led to 'social advances' for disabled people, and therefore should remain, it is not an accurate reflection of UPIAS' intended re-definition of disability. Thomas (2004:572) outlines how Vic Finkelstein later explained the social theory he had in mind, one with a focus upon the 'material aspects of social relations' reflecting his materialist orientation. It is the social relational aspects of Finkelstein's work which appears to have received less attention within the field. Thomas (2004) goes on to suggest both macro and micro scale examinations of the social relational aspects of disability between impaired and non-impaired people is needed. The approach advocated by Thomas (2004) maintains a focus upon disability as a form of social oppression, but which moves away from a definition based solely upon restricted activity to one where disability can be understood as:

> ' … a form of social oppression involving the social imposition of restrictions of activity on people with impairments and the socially engendered undermining of their psycho-emotional wellbeing.' (Thomas, 2004:60)

It is the forms of 'oppressive social responses' to people with impairments that are of concern, rather than simply restricted activity. A social relational approach would acknowledge that impairments do place restrictions upon disabled people, whilst also focussing attention upon social reactions and how these oppress disabled people.

Thomas (2006) highlighted the scope for future research within disability studies to take account of impairment and disability, although warns against research that might take the focus off 'disablism' (the social oppression of disabled people) and lose sight of the need to make a contribution to support disabled people's equality and social justice.

Corker (1999) argues for a post-modern understanding of disability and impairment, where the emphasis is upon the:

> 'relational, mediatory and performative role of discourse [and] the increasing importance of local knowledge in shaping the social and political world.'

to better understand the lives of disabled people (Corker, 1999:627). Corker (1998) suggests it is essential to consider disability within the realities of the post modern world, to recognise the relationship between impairment and disability, to connect with others who may otherwise be marginalised within the disability movement, and to understand the social construction of disability in order to consider discourse as an important element of the experience of disability.

Whilst Corker (1999) and Thomas (2004) recognise the political and pragmatic value of the social model for disabled people and the importance of maintaining links between disability studies and disabled people's activism, Corker believes there is scope to both critique the dominant social model, and explore alternative strands to contribute to the development of a social theory of disability. Corker argues for a:

> 'critical analysis of the slippage in personal and social meaning that is created when we begin to examine the mutual constitution of disability and impairment more closely at the theoretical level can be actively employed in [disabled people's] political struggles.' (Corker, 1999: 639)

Looking at the individual and society rather than either the individual or society can enable marginalised voices to be fore grounded and to further challenge dominant cultures (Corker, 1998).

Agreeing with Leonard (1997), Corker argues for the addition of:

> 'a "paradigm of communication" rooted in discursive strategies...[in addition] to the Marxist "paradigm of production" and its preoccupation with structure.' (Corker, 1999: 639)

Such a paradigm would 'emphasise that disability is produced in the relationships between impairment and oppression', and would enable research to further explore issues of disabled people's social agency, notions of language and difference, and importantly explore those aspects of experience which a materialist approach cannot explain fully (Corker, 1999: 640).

We are not arguing against the social model of disability, or the material focus of much of disability studies research. Rather, we are following Thomas (2004) and Corker (1999) in their assertion that there may be additional ways of 'deploying a range of theoretical perspectives' which can enrich our understanding and research of disability (Thomas, 2004), and bring the theorisation of disability into more contemporary approaches to researching the social world (Corker, 1999). As Musson and Duberley (2007) note:

> 'humans need access to symbolic and material resources and authority to make themselves heard, and legitimize their respective projects.' (2007:146)

Taking forward a critical, social, relational and communicative focus could answer such a call, be part of the fluidity of paradigmatic approaches to disability, offer different insights and enrich our understanding of experiences of disability (Meekosha, 2004).

Developing a methodology

The critiques discussed above have led us to seek a methodology which enables an exploration of a critical social relational and communication orientated understanding of disability, and which can contribute to our knowledge of the experiences of deaf students in Higher Education. However, the aim of the research is not to lose sight of the emancipatory call of UPIAS (1975) nor of the need to maintain links between the academy and the disabled people's movement (Corker, 1999, Germon, 1998). As such, an important element of the methodology will be considering the research methodologies promoted within disability studies to assist researchers in maintaining these links.

A central tenant of disability studies is an emancipatory (or at least participatory) research methodology which seeks to avoid positioning disabled people as 'passive research subjects' or reproducing within its processes social practices which fail to ensure disabled people are active partners (Priestley, 1997:89). For Vernon (1997:163) emancipatory research can be best described as research 'which seeks to alleviate oppression... in exposing the mechanisms for producing, maintaining and legitimizing social inequities'. Kitchin explains the distinction between emancipatory and participatory approaches as they are broadly used within disability studies as:

> 'emancipatory (seeking "positive" societal change) and empowering (seeking "positive" individual change through participation).' (Kitchin, 2001:62)

For the purposes of this chapter, the term used by original authors will be used, although in recognition that some authors move fluidly between the two terms, or use 'emancipatory' to refer to both approaches.

Barnes (2003) suggests six 'core principles' upon which emancipatory disability research should be based:

- Accountability – to the disabled community, noting the tendency in research to position disabled research participants as 'passive subjects';
- The social model of disability: emancipatory research should adhere to the model;
- The problem of objectivity: researchers should recognize the extent to which sociological judgments are coloured by personal experience, propositions limited by meanings in language used, and observations theory laden. Researchers should clearly state their 'ontological and epistemological positions' and 'research methodology and data collection strategies are logical, rigorous and open to scrutiny' (Barnes:2003:11-12);
- The choice of methods: that whilst qualitative methods favour the collection of the 'complexity of the every day experiences of disabled people' it is the uses methods are put to that is of central importance- that is, recognition of the value laden nature of research methods (Barnes:2003:12);
- The role of experience: whilst focusing upon the experiences of disabled people, sight is not lost of the 'environment in which those experiences are shaped and, in so doing, simply re-emphasise...the personal tragedy theory of disability' (Barnes, 2003:13);
- Practical outcomes: aim to disseminate key data or outcomes, to make a contribution to the wider disabled peoples' movement.

Emancipatory disability research should be judged by its ability to 'empower disabled people through the research process' albeit with acknowledgement that this is not an easy aim to achieve (Barnes:2003:16). Routledge (cited by Kitchin (2000:44) suggests participatory and emancipatory research constitutes a 'third space', a place 'between researcher and researched, academic and activist, [which] can be occupied' when carrying out research as critical engagement.

In addition, there are a number of further issues raised, mostly by disabled researchers in the field, which need to be considered. The exclusion of disabled people from the role of researcher has long been a concern in the field, with significant levels of research being carried out by non-disabled people (Barnes, 2003; Barnes and Mercer, 1997; Kitchin, 2000; Linton, 1998; Oliver, 1993). It is suggested that such levels of exclusion leads to research that is not wholly representative of 'disabled peoples' experiences and knowledges' (Kitchin, 2000:26). The issue of concern is that much research addresses the concerns and interests of the 'non-disabled researcher and … funding agencies' rather than disabled communities (Kitchin, 2000; Oliver, 1993:63). That research should attempt to break from the 'positivist tradition … [and] no longer be carried out in isolation from disabled people themselves' is of clear importance (Oliver, 1993:66). Vernon quotes Oliver (1992) in focusing upon three 'essential principles of emancipatory disability research … reciprocity, gain and empowerment' (Vernon, 1997:168). Reciprocity being two fold; to be prepared to answer participant questions about personal experiences, to be aware that this may lead to some level of self-exposure (Vernon, 1997:169).

The benefits to this approach are mutual with gains for both researcher and participant. The researcher gains rich data, within their career, and personally, if they are researching around experiences they share with research participants. Gain for participants may be to have the opportunity to be fully listened to, to obtain feedback on non-research related matters they bring to the research situation and also by being involved in the research.

Vernon (1997) suggests empowerment is 'something people do for themselves', with the researcher encouraging participants by treating them as equals in the research process, and 'take steps towards empowerment' by allowing them to 'speak for themselves about their experiences and concerns…engendering a feeling of being valued' (Vernon:1997:171). For Vernon, where people live as a minority within a minority (for example Black disabled people), sharing of experiences itself may be empowering.

In summary, working towards an emancipatory or participatory research strategy is an important principle when researching experiences of disability and can be interpreted as a set of standards against which research strategies can be assessed. We believe that the following principles can be adopted from this agenda to inform research on deaf student experiences:

1. Aiming to work with disabled people as research partners who are involved throughout, and adopting a research strategy which:

- recognises research as a social practice;
- offers the opportunity for empowerment, or at least recognises the need to share power;
- focuses upon raising voices and value (or gain) for participants.

2. The importance of reflexivity in addressing issues of researcher voice and gain, and drawing the researcher towards contextual factors for both themselves and research participants.

3. Research should be carried out from a social model perspective, understanding that impairment is not the cause of disability, and acknowledging the importance of examining social responses towards people with impairments. In other words, acknowledging that disability is socially constructed.

Narrative approaches to researching organizational experiences

The use of narrative in organizational research is well established. Rhodes and Brown (2005) outline a growth in narrative approaches to management and organization research, and a range of applications to areas such as sense-making, communication, learning/change, politics and power, and identify and identification. Narrative have been used to research a range of organizational environments and experiences including public administration (Feldman et al, 2004), organizing in a public health environment (Currie and Brown, 2003), indignation (Sims, 2005) knowledge acquisition (Patriotta, 2003) organizational change (Garcia-Lorenzo, 004). Within these studies, narrative is recognised as making contributions to organizational theory and methodology, that narrative approaches enable researchers to 'engage with the lived realities of organizational life' (Rhodes and Brown, 2005), and that they highlight the importance of paying attention to organizational stories.

Narrative research is perceived as different to other qualitative approaches to research, in that research accounts, or texts, produced are valued as co-constructions between researcher and participants, where research participants are placed centre stage, and social relations between researcher and research participants are problematised (Chase, 2005).

One of the central concerns of narrative researchers is that of voice; the voices of research participants, the researcher's interpretive voice and how these should shape and be represented (Chase, 2005; Czarniawska, 2004; Hoskins and Stoltz, 2005). McNamee and Hosking (2006) cite narrative inquiry as means to 'articulate muted, suppressed, and excluded voices, and in this way to re-situate dominant voices/stories' (McNamee and Hosking, 2006: 149).

This encourages an emphasis in narrative research upon creating a research environment where participants are encouraged to talk about issues and events which are relevant to them. This relationship can be seen in approaches adopted in narrative interviewing, with an emphasis upon treating research interviews as a 'conversation of equals' , creating space for narrators, for researchers to 'get out of their way' (McNamee and Hosking, 2006:149) and to understand the interview relationship as one of narrator and listener (Chase, 2005). Mishler sees narrative interviewing as a 'means of empowerment of respondents' (Mishler 1986 cited in Czarniawska, 2004:663-664).

Whilst researchers may have theoretical interests (Czarniawska, 2004; Riessman, 1993), and as such prompt for narratives (Czarniawska, 2004; Chase, 2005), Riessman (2002:3) suggests narrative interview techniques enable participants to maintain their own way of organising meaning, and require the researcher to 'give up communicative power, and follow participants down their diverse trails', in other words changing the power balance of the researcher/participant relationship to ensure that the researcher has no preconceived ideas of the direction the narrative will take, thus allowing participants to shape the research agenda.

However, Hoskins and Stoltz (2005:99) highlight the importance of ensuring that research reports are not 'awash in content' at the expense of meaning and the importance of ensuring researcher voice and interpretive analysis are present, an issue many narrative researchers struggle with. The solutions proposed by Hoskins and Stoltz are to consider narrative research within a network metaphor, recognising a holistic understanding of the research and focusing not only on the relationship between researcher and researched as conflictual, but as part of a whole, enabling other 'entities' to be brought into focus, for example those to whom the research should be disseminated. Secondly to consider the moral aspects of methodological choices, when participant collaboration and interpretation ends, the researcher can chose approaches which do not objectify and categorise participants experiences, rather those which offer more 'holistic, descriptive accounts of human experience', citing narrative, social constructionism and constructivism as examples (Hoskins and Stoltz, 2005: 108).

Narrative inquiry can report 'the voices of the field', it can produce a many voiced story, where there is no aim to identify one 'correct' version of experience, to totalise, or to follow only dominant plots (Czarniawska, 2004). Rather the author is encouraged to take responsibility to carry out a 'novel reading' of narratives produced (DeVault, 1990 in Czarniawska, 2004), and to recognise their role in decontextualising and recontextualising these voices to their own narrative, that is their research report (Rorty, 1991 in Czarniawska, 2004). Addressing issues of power and empowerment is a 'strain within most narrative research' (Hoskins and Stoltz, 2005). Rather than losing the researcher interpretive voice, 'a degree of expert knowing on the part of the researcher is acceptable if it is paired with a commitment to accountability and transparency.' (Hoskins and Stoltz, 2005:108).

We might consider such an approach in support of epistemological and methodological reflexivity. Epistemic reflexivity directs the researcher to reflect upon their own socio/political and cultural influences, their social location, thus the role of the researcher and the nature of research itself upon how knowledge is created:

> 'Epistemic reflexivity entails systematic reflection by the researcher aimed at making the unconscious conscious and the tacit explicit so as to reveal how the researcher's social location forms a sub - text to the research.' (Bryans, Mavin and Waring, 2002:2)

Narrative inquiry leads to the articulation of 'local and practical concerns' (McNamee and Hosking, 2006:148).

Methodological reflexivity draws the researcher's attention to the social relations between researcher and research participants, the level of collaboration and involvement in the research project and in particular in the interpretation of data; that is to critically appraise our own practices. This can be evidenced by practices such as discussing research aims and agreeing in advance research relationships with participants, enabling participant reflexivity (by passing back data before, during and after interpretation), enabling participants to make changes or raise their own issues of importance (Bryans, Mavin and Waring, 2002).

Hoskins and Stoltz (2005) note the emphasis placed in narrative research on researchers and research participants working in partnership, empowerment, developing understanding, social change and the dissemination of research. Chase (2005) further makes the case for narrative inquiry as enabling a social change agenda, highlighting key questions for researchers considering this issue:

> 'What kinds of narratives disrupt oppressive social processes? How and when do researchers' analyses and representations of others' stories encourage social justice and democratic processes? And for whom are these processes disrupted and encouraged? Which audiences need to hear which researchers' and narrators' stories?' (Chase, 2005:667)

Acknowledging that social change can begin with the individual, where 'the act of narrating a significant life event itself facilitates positive change', self-emancipation, 'better' stories of life, and the benefits of others hearing ones story (Chase, 2005:667-8), Chase goes on to highlight that whilst there is a the long history in narrative research of 'giving voice' and 'naming silent lives', there is scope to extend the potential social impact of narrative research. Researchers can use their interpretive strategies to highlight not only the narrator's story, but also how:

> 'it is constrained by, and strains against, the mediating aspects of culture (and of institutions, organizations, and sometimes the social sciences themselves).' (Chase, 2005:668)

The voice of the researcher is thus making a contribution to the social change agenda.

Conclusions

It is important to consider the timing of bringing narratives into focus when aiming for social change, to when narratives can be 'more effective ... in challenging oppression' (Naples, 2002: 1152 in Chase, 2005: 669) and when others in different social locations are ready to move beyond empathetic listening to action. Changes to the UK legislative framework on disability equality suggest we are now entering a period when audiences in Higher Education may be ready to listen. The UK recently enacted the Disability Equality Duty for public sector organizations, introducing a wide range of positive duties on Higher Education with a requirement to consider the experiences of deaf students, and to take action as a result.

This chapter aims to encourage institutions to not just rely on the traditional methods of obtaining quality information but to enhance their existing systems with a more innovative approach to data collection to understand deaf student experiences. For this to happen the student/institution relationship needs to shift and the power balance needs to be redressed. Pushing the boundaries, taking risks and challenging existing practices should result in degrees of innovation and testing out new ways of working can only result in more in-depth learning and knowledge of the student experience.

This chapter has also demonstrated that working from a disability studies approach to deaf student experiences and using a narrative methodology may provide a more effective conduit by which the views and opinions of deaf students can be raised. As an under-researched and under-represented group in Higher Education, deaf students would then be able to contribute to developing our knowledge and understanding of their everyday experiences and be active participants in the further development of services and support across institutional activities.

It may be tempting to predict how narrative inquiry will contribute to the development of future services and inclusive practices for deaf students. However, this would undermine the whole premise of what a narrative approach offers. To attempt to provide the answers would privilege our voices over those of deaf students. We cannot know the answers until we have listened to the broad and unrestricted accounts of deaf students lived experiences of Higher Education. If we listen, deaf students will tell us what the future of support services and an inclusive Higher Education environment should be.

Key considerations

1. The type of services available within any one Higher Education Institution will depend upon a number of factors, noted above. Whilst a Higher Education Institution operating alone may struggle to offer a cohesive range of services it may be possible to develop collaborative partnerships between Higher Education Institutions and Furth Education Colleges in geographically close areas to improve the range of services available to deaf students.
2. When seeking student feedback on service provision practitioners should aim to ensure student involvement opportunities do not exclude deaf students, and where possible are representative of all disabled student groups.
3. Where feedback or involvement exercise outcomes are limited due to small numbers of students from representative groups,

for example deaf students, Higher Education Institutions could consider using more in depth or alternative forms of involvement and analysis, for example working with a narrative approach to explore the student experience in detail.

4. Practitioners using more in depth forms of involvement and analysis may find they gain access to rich accounts of student experiences which were not previously highlighted, and which can inform future provision for deaf students.

Further reading

Barnes, C. 2003 'What a difference a decade makes: reflections on doing 'emancipatory' disability research'. *Disability and Society*, 18, 1:3-17.

Barnes, C. & Mercer, G. (eds.) 1997 *Doing disability research.* Leeds: The Disability Press.

Brennan, M, Grimes, M and Thoutenhoofd, E 2005 *Deaf students in Scottish Higher Education.* University of Edinburgh

Bryans, P., Mavin, S. & Waring, T. 2002 *Reflexivity - what is it?.* Working paper.

Building on Strengths: HEFCE funded initiative at the Nottingham Trent University 1996 – 1999 deaf students in Higher Education: developing and improving specialist support provision

Chase, S. 2005 'Narrative inquiry; multiple lenses, approaches, voices', in Denzin, N. K. & Lincoln, Y. S. (eds.) *The Sage handbook of qualitative research.* London: Sage Publications Inc: 651-679.

Corker, M. 1998 'Disability discourse in a post-modern world', in Shakespeare, T. (ed.) *The disability reader.* London: Cassell: 221-233.

Corker, M. 1999 'Differences, conflations and foundations: the limit to "accurate" theoretical representation of disabled people's experience?' *Disability and Society*, 14, 5:627-642.

Currie, G. & Brown, A. D. 2003 'A narratological approach to understanding processes of organizing in a UK hospital'. *Human Relations*, 56, 5:563-586.

Czarniawska, B. 2004 'The uses of narrative in social science research', in Hardy, M. & Bryman, A. (eds.) *Handbook of data analysis.* London: Sage Publications:649-670.

DeVault, M., L 1990 'Novel readings: The social organization of interpretation' cited in Czarniawska, B. (2004) 'The uses of narrative in social science research', in Hardy, M. & Bryman, A. (eds.) *Handbook of data analysis*. London: Sage Publications: 649-670..

Durham University 2006 'Diversity annual report 2004/5' [Online]. Available at: http://www.dur.ac.uk/resources/diversity.equality/Diversity%20Annual%20Report%202005%20FINAL%20REPORT%2022nd%20May%202006.pdf (Accessed: 20th August 2006).

DRC 2006 'Disability briefing - March 2006' [Online]. Available at: http://www.drc-gb.org/PDF/10_783_Disability%20Briefing%20%20March%20%202006.pdf (Accessed: 4th April 2006).

Elliott, J. 2005 *Using narrative in social research. Qualitative and quantitative approaches*. London: Sage Publications Ltd.

Feldman, M. S., Skoldberg, K., Brown, R. N. & Horner, D. 2004 'Making sense of stories: A rhetorical approach to narrative analysis', *Journal of Public Administration Research and Theory*, 14, 2:147-170.

Gabel, S. & Peters, S. 2004 'Presage of a paradigm shift? Beyond the social model of disability toward resistance theories of disability', *Disability and Society*, 19, 6:585-600.

Garcia-Lorenzo, L. 2004 '(Re)producing the organization through narratives: The case of a multinational', *Intervention Research*, 1:43-60.

Germon, P. (1998) 'Activists and academics: Part of the same or a world apart', in Shakespeare, T. (ed.) *The disability reader*. London: Cassell, pp. 245-255.

Hall, J. & Tinklin, T. 1998 *Students first: the experiences of disabled students in Higher Education*, Edinburgh, Scottish Council for Research in Education.

Hardy, C., Palmer, I. & Phillips, N. 2000 'Scaling up and bearing down in discourse analysis: questions regarding textual agencies and their context' cited in Musson, G. & Duberley, J. 2007 'Change, change or be exchanged: The discourse of participation and the manufacture of identity', *Journal of Management Studies*, 44, 1:143-164.

Holloway, W. & Jefferson, T. 2000 *Doing Qualitative research differently: free association, narrative and the interview method.* London: Sage.

Hosking, D., M & McNamee, S. (eds.) 2006 *The social construction of organization.* Malmo: Liber and Copenhagen Business School Press, Advances in Organization Studies

Hoskins, M. & Stoltz, J.-A. 2005 'Fear of offending: disclosing researcher discomfort when engaging in analysis', *Qualitative Research*, 5, 1:95-111.

Kitchin, R. 2000 'The Researched Opinions on Research: disabled people and disability research', *Disability and Society*, 15, 1:25-47.

Kitchin, R. 2001 'Using participatory action research approaches in geographical studies of disability: Some reflections', *Disability Studies Quarterly* 21, 4

Leonard, P. 1997 *Postmodern welfare*. London: Sage.

Linton, S. 1998 'Disability Studies/Not Disability Studies', *Disability and Society*, 13, 4:525-540.

McNamee, S. & Hosking, D.M. 2006 'Intermezzo: Narrative approaches to inquiry' in Hosking, D.M., & McNamee, S. 2006 *The Social construction of organization.* Liber, Liber and Copenhagen Business School Press, Advances in Organization Studies.

Mauthner, N. & Doucet, A. 1998 'Reflections on a voice-centred relational method: analysing maternal and domestic voices' in Ribbens, J. & Edwards, R. (eds.) *Feminist dilemmas in qualitative research: public knowledge and private lives.* London: Sage: 119-146.

Meekosha, H. 2004 'Drifting down the Gulf Stream: navigating the cultures of disability studies', *Disability and Society*, 19, 7: 722-733.

Mishler, E. G. (1986) *Research interviewing. context and narrative.* London: Harvard University Press, p142-3 in Czarniawska, B. (2004) 'The uses of narrative in social science research', in Hardy, M. & Bryman, A. (eds.) *Handbook of data analysis.* London: Sage Publications, pp. 649-670.

Morris, H. 2003 'Changing communities at work in academia', *Work, Employment and Society*, 17, 3:557-568.

Musson, G. & Duberley, J. 2007 'Change, change or be exchanged: The discourse of
participation and the manufacture of identity', *Journal of Management Studies*, 44, 1:143-164.

Naples, N. 2003 'Deconstructing and locating survivor discourse: Dynamics of narrative, empowerment, and resistance for survivors of childhood sexual abuse' *Signs: Journal of Women in Culture and Society*, 28:1151-1185.

O'Day, B. & Killen, M. 2002 'Research on the lives of persons with disabilities' *Journal of Disability Policy Studies*, 13, 1:9-15.

Oliver, M. 1992 'Changing the social relations of research production' *Disability, Handicap and Society*, 7, 2:101-114.

Oliver, M. 1993 'Re-defining disability: a challenge to research', in Swain, J., Finkelstein, V., French, S. & Oliver, M. (eds.) *Disabling barriers - enabling environments*. London: Sage Publishing Ltd: 61-67.

Patriotta, G. 2003 'Sensemaking on the shop floor: Narratives of knowledge in organizations', *Journal of Management Studies*, 40, 2: 349-375.

Priestley, M. 1997 'Who's research ?: A personal audit', in Barnes, C. & Mercer, G. (eds.) *Doing Disability Research* Leeds: The Disability Press: 88-107.

Rhodes, C. & Brown, A. D. 2005 'Narrative, organizations and research' *International journal of management reviews*, 7, 3: 167-188.

Riessman, C. K. 1993 *Narrative analysis*. London: Sage Publications, Qualitative Research Methods Series 30.

Riessman, C. K. 2002 'Analysis of personal narratives' in Gubrium, J. F. & Holstein, J. A. (eds.) *Handbook of interview research: Context and method.* Thousand Oaks: Sage Publications Ltd: 695-710.

Rorty, R. 1991 'Inquiry as recontextualization: An anti-dualist account of interpretation' in *Philosophical Papers 1. Objectivity, relativism and truth.* New York: Cambridge University Press: 93-110.

Routledge: 1996 'The third space as critical engagement' *Antipode*, 28, 4: 399-419.

Shah, S. 2005 *Career success of disabled high-flyers*. London: Jessica Kingsley Publishers.

Shakespeare, T. 2006 *Disability rights and wrongs*. London: Routledge.

Sims, D. 2005 'You bastard: A narrative exploration of the experience of indignation within organizations, *Organization Studies*, 26, 11: 1625-1640.

Smith, A. & Twomey, B. 2002 'Labour market experiences of people with disabilities' London: Office for National Statistics [Online]. Available at: http://www.statistics.gov.uk/cci/article.asp?ID=238&Pos=3&ColRank=2&Rank=192 (Accessed: 23rd March 2003).

Thomas, C. 1999 *Female forms: experiencing and understanding disability*. Buckingham: Open University Press.

Thomas, C. 2004 'How is disability understood? An examination of sociological approaches' *Disability and Society*, 19, 6: 569-583.

Thomas, C. 2006 *Disability Studies Association conference*, 19th September 2006.

Tinklin, T, Riddell, S and Wilson, A 2004 'Policy and provision for disabled students in Higher Education in Scotland and England: the current state of play' *Studies in Higher Education* 29, 5

Tinklin, T. & Hall, J. 1999 'Getting round obstacles: disabled students' experiences' in *Higher Education in Scotland: Studies in Higher Education* 24: 183-194.

Trowler, P. and Turner, G. H. 2002 'Exploring the hermeneutic foundations of university life: Deaf academics in a hybrid 'community of practice' *Higher Education* 43: 227-256.

UPIAS 1975 'Fundamental principles of disability' [Online]. Available at: http://www.leeds.ac.uk/disability-studies/archiveuk/UPIAS/UPIAS.pdf (Accessed: 5th February 2007).

Vance (ed.) (Forthcoming) *Multiple voices and identities in Higher Education: Writings by disabled faculty and staff in a disabling society*. Huntersville: Association of Higher Education And Disability.

Vernon, A. 1997 'Reflexivity: The dilemmas of researching from the inside' in Barnes, C. & Mercer, G. (eds.) *Doing disability research*. Leeds: The Disability Press:158-176.

Glossary of acronyms

AHEAD	Association for Higher Education and Disability
AVCE	Advanced Vocational Certificate of Education
BSL	British Sign Language
BTEC	Business and Technology Education Council
CDA	Critical Discourse Analysis
CSW	Communication Support Workers
DDA	Disability Discrimination Act
DED	Disability Equality Duty
DES	Disability Equality Scheme
DfES	Department for Education and Science
DRC	Disability Rights Commission
DSA	Disabled Students' Allowances
ECU	Equality Challenge Unit
ENT	Electronic notetakers
FDP	Federation of Deaf People
FHE	Further and Higher Education
GCSE	General Certificate of Secondary Education
HEA	Higher Education Academy
HEFCE	Higher Education Funding Council for England
HEI	Higher Education Institutions
HND	Higher National Diploma
ILTHE	Institute for Learning and Teaching in Higher Education
LSC	Learning and Skills Council
LTSN	Learning and Teaching Subject Networks
NADO	National Association of Disability Officers
NADP	National Association of Disability Professionals
NATED	National Association for Tertiary Education for Deaf people
NIC	National Innovations Centre
NUS	National Union of Students
NVQ	National Vocational Qualification
PhD	Doctor of Philosophy
QAA	Quality Assurance Agency
SENDA	Special Educational Needs and Disability Act
SHEFC	Scottish Higher Education Funding Council
UCAS	Universities and Colleges Admissions Service
UCLan	University of Central Lancashire, Preston, United Kingdom

Index

Deaf Students in Higher Education: current research and practice